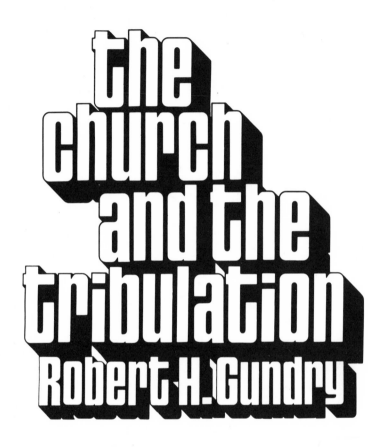

the church and the tribulation

Robert H. Gundry

ZONDERVAN PUBLISHING HOUSE OF THE ZONDERVAN CORPORATION
GRAND RAPIDS, MICHIGAN 49506

THE CHURCH AND THE TRIBULATION

Copyright © 1973 by The Zondervan Corporation

Grand Rapids, Michigan

Library of Congress Catalog Card Number 73-8359

Grateful acknowledgment is made to the following:

   Bibliotheca Sacra for permission to quote from various articles in that journal.

   Wm. B. Eerdmans Publishing Co. for permission to quote from Robertson and Donaldson's edition of the *Ante-Nicene Fathers*.

   The Lockman Foundation, La Habra, California, for permission to quote from the *New American Standard Bible* © 1960, 1962, 1963, 1968, 1971.

Printed in the United States of America

To

Bernard Dell

Contents

ABBREVIATIONS

(See Bibliography for further information.)

Alford = Henry Alford, *The Greek Testament*
BAG = W. Bauer, W. F. Arndt, and F. W. Gingrich, *A Greek-English Lexicon of the New Testament and Other Early Christian Literature*
BibSac = *Bibliotheca Sacra*
Biederwolf = William Biederwolf, *The Millennium Bible*
Chafer = Lewis Sperry Chafer, *Systematic Theology*
Deissmann, *LAE* = Adolf Deissman, *Light From the Ancient East*
Douty = Norman F. Douty, *Has Christ's Return Two Stages?*
Ellicott = Charles J. Ellicott, *St. Paul's Epistles to the Thessalonians*
English = E. Schuyler English, *Re-Thinking the Rapture*
EGT = *Expositor's Greek Testament*
Frost = Henry W. Frost, *Matthew Twenty-Four and the Revelation*
Kittel = *Theological Dictionary of the New Testament*
Ladd = George Eldon Ladd, *The Blessed Hope*
Linton = John Linton, *Will the Church Escape the Great Tribulation?*
LSJ = Liddell, Scott, and Jones, *A Greek-English Lexicon*
Ludwigson = R. Ludwigson, *Bible Prophecy Notes*
LXX = the Septuagint
MM = Moulton & Milligan, *The Vocabulary of the Greek Testament*
NBC = *New Bible Commentary: Revised*
NT = New Testament
OT = Old Testament
Payne = J. Barton Payne, *The Imminent Appearing of Christ*
Pentecost = J. Dwight Pentecost, *Things to Come*
Robertson = A. T. Robertson, *A Grammar of the Greek New Testament in the Light of Historical Research*
SRB = *Scofield Reference Bible*
Stanton = Gerald B. Stanton, *Kept From the Hour*
Strombeck = J. F. Strombeck, *First the Rapture*
Thayer = Joseph Henry Thayer, *A Greek-English Lexicon of the New Testament*
Thiessen = Henry C. Thiessen, *Will the Church Pass Through the Tribulation?*
Thiessen, *Theology* = Henry C. Thiessen, *Lectures in Systematic Theology*
Walvoord = John F. Walvoord
Walvoord, *MK* = John F. Walvoord, *The Millennial Kingdom*
Walvoord, *RQ* = John F. Walvoord, *The Rapture Question*
Walvoord, *Thess* = John F. Walvoord, *The Thessalonian Epistles*
Wood = Leon J. Wood, *Is the Rapture Next?*

N.B.: In citing journals, numbers preceding the colon represent volumes; numbers following the colon represent pages.

Scripture quotations are taken from the *New American Standard Bible* unless otherwise indicated. All emphases in Scripture quotations are mine.

1

Approaching the Issue

The issue which we are approaching has to do with the possibility of Jesus' return to evacuate the Church from the earth before a future period of intense tribulation. If we favor the possibility of such a pretribulational rapture, it becomes incumbent to stand in constant readiness for the event. However, if Jesus will return solely after the tribulation, that readiness should include mental and moral preparation for prior experience of the tribulation itself. The exhortation to "endure to the end" and the special warning about the leading astray of, "if possible, even the elect" (Matt. 24:12, 13, 24) highlight the danger of dismay and loss of faith on the part of whatever saints do find themselves in the last great time of testing.

Ten to twenty years ago this issue peaked on the American evangelical scene, and then abated. But recent events in the Middle East have revived interest in biblical prophecy concerning the future. It therefore seems appropriate to reconsider the chronology of the rapture—the more so since in the last spate of publications on the topic posttribulationism gained neither the volume of press nor the exegetical backing which were given to pretribulationism. George Ladd's *The Blessed Hope,* written in a popular style, takes a largely historical approach. And the standard posttribulational polemic by Alexander Reese has long been out of date, not to mention its embarrassingly bombastic style.

This work moves within the ambit of conservative evangelical

9

premillenarianism apart from questions of realized versus consistent eschatology and higher critical issues of various sorts, all of which would need discussion in a larger frame of reference. It should (but cannot) go without saying that in matters of disagreement the appearance here of the names of writers on the topic at hand ought not to be taken as personal attack, but only as means of documentation. The attempt has been to evaluate normative views as represented by acknowledged leaders in the field. However, for the sake of comprehensiveness, some idiosyncratic arguments by other writers occasionally receive attention. There is no implication that such arguments or their refutation settles the issue as a whole. In the same vein, general statements to the effect that "pretribulationists say . . ." do not necessarily impute the following view to *all* pretribulationists. The same holds true for statements concerning the views of posttribulationists.

The present thesis is threefold: (1) direct, unquestioned statements of Scripture that Jesus Christ will return after the tribulation and that the first resurrection will occur after the tribulation, coupled with the absence of statements placing similar events before the tribulation, make it natural to place the rapture of the Church after the tribulation; (2) the theological and exegetical grounds for pretribulationism rest on insufficient evidence, *non sequitur* reasoning, and faulty exegesis; (3) positive indications of a posttribulational rapture arise out of a proper exegesis of relevant Scripture passages and derive support from the history of the doctrine.

In the terminology of this book, "Christian" and "Church" refer to saints of the present age. "Church" is capitalized when used in the generic or universal sense by way of distinction from "Israel." "Israel" refers to the physical descendants of Abraham through Isaac and Jacob, either nationally considered or ideally considered as a spiritual body of redeemed people. Context determines the particular reference of the general term "saints." The "tribulation" points to the future period of Daniel's seventieth week and the Antichrist's career, although, strictly speaking, the term should refer to the persecution within that period of time rather than the period of time itself.[1] The terms "second com-

---

[1] Pentecost erroneously generalizes in stating that posttribulationists deny the futurity of Daniel's seventieth week (165, 170ff.). Those who hold to the historical view of the seventieth week should be designated a-tribulationists; for although they may allow for a few events necessarily prior to the second

ing," "return," "advent," and "Parousia" all refer to the posttribulational return of Christ with attendant events unless qualified otherwise by the immediate context. The alleged pretribulational advent, resurrection, translation, and rapture of the Church are always so qualified by modifiers or by context. As used here, "Armageddon" refers to the final crisis at which Christ will come, not to preceding campaigns or battles.

It is hoped that the following pages will contribute to an understanding and appreciation of the posttribulational position and that it will do so in a manner characterized by "the wisdom from above . . . first pure, then peaceable, gentle, reasonable, full of mercy and good fruits, unwavering, without hypocrisy" (James 3:17).

---

coming, they squeeze them into such a short space of time that for all practical purposes the question whether Jesus will come beforehand or only afterwards holds little meaning.

2

The Dispensational-Ecclesiological Backdrop

In the chronological question concerning the rapture, the dispensational issue centers in the field of ecclesiology. An absolute silence in the OT about the present age, a total disconnection of the Church from the divine program for Israel, and a clean break between dispensations would favor pretribulationism: the Church would not likely be related to the seventieth week of Daniel, or tribulation, a period of time clearly having to do with Israel. But a partial revelation of the present age in the OT, a connection (not necessarily identification) between Israel and the Church, and a dispensational change involving a transitional period open the door to the presence of the Church during the tribulation.

THE NATURE OF THE CHURCH AS A MYSTERY

In pretribulationism the dealings of God with the Church are severed from His dealings with Israel. Justification for the severance derives from the designation as "mysteries" of certain churchly doctrines missing in the OT. These mysteries sharply set apart the Church. So runs the reasoning. However, we might well be chary of deducing the absence of the Church from the tribulation in such fashion. Both parties agree that a large number of

Gentile saints (whether or not they will belong to the Church) will live on earth during the tribulation (so, clearly, Rev. 7:9-17). But do any tribulational passages in the OT mention those Gentile saints? No such passages are adduced.[1] If none exist, pretribulationists should hardly argue from a mysterious silence in the OT concerning the Church, because the OT remains silent also concerning the Gentile saints whom we know to be on earth during the tribulation.

None of the "mysteries" distinctive of the Church—such as the equality of Jews and Gentiles in one Body, the Church as the bride of Christ, and Christ's indwelling of believers—are ever applied specifically to tribulational saints.[2] But this acquires significance as an argument for pretribulationism only on the premise that the burden of proof rests on posttribulationists to show that tribulational saints will belong to the Church. If the burden of proof rather rests on pretribulationists to show that tribulational saints will *not* belong to the Church, the "failure" of NT writers to single out a tribulational generation of the Church on earth as possessive of the "mysteries" weighs nothing—the application of the "mysteries" to all generations of the Church is a matter of course. Besides, for all the NT writers knew, their own generation, to whom they explained the "mysteries," might turn out to *be* the last. Neither side gains an argument of independent value, then, because the matter reduces to assigning the burden of proof *on other grounds.*

More specifically, the mysterious character of several churchly doctrines that were not revealed until the NT divorces the Church neither from OT prophecy and the chronology of Israel in general nor from the seventieth week of Daniel, the tribulation, in particular. For, in actuality, a number of the truths designated by the term "mystery" transgress the intercalary boundaries of the Church age (as pretribulationists have drawn them) by operating outside those boundaries and sometimes even culminating within the tribulation:

"The mystery of lawlessness," even now working, will culminate in the tribulation (2 Thess. 2:7).

"The mystery of God" will be finished late in the tribulation (Rev. 10:7).

The mystery of the harlot BABYLON will continue through the tribulation (Rev. 17:5-7).

---

[1] See Walvoord, *RQ*, 38, 39, for a relevant discussion.
[2] *Ibid.*

The mysteries of the incarnation and earthly ministry of Jesus antedate the Day of Pentecost (the start of the Church age according to most pretribulationists) and surely relate to all dispensations, since they form the basis for the entire salvific program of God (Col. 2:2, 3; 1 Tim. 3:16).

The mystery of God's summing up all things in Christ in the fulness of times—"things in the heavens and things upon the earth" (Eph. 1:9, 10)—will extend far beyond the present age.

We can therefore be certain that the mysterious nature of several churchly truths does not require an exclusiveness between the chronology of Israel and that of the Church. Further, any argument for exclusiveness on such a ground runs up against the fact that the Church *as such* is never designated a mystery. Neither are the rapture and the totality of churchly truth (although Paul calls one aspect of the rapture, the translation of saints living at the time, a "mystery" in 1 Cor. 15:51, 52). So far as terminological usage is concerned, the mysteries which will operate during and throughout the tribulation raise the possibility that mysteries concerning the Church will likewise continue to function at that time.

The Present Age and the OT

Besides dispensational breadth in the usage of the term "mystery," there are OT prophecies which specifically mention and imply the present age. These prophecies provide support for a connection between Israel and the Church, between OT prophecy and the present age.

The current session of Christ at the Lord's right hand fulfills the Messianic prediction in Psalm 110:1 (see especially Acts 2:34, 35).

The Church now occupies a period of time foretold concerning Israel, viz., the period of Israel's world-wide dispersion (Deut. 28:25, 64, 65; 30:1-4). Dispensationally speaking, if the Church presently occupies the predicted time of Israel's dispersion, she may also occupy the predicted time of Israel's final tribulation.

"Then after the sixty-two weeks the Messiah will be cut off" (Dan. 9:26). "The anointed one, or the Messiah, is cut off after the sixty-ninth week, but not in the seventieth. Such a circumstance could be true only if there were a time interval between these two periods."[3] We see, then, an indication in the OT of the present hiatus between the sixty-ninth and seventieth weeks of Daniel. Furthermore, if an event such as the destruction of Jerusalem prophesied in the OT (Dan. 9:26) fell within the Church age (A.D. 70), from the dispensational standpoint other events foretold in the OT and relating to Israel, such as tribulational events, might equally well fall within the Church age.

Although they appear in the NT, the statements of Jesus which intimate the present age (outstandingly, Matt. 16:18) came to expression under the old dispensation, before the finalization of Israel's rejection. Hence again, the present age is neither unforeseen in the preceding age nor unrelated to the chronology of Israel as revealed in the OT.

Not only did the OT predict the present age, but the NT applies OT prophecy to the Church. The applications are more than analogical; i.e., they do more than draw comparisons. They affirm at least partial fulfillments of the OT in the Church and the present age.

Peter says, "This is what was spoken of through the prophet Joel . . ." (Acts 2:16-21). A stronger equation between OT prophecy and fulfillment in the Church age could not be stated. We do not read, "This is *like* what was spoken," but, "This *is* what was spoken." Whatever future and greater fulfillment may yet come, we can hardly evade the simple, direct force of Peter's declaration that the Pentecostal outpouring of the Holy Spirit fulfilled Joel's prophecy. Nor was Peter speaking of an incidental detail in the events on the day of Pentecost. The baptism in the Spirit constituted the crux among those events. If then the main event on the very birthday of the Church was prophesied in an OT passage within an Israelitish context, it should not seem strange that the Church bears a relationship also to end-time events similarly prophesied in the OT, even though they are Israelitish in cast. In fact, since the beginning of the Church age bears a marked relationship to OT predictions concerning Israel, we are not hindered dispensationally from presuming that the same will be so at the end of the Church age.

In Galatians 3:16, Paul, directly quoting Genesis 13:15; 17:8 ("And to your seed"), applies the promise of the land of Palestine to Abraham's *spiritual* seed, i.e., all who believe. He quotes not merely from God's promise of *general* blessing upon

---

[3] Walvoord, *RQ*, 25.

all families of the earth (Gen. 12:3), but from the later promise specifically concerned with the land itself. Plainly, the OT promise to Abraham and his seed finds a fulfillment now among believers who belong to the Church.

Paul bases his turning to the Gentiles on an OT prediction of Gentile salvation found in Isaiah 49:6 (Acts 13:46, 47; cf. 26:22, 23). We might think that the prophecy in Isaiah has to do with salvation of Gentiles during the millennium, to which Gentile salvation now is only analogous. But a mere analogy could hardly form the basis of a command for the evangelization of Gentiles in this age. Paul declares, "For thus has the Lord *commanded* us, I have placed You as a light for the Gentiles . . . ." A command is more than an indirect comparison. It is an imperative addressed to those for whom it was meant. If not meant also for us in this age, it loses the force of a command.

Paul establishes the duty of Jewish and Gentile Christians to receive one another (Rom. 15:7-13) by quoting four separate OT prophecies (2 Sam. 22:50, parallel Ps. 18:49; Deut. 32:43; Ps. 117:1; Isa. 11:10), which he applies to the present conversion of Gentiles. One of these prophecies, Isaiah 11:10, comes from a prominent millennial passage. Hence, the evangelization of Gentiles predicted in the OT has a fulfillment in the present dispensation as well as in the millennium. The subsequence of the revelation that Gentile converts should compose one body with the Jews (Eph. 3:3, 6) does not alter the fact that OT prophets predicted the salvation of Gentiles during the Church age.

Peter writes that the prophets foretold "the grace that would come to you . . ." (1 Pet. 1:10-12). By occurring no fewer than four times in these three verses, the phrase "to you" underscores a direct relevance to Christian believers. Although the prophets themselves did not fully understand the chronology of their own predictions, the "grace" and "salvation" of which they prophesied make the very foundation of the Church's economy.

Jeremiah prophesied the new covenant under which the Church now stands (Jer. 31:31-34). Some dispensationalists separate the new covenant for Israel of which Jeremiah spoke from an unpredicted covenant for the Church.[4] However, that view seems defective. Scripture makes no explicit distinction between two different new covenants. The identity of terminology therefore creates a presumption in favor of only one. A number

---

[4] For example, Walvoord, *BibSac,* 103:20ff.; cf. Walvoord, *MK,* 218f.

of parallel details exist between the new covenant as described in Jeremiah and the new covenant as it appears in the NT. The title is the same—"new covenant." In Jeremiah, the Lord institutes the covenant; in the NT, the Lord Jesus Christ does so (Matt. 26:28). Both contrast with the Sinaitic covenant (Gal. 4:24ff.). In both, God places His law in the heart (cf. Rom. 8:4). In Jeremiah we read of "their God" and "my people"; in 1 Peter 2:9 the apostle portrays Christians as "a holy nation, a people for God's own possession." Forgiveness of sin becomes the gracious provision in both. And the new covenant is unbreakable and everlasting in both Jeremiah and the NT (Heb. 13:20).

The quotation of Jeremiah 31 in Hebrews gives great weight to these likenesses. The author of Hebrews applies the prophecy to believers of the Church age (Heb. 8:8-13; 10:15-17). If there were a distinction between two new covenants, we might expect it to be stated here. But the author of Hebrews passes from the new covenant of the Church to the quotation from Jeremiah with no apparent shift of reference. It is sometimes maintained that the only purpose in the quotation of Jeremiah is to prove that the OT taught a new covenant which was to nullify the Mosaic covenant. To say this, however, is to miss the contextual flow of thought in Hebrews. The real point is that the Hebrew Christians are themselves under the new covenant, and therefore cannot go back to the old. This requires an identification of Jeremiah's new covenant with the new covenant in force during the present age. In introducing the quotation in 10:15, the author of Hebrews writes, "And the Holy Spirit also bears witness *to us.*" A context precedes in which believers *of this age* are put under the new covenant (vv. 8-14). In the following context (vv. 19ff.) the argument for *our* boldness to enter into the holy place rests on the new covenant just described in the quotation from Jeremiah. "Since *therefore,* brethren, we have confidence to enter the holy place by the blood of Jesus . . ." (v. 19).

The objections to a single new covenant stem mostly from certain features of the new covenant in Jeremiah 31 which do not find fulfillment in the Church age. That Jeremiah's account contains many details identical with the new covenant as delineated with reference to the Church and some details applicable only to Israel is exactly what we might expect because Jeremiah, an OT prophet, had Israel primarily in view. But the identical details together with the quotations in Hebrews are enough to show the singleness of the new covenant. The contrasting details simply manifest a necessary and understandable difference between applications to the Church and to Israel, respectively.[5]

Logically, the position that the Church and her chronology are altogether mysterious to the OT stands in danger of lapsing into hyperdispensationalism. For if we aver that the Church is wholly other from anything foreseen in the OT and at the same time admit the full force of citations of fulfilled OT passages in Acts and the pre-prison epistles of Paul, we can only deduce that the present dispensation began not until the close of Acts. To avoid such a conclusion, we must either minimize NT citations of fulfilled OT Scriptures—an invalid procedure—or we must acknowledge that the Church is not entirely unrelated to OT prophecy which pertains to Israel. Such an acknowledgement opens a dispensational door to posttribulationism by allowing, in principle, the possibility of the Church's presence on earth during a period of time predicted in the OT, such as is the tribulation.[6]

---

[5] Walvoord writes that the phrase "after those days" (Jer. 31:33) means "after the days of judgment and affliction described in the preceding context." However, the burden of the previous thirty verses is the millennial blessedness of Israel, not her tribulational affliction. The phrase probably refers to the days of the Sinaitic covenant described in the immediately preceding verse. Walvoord further argues that not "all" know the Lord today as Jeremiah pred cts they will and that the fulfillment of Jeremiah's new covenant is conditional upon Israel's regathering and permanent establishment in the land (Jer. 32:34, 37-41). It is true that these aspects of Jeremiah's prophecy have not yet found fulfillment. But neither was *all* of Joel's prophecy fulfilled at Pentecost—where were the "blood, and fire, and vapor of smoke"? This consideration demonstrates only that the present fulfillments in the Church are partial.

[6] But it does not endanger a consistent and balanced premillennialism: "It would be one-sided to say that the Old Testament kingdom prophecies never speak of the blessings which we enjoy in the present age of the gospel. This would in no way do justice to the manner in which the New Testament cites the Old Testament prophecies. On the other hand it would be likewise one-sided to declare that, because they speak of these now present blessings, henceforth no further, and perhaps still larger, fulfillment than the present can come. . . . The one would stand in opposition to the New Testament way of applying Old Testament prophecy; the other to the Old Testament text itself . . ." (E. Sauer, *From Eternity to Eternity*, 171).

Although a number of other OT quotations in the NT might have been considered (notably Acts 15:15-18, which also contains a probably insoluble textual problem in the crucial first phrase), we have looked only at those quotations which cannot be satisfied by a mere analogy between the present age and the millennial kingdom.

DISPENSATIONAL TRANSITIONS

Other things being equal, a clean break between dispensations at Pentecost would make easy the establishing of another clean break between the end of the Church age and the beginning of Daniel's seventieth week. However, without belittlement to the significance of the day of Pentecost and the baptism in the Spirit on that day, there are clear indications that the change from Israel to the Church took place over a prolonged period of transition dating from early in Jesus' ministry to a time posterior to Pentecost.

In Mark 2:21, 22 where the scribes and Pharisees ask Jesus why His disciples do not fast, Jesus defends the disciples by saying that the old dispensation is now passing away and the new coming in. His defense rests on the currency of the dispensational shift, for a future change would not excuse their action at the time.

According to Matthew 11:13 (cf. Luke 16:16), "the prophets and the Law" ceased with John the Baptist. According to John 1:17, "grace and truth were realized through Jesus Christ." The beholding by the fourth evangelist and by other eyewitnesses of Jesus' "glory . . . full of grace and truth " encompassed the whole public ministry of Jesus (so the context). Therefore, the dispensational exit of the law with John the Baptist and the entrance of grace and truth by Jesus Christ commenced long before Pentecost.

In Mark 7:18, 19, Jesus "declared all foods clean" some time before His passion, exaltation, and giving of the Spirit. The statement indicates an abrogation of at least part of the Mosaic law, according to which *not* all foods were clean. A prolonged period of transition enabled Jesus to anticipate His nailing to the cross the old ordinances, including taboos concerning "food and drink" (Col. 2:14, 16).

Jesus revealed to the apostles His future building of the Church (Matt. 16:18) and even gave them instructions concerning church discipline (Matt. 18:15-18). The transitional nature of His public ministry enabled Him to prepare the ground for the Church while still dealing with the nation of Israel. He also chose and trained the twelve apostles to become the foundation of the Church (Eph. 2:20; cf. Rev. 21:14). In the apostles we find the Church in embryo until its actual birth on the day of Pentecost.

Our Lord Jesus Himself originally spoke the salvific message of the present age (Heb. 2:3). This shows that the beginnings of the present dispensation reach back to a time prior to Pentecost. Even more pointedly, Paul makes the "sound words . . . of our Lord Jesus Christ" the standard of orthodoxy for Christian "doctrine" (1 Tim. 6:3). In view of the apostle's distinction between his own words, authoritative though they be, and those of the Lord (1 Cor. 7:10, 12, 25), the "sound words . . . of our Lord Jesus Christ" must refer to the teachings of Jesus during His earthly ministry, prior to Pentecost yet basic to the economy of the Church.[7]

Moving to the day of Pentecost and beyond, we discover transitional features in much of the period covered by the book of Acts even though the Church had already come fully into existence. In explaining the necessity for a transitional period, Roy L. Aldrich writes,

> It is simply the necessity of a prolonged time period to reach all the living believers of the former age with the Pentecostal message. . . . Only 120 received the initial baptism at Pentecost. There is no record of any simultaneous coming or outpouring of the Spirit upon individuals or groups in other places. . . . The evidence seems to point to the conclusion that all living believers, except those at Jerusalem in the upper room, passed into the new dispensation without the baptism of the Spirit. The Spirit was ministered to them later as they came in contact with the apostles or their associates. Paul speaks of one who had ministered the Spirit and worked miracles among the Galatians (Gal. 3:5).[8]

The historical process of baptism in the Spirit required a period of dispensational transition.

Upon healing the lame man, Peter addressed the "men of Israel" (Acts 3:12) in the following words:

> Repent therefore and return, that your sins may be wiped away, in order that times of refreshing may come from the presence of the Lord; and that he may send Jesus, the Christ appointed for you, whom heaven must receive until the period of restoration of all

---

[7] A further, slight suggestion of a transitional period crops up in the gap between the end of Daniel's sixty-ninth week (at the Triumphal Entry according to Sir Robert Anderson's calculations, generally accepted by pretribulationists) and the day of Pentecost.

[8] *BibSac*, 114:237, 238.

things, about which God spoke by the mouth of His holy prophets from ancient time (Acts 3:19-21).

The evident meaning of Peter's words is that if the men of Israel will turn to their Messiah, God will send Him back to earth for the promised restoration. This dramatic declaration had no relevance to the men whom Peter was addressing apart from the possibility of an immediate, or nearly immediate, restoration of the kingdom to Israel.[9] To explain how such an offer could have been made in good faith after the Church had come into existence, it is necessary to posit a transitional period during which God was dealing simultaneously with Israel and with the Church. Again, by means of the destruction of the temple in A.D. 70, God forcibly caused the outmoded sacrifices to cease and inaugurated the national and continuing chastisement of Israel for their rejection of Jesus the Messiah. This shows that well into the present age God was dealing with the nation of Israel in relation to the OT economy by bringing to an end the last vestige of that bygone era.

That the change in dispensations at the dawn of the Church age was gradual, extending over a period of years, rather than immediate and clean-cut may lead us to expect a similar transitional period in the twilight of the Church age. This future period of transition might well be the tribulation, during which God finishes His dealings with the Church and prepares Israel and the nations for the millennial kingdom of Christ.

UNIQUENESS AND UNITY

In an attempt to disconnect the Church from God's workings with Israel and the nations, emphasis frequently falls on the uniqueness of the Church. To be sure, many features about the Church and this age are unique. However, the Scriptures also teach the essential unity of all saints. Dispensational distinctions between God's people are economical and transitory. At a deeper level, all saints enjoy unity in Christ. That unity allows the possibility of, indeed provides the basis for, an overlapping of dispensations.

Evidence abounds that the Church merges with God's people

---

[9] See further J. S. Baxter, *Explore the Book*, VI, 13-20.

of all ages. Paul calls Abraham, himself an OT saint and the pro-
genitor of the Israelite nation, "the father of *all* who believe"
(Rom. 4:11; cf. vv. 12, 16). Paul also emphasizes the unity of
Abraham's seed through union with Christ: all believers, regardless of dispensation, compose one race—the seed of Abraham,
the corporate Christ (Gal. 3:16). The unity of all saints arises
out of the theological necessity for union with Christ, the sole
means by which the imputation of His righteousness takes place.
(Of course, OT saints received salvation in anticipation of the
historical accomplishment of redemption—Rom. 3:25, 26.)

God has grafted Gentile believers, belonging to the Church, as
wild branches into the olive tree of Israel (Rom. 11:16ff.).
Paul describes current believers from among the Gentiles as once
"excluded from the commonwealth of Israel, and strangers to the
covenants of promise," but now "brought near by the blood of
Christ" (Eph. 2:11-13). The description scarcely bespeaks a
discrete position for the Church.

Concerning OT believers, the author of Hebrews writes,
"Apart from us they should not be made perfect" (Heb.
11:40). Our relation of perfection and completion to OT saints
requires an underlying unity. Moreover, they share with current
believers a heavenly goal and destiny:

> He [Abraham] was looking for the city which has foundations,
> whose architect and builder is God. . . . All these died in faith, . . .
> having confessed that they were strangers and exiles on the
> earth. . . . But as it is, they desire a better country, that is a heav-
> enly one, . . . for He [God] has prepared a city for them (Heb.
> 11:9, 10, 13-16, against the opinion that the programs for Israel
> and the Church remain entirely distinct in that one is earthly, the
> other heavenly[10]).

John's description of the New Jerusalem provides the consummating evidence for the unity of all saints. On the gates of the
city are inscribed the names of the twelve tribes of Israel, encompassing the saved who belong to that company, and upon the
foundations the names of the twelve apostles, encompassing the
saved who belong to the Church (Rev. 21:12, 14). Thus the
final destinies of Israel and the Church converge.

The distinctiveness of the Church tends toward pretribula-

---

[10] Chafer, IV, 34; Strombeck, 58.

tionism. The oneness of the Church with saints of other dispensations tends toward posttribulationism. The scriptural equipoise leaves open—at this point—the chronological question concerning the rapture.

THE ECONOMY OF THE TRIBULATION

If the Church is to go through the tribulation, God will work simultaneously with two groups of covenant people, Israel and the Church. Millenarians of all varieties, including pretribulationists, should find the possibility of such simultaneous workings hard to deny. For during the millennium the Church will rule with Christ upon the earth (1 Cor. 6:2; Rev. 5:10) along with all other saints, those from the OT period and those martyred during the tribulation, even though by pretribulational standards the latter, also, do not belong to the Church (Rev. 20:4, 6). In addition to dealing with the different groups of saints who will rise in the first resurrection, God will work with Israelites living on earth in their natural bodies as subjects of the Davidic kingdom.

We already have a hint of God's simultaneous dealings with the Church and Israel in the return of the Jews to Palestine at the present time. They are returning in unbelief but they *are* returning. And that is a necessary prelude to the foretold tribulation. If the dispersion of Israel beginning in the first and second centuries A.D. and the reestablishment of Israel in Palestine have both occurred within the era of the Church, doubt settles over the contention that God cannot deal with two groups at the same time.

But it is not merely a matter of dealing with two groups at once. It is a matter of dealing simultaneously with, and through, two groups of *redeemed people* and *witnesses*. Will two diverse groups of saints, those who belong to the Church and those who belong to Israel coexist on earth and perhaps live according to different regulations? If so, will the tribulational Church be composed exclusively of Gentile believers? Will two distinct companies of witnesses preach the Gospel, maybe variations of it? Such questions arise quite naturally if we take the tribulation as transitional. But the mere existence of these questions does not preclude the possibility of the presence of the Church in the tribulation. For we might ask similar questions about the saints who we know came out of the Mosaic dispensation into the Church.

The following suggestions may help to solve the problematical nature of our understanding the tribulation as a transitional period during which both Israel and the Church share divine attention.

The tribulation knows only one group of redeemed people, the Church. The regenerate Jewish remnant will belong to the Church then as now (Rom. 11:5) and will be raptured at the posttribulational advent of Christ. That unconverted part of the Jewish nation who by God's special protection will physically survive the tribulation (Rev. 7:1-4) will repent, believe, and be saved as they see their Messiah descending. But they will have missed the rapture. Instead, they will enter the millennium as the natural-bodied subjects of the restored Davidic kingdom.

Indications are strong that the conversion of those Jews who will form the nucleus of the Davidic kingdom will take place suddenly at Jesus' return following the tribulation. The iniquity of the land will be removed "in one day" when "the Branch" comes forth (Zech. 3:8, 9). Nationwide repentance will take place when the Lord descends to deliver Jerusalem from her enemies, for the families of besieged Israel will not be able to mourn in repentance throughout the land until Messiah has come and smitten the invaders:

> . . . when the siege is against Jerusalem. . . . in that day . . . I will set about to destroy all the nations that come against Jerusalem. And I will pour out on the house of David and on the inhabitants of Jerusalem the Spirit of grace and of supplication, so that they will look on Me whom they have pierced; and they will mourn for Him, as one mourns for an only son. . . . And the land will mourn, every family by itself; . . . all the families that remain. . . . In that day a fountain will be opened for the house of David and for the inhabitants of Jerusalem, for sin and for impurity (Zech. 12:1-14:8).

The Lord will purify Israel when He suddenly comes to His temple (Mal. 3:1-5). Judgment and tribulation for Israel precede cleansing and deliverance (Jer. 30:7-11). "And a Redeemer will come to Zion, and to those who turn from transgression in Jacob" (Isa. 59:20). "All Israel will be saved; just as it is written, 'The Deliverer will come from Zion, He will remove ungodliness from Jacob.' 'And this is My covenant with them, when I take away their sins' " (Rom. 11:26, 27). Thus, the removal of "ungodliness from Jacob" when "all Israel will be saved" will occur at the inception of the Messiah's earthly rule, immediately upon His second advent.

During the tribulation the Mosaic system will be reinstituted in the land of Israel, and the presence of the temple, the offering of sacrifices, and the sabbath law give evidence (Matt. 24:15, 20; 2 Thess. 2:4). *But the reinstitution of the Mosaic system in Israel during the tribulation will not enjoy divine sanction.* General unbelief will still characterize Israel. God will not approve of Judaistic practices then any more than He approved of them during the period from the crucifixion of Christ to the destruction of the temple in A.D. 70. Worship in the temple will receive its sanction, not from God, but from the Antichrist, who "will make a firm covenant" with the Jews only to break it by putting "a stop to sacrifice and grain offering" (Dan. 9:27).

We may list the primary distinctive features of the Church's economy, in contrast to the Mosaic economy, as follows: (1) replacement of a forward-looking soteriology in the sacrificial system by a backward look to Christ's once-for-all sacrifice (Heb. 10:1-10); (2) emancipation from the Mosaic law as a way of life for believers (John 1:17; Rom. 6:14; Gal. 2:16-5:1); (3) change from a national to an individual emphasis, which will continue into the millennial economy (Jer. 31:29, 30); (4) abolition of the distinction between Jew and Gentile within the one body of Christ (Eph. 2:11-3:13); (5) world-wide evangelistic emphasis (Matt. 28:18-20 *et passim* in the NT); (6) the baptizing work and fulness of the Spirit for all believers on the basis of Christ's crucifixion, resurrection, and exaltation (Acts 2:32, 33, 38); (7) the personal presence of Christ in the believer (John 14:20, 23; Col. 1:26, 27); and (8) change from the Aaronic priesthood to the priesthood of Christ after the pattern of Melchizedek (Heb. 7:1-22). A posttribulational understanding such as that outlined in the preceding paragraphs need not weaken any of the listed dispensational distinctives.

In another approach to the economy of the tribulation we may consider whether the Jewish cast of the seventieth week precludes the presence of the Church. As an initial observation, the truism that Daniel's seventieth week relates to Israel would seem to require the absence of the Church no more than it requires the absence of the large host of Gentile saints whom preas well as posttributionists see in the tribulation. The Church did not figure in the first sixty-nine weeks, but neither did a group of Gentile saints comparable to those who will be on earth during the seventieth week. Nor had the Church yet come into existence. In that respect we can hardly compare the sixty-nine weeks with the seventieth week.

But we need further inquiry into the distinctive nature of the seventieth week. It is not merely that God will be dealing again with the nation of Israel, something He had begun to do many centuries before Daniel's vision. Rather, the seventy weeks represent a period of time during which God will work for Israel's cleansing, conversion, and righteousness (Dan. 9:24). Thus, despite the Messiah's being cut off, despite the destruction of the city and sanctuary, and despite the Antichrist's breaking a covenant with the Jews and perpetrating the abomination of desolation—by the end of the period God will have brought Israel to the place of finished transgression, reconciliation, and everlasting righteousness. Nothing intrinsic to the promise would prevent God's dealing with the Church during the seventieth week while at the same time bringing Israel toward the stated goals. Insofar as the desecration and destruction of the temple during the Church age (A.D. 70) precursively fulfill the prophecy of the Antichrist's abomination of desolation (Dan. 9:27), the contention that Jewish elements in the seventieth week exclude the Church falls to the ground. It seems more natural that the final fulfillment should follow the precursive pattern by likewise falling within the Church age.

Again within a posttribulational understanding of the tribulation, the Church will be God's sole witnessing body during the tribulation. For all the redeemed of that period, Jews and Gentiles, will belong to the Church (see above). Not until their conversion at the Parousia, which inaugurates Christ's millennial reign, will God reinstate the nation of Israel as His witness to the nations. *Prima facie,* it is reasonable that the Church rather than Israel should represent God to the world during the time Israel undergoes final, bitter chastisement.

But will not the 144,000 Jews evangelize the world by heralding the Gospel of the kingdom during the tribulation? Not a single statement in Scripture supports this common tenet. Jesus said that "this gospel of the kingdom shall be preached in the whole world for a witness to all the nations" (Matt. .24:14), but He did not identify the preachers with the 144,000. Furthermore, we do not need to look upon "the gospel of the kingdom" preached in the whole world as a special message committed to Jews. It is simply the one Gospel known and preached already: in Rome Paul proclaimed "the kingdom of God" as "gospel" after turning from the Jews to the Gentiles (Acts 28:30, 31, especially in the Greek text).

The two passages which speak of the 144,000 (Rev. 7:1-8; 14:1-5) say nothing about evangelistic activity during the tribulation. An angel dubs them "servants" (7:3), but offers no further explanation. In the second passage there follows a vision of an angel with the everlasting gospel (14:6, 7), but nothing is said which would link the 144,000 with the preaching of the everlasting gospel. To the contrary, the possibility of such a connection seems to be precluded by the fact that the 144,000 are standing with the Lamb on Mount Zion and singing "before the four living creatures and the elders"—surely indicative of a posttribulational scene—whereas the angel has good tidings for people still in the tribulation. (Isaiah 43:10—"You are My witnesses"—sometimes appears in argument for the theory that the 144,000 will evangelize; however, the context shows that "witnesses" there means "spectators" of the Lord's mighty works, not "preachers" of the Gospel.)

In summary, then, we do wrong to think that the Church and this age are mysteries, that the mysterious character of a truth sets it apart dispensationally and chronologically from prophecy pertaining to Israel, that dispensations are broken cleanly, and that the presence of the Church in the tribulation would cause confusion in God's redemptive economy. We ought rather to recognize the connection of the Church with other dispensations and saints. This connection becomes possible and actual in the broad use of the term "mystery," in specific OT indications of this age, in NT applications of OT prophecies to the Church, in the prolonged period of transition during which the old economy faded away and the new began, in the oneness of all the redeemed in Christ, and in the united, heavenly goal of both Israel and the Church.[11] With the Church as the sole body of redeemed during the tribulation and with the conversion and reinstatement of Israel not until the second coming itself, there results neither weakening nor blurring of the distinctive features of the present economy or of the Jewish features of Daniel's seventieth

---

[11] In his final article in "The Millennial Series" (*BibSac*, 115: 291-301), Walvoord concedes much ground along this line. The concessions undermine his whole dispensational foundation for pretribulationism.

week. Posttribulationism accords well with a scripturally measured dispensationalism. Conversely, a scripturally measured dispensationalism gives no advantage to pretribulationism.[12]

---

[12] Hopefully the foregoing treatment of dispensationalism corrects the following statements: "(1) Posttribulationism must be based on a denial of dispensationalism and all dispensational distinctions. . . . (2) Consequently, the position rests on a denial of the distinctions between Israel and the church" (Pentecost, 164).

3

Expectation and Imminence

How shall Christians look for the return of their Lord if the tribulation must precede it? How can the prospect of that return exercise a purifying influence on the Church if the event cannot take place at any moment? These are the basic questions which face posttribulationists with regard to the alleged imminence of the Parousia.

We should first of all note a lack of identity between belief in imminence on the one hand and pretribulationism on the other. By common consent imminence means that so far as we know no predicted event will *necessarily* precede the coming of Christ. The concept incorporates three essential elements: suddenness, unexpectedness or incalculability, and a possibility of occurrence at any moment.[1] But these elements would require only that Christ *might* come before the tribulation, not that He must. Imminence would only raise the possibility of pretribulationism on a sliding scale with mid- and posttribulationism. It is singularly strange that the most popularly cherished argument for pretribulationism should suffer such an obvious and critical limitation.

The limitation of imminence aside, an expectant attitude toward the Lord's return does not contradict a posttribulational belief in necessarily preceding events. If imminence is to be established,

---

[1] Cf. Linton, 12.

it must be done on grounds other than NT admonitions to watch for the Parousia. Indeed, such admonitions regularly pertain to the coming of Christ after the tribulation. These assertions need justification.

NT TERMINOLOGY FOR EXPECTANCY

The words used in the NT for an attitude of expectancy toward the Parousia occur in all branches of Greek literature, sometimes with reference to an imminent event but sometimes not so and at yet other times with reference to a general attitude unrelated to any event. If a particular goal does come into focus, the vocabulary of expectancy does not indicate whether or not other events will necessarily intervene. Therefore, as such, the terminology of watchfulness cannot decide the issue for or against imminence.

The following examples from the various branches of Greek literature demonstrate that the NT words for expectancy appear in passages where one or more of the ideas of suddenness, incalculability, and possibility of occurrence at any moment—the loss of any one of which subverts an appeal to imminence—are absent (OT references are to the LXX):

Προσδέχομαι (*wait for, expect*) concerns the second coming in Luke 12:36; Titus 2:13; and perhaps Jude 21. Yet Paul uses προσδέχομαι in saying that he "looks for" the resurrection, including that of the "unjust" (Acts 24:15) which takes place in a premillennial scheme not until after the millennium. The Jewish expectation of Israel's Messianic deliverance carried with it the recognition of necessarily preceding signs, such as the ministry of a herald (Isa. 40:1ff.; Mal. 4:5), but προσδέχομαι also describes that expectation (Luke 2:25, 38). In Ruth 1:13 an interval of many years comes into view: "Would you therefore wait until they [yet unborn sons of Naomi to be husbands for Orpah and Ruth] were grown?" "Let Lucia wait until the year [expires]" (MM). "We will wait here many a day" (Homer, *Odyssey* 2.205; also 2.186 and *Iliad* 19.234). See also 4 Macc. 5:37.

Ἀπεκδέχομαι (*await eagerly*) finds the second coming and coincident events as its objects in Romans 8:23, 25; 1 Corinthians 1:7; Galatians 5:5; Philippians 3:20; and Hebrews 9:28. The word cannot imply imminence in Romans 8:19, because there Paul writes that the physical creation longingly awaits the manifestation of the sons of God. Then the curse will be lifted. Yet during the tribulation the earth will undergo intense suffering because of sin. Hence her earnest expectation concerns a posttribulational deliverance and cannot connote imminence. Peter uses ἀπεκδέχομαι (1 Pet. 3:20) of God's waiting with longsuffering in Noah's day. But the Flood was not imminent, for God had longsufferingly prescribed an interval of one hundred and twenty years (Gen. 6:3).

Ἐκδέχομαι (expect, wait for) refers to the second coming in James 5:7, where James likens the expectancy of believers to that of a husbandman who patiently waits through the prolonged period of the early and latter rains until the harvest. We could hardly find a more nonimminent usage. Luke uses ἐκδέχομαι also for Paul's waiting in Athens for Silas and Timothy although Paul knew they could not arrive until sufficient time for travel had elapsed (Acts 17:15, 16). Cf. 1 Corinthians 16:10, 11; and Hebrews 10:13.

In Matthew 24:50 and Luke 12:46 Jesus uses προσδοκάω (wait for, look for, expect) in connection with His Parousia. Again, although the (initial) coming of the Messiah was not an imminent, unheralded event, προσδοκάω describes Jewish expectation of it (Matt. 11:3; Luke 3:15; 7:19, 20). Peter exhorts Christians to look for the day of God and the new heavens and earth, which will not come into being until at least the close of the tribulation and probably not until the close of the millennium. Consequently, the expectancy enjoined cannot possibly depend upon, or even be accompanied by, imminence (2 Pet. 3:12-14). At the same time, the exhortation to purity—"be diligent to be found by Him in peace, spotless and blameless"—demonstrates the needlessness of imminence for the purifying effect of the blessed hope. See also Ps. 103(104):27; 24(25):3; 2 Macc. 7:14; 12:44; 3 Macc. 5:24 ("waited impatiently for the dawn"); Isa. 38:18; Lam. 2:16.

Νήφω (be sober, self-controlled, free from excess) designates an attitude appropriate to believers at the second coming (1 Thess. 5:6, 8 and 1 Pet. 1:13; 4:7) but neither demands nor supplies the thought of imminence. In 2 Timothy 4:5 the word occurs apart from any event, imminent or otherwise: "Be sober in all things, endure hardship. . . ." Similarly, "I will send you the letter by Syrus in order that you may read it in a sober mood and be self-condemned" (citation in MM). " Νήφω is found along with ἁγνεύω to mark the proper state of intending worshippers . . ." (MM).

Γρηγορέω, used with reference to the second coming in Matthew 24:42, 43; 25:13; Mark 13:34, 35, 37; Luke 12:37, 39;

1 Thessalonians 5:6, 10; Revelation 16:15; and perhaps 3:2, 3, means *to be* or *keep awake*. Not dependent on imminence, it denotes alertness in prayer (Matt. 26:38, 40, 41; Mark 14:34, 35, 37; Col. 4:2). See Lamentations 1:14; Daniel (Theod.) 9:14; Baruch 2:9.

'Αγρυπνέω (*be* or *keep oneself awake, be on the alert*) relates to the second coming in Mark 13:33 and Luke 21:36. Imminence is irrelevant to the two other passages where the term appears in the NT: Paul exhorts to wakefulness in prayer (Eph. 6:18) and the author of Hebrews urges watchfulness in the care of the church (Heb. 13:17). See 2 Kings 12:21; Job 21:32; Psalm 101(102):7; Canticles 5:2; 1 Esdras 8:59; and compare the meaning "to lie awake" or "pass sleepless nights" (Thgn. 471, Hp. l.c., Pl. *Lg.* 695a—LSJ).

Βλέπω (*see, look at*) has the second coming in view in Mark 13:33 and Hebrews 10:25. This word appears over 130 times elsewhere in the NT and not once with the implication of imminence. See also Genesis 45:12; 48:10; Joshua 18:14; Judges 9:36; 1 Kings 3:2; 4:15; Nehemiah 2:17; Psalm 9:32(10:11); Proverbs 4:25; and numerous other references, and further, MM.

'Αναμένω(*wait for, expect*) has to do with the second coming in 1 Thessalonians 1:10. That constitutes its only occurrence in the NT. Usage outside the NT does not require imminence. See Judith 7:12 ("Remain in your camp"); Sirach 2:7; 5:7; 6:19; 2 Macc. 6:14 ("The Lord patiently forbears"); and 1 Kings 13:8 and Psalm 24(25):5 in the version of Symmachus. The word is used of "debtors who are to pay up without 'waiting for' the time allowed them" (MM) and of "awaiting the dawn" (Homer, *Odyssey* 19.342). The end of a stated period for payment of debts and the dawn hardly represent the incalculability and capability of occurrence at any time which an implication of imminency in ἀναμένω would require.

Although ἐγγύς (*near*) and the phrase "at the door" do not describe our expectancy, it is sometimes thought that these expressions denote imminence in Philippians 4:5 ("The Lord is near") and James 5:8, 9 ("the coming of the Lord is at hand. . . . the Judge is standing right at the door"). However, Paul's statement may refer, not to the second coming, but to the personal nearness of Christ to His children in adversity (cf. the context). Even otherwise, both expressions occur in Matthew 24:33 and Mark 13:29 concerning Jesus' *post*tribulational coming, just described in preceding verses, and alongside the illustration of the fig tree, which teaches that Jesus will return only after the signalling events of the tribulation have occurred: "even so you too, *when you see all these things*, recognize that He is near, right at the door." In Philippians 4:5 Paul fails to mention precursory signs simply because he does not purpose to teach the details of eschatology in this passage. The illustration of the husbandman waiting for the early and latter rains further cancels any implication of imminence in James 5.

'Εγγύς also describes the Jewish feasts, which, far from being sudden or incalculable, fell on set dates (John 2:13; 6:4; 7:2; 11:55). Neither does the verb ἐγγίζω, which relates to the second coming in Romans 13:12; Hebrews 10:25; and James 5:8; necessitate imminence, suddenness, unexpectedness. For it also refers to the posttribulational advent in Luke 21:28 and to "the end of all things" in 1 Peter 4:7. And Jesus uses it concerning the seasons of the year (Matt. 21:34; 24:32; Mark 13:28; Luke 21:30. In the same fashion we say that a holiday is "near," although it may be some days or weeks in the future. The nearness of Christ's coming, then, does not imply its imminence.

Since the words for expectancy do not resolve the question of imminence one way or the other, their contexts become decisive. We need therefore to examine contexts in order to discover whether features in them besides the watching itself present the Parousia as imminent.

ADMONITIONS TO WATCH

The first admonition to watch appears in Luke 12:35-48. Jesus describes neither a posttribulational advent nor an alleged pretribulational advent. Watchfulness constitutes the sole theme. It is noteworthy, however, that Jesus gives a hint of delay in His return by the words, "Whether he comes in the second watch, or even in the third . . ." (v. 38). The phraseology and the parables are almost identical to those in the Olivet Discourse. Therefore we are probably to understand these exhortations in the same fashion as those, to which we now proceed.

The strongest and most extensive warnings to watch in the entire NT appear in the Olivet Discourse (Matt. 24:32-25:30; Mark 13:28-37; Luke 21:28-36). There Jesus gives not the slightest hint of a pretribulational rapture in the chronological outline of events which occupies the first section of His discourse. Yet a very full description of the posttribulational Parousia forms the climax. If, in accordance with the context, we attach the admonitions to watch to the posttribulational advent, which is not imminent, there is no reason to infer an imminent coming before the tribulation from similar admonitions in the epistles. If expectancy in the Olivet Discourse finds its object in an event at the close of the tribulation, expectancy in the epistles may do the same. In the epistles the comparative isolation and brevity of admonitions to watch aggravate the difficulty of inferring imminence from them but not from fuller admonitions in the Olivet Discourse.

On the other hand, it may be suggested that, despite context, the exhortations from Olivet do not refer to the posttribulational advent of Christ, but anticipate His pretribulational coming revealed later in the epistles.[2] But a glance at the flow of thought in the Olivet Discourse will reveal how violently such an interpretation wrests the section on watching from the section which treats the posttribulational advent and precursive, including tribulational, events:

> When you see all these things [the tribulational signs minutely delineated], recognize that He is near, right at the door. . . . But of that day and hour no one knows ["that" necessarily has its antecedent in the previously described Parousia]. . . . For the coming [Parousia, as in v. 27] of the Son of man will be just like the days of Noah. . . . Therefore be on the alert ["therefore" connects the admonition with the preceding context about the posttribulational advent]. . . . For this reason you be ready. . . . Be on the alert then, for you do not know the day nor the hour (excerpts from Matt. 24:32-25:13).

The parable of the fig tree and Luke 21:28 conclusively establish the connection of the admonitions to watch with the posttribulational advent and percursive signs:

> But when these things begin to take place, straighten up and lift up your heads, because your redemption is drawing near.

Luke 21:28 does *not* teach that the *redemption* of those who watch will take place at the beginning of "these things."[3] Rather,

[2] Wood, 96-99.
[3] *Pace* Wood, 103, 104.

at the beginning of these things disciples of Christ are to recognize that their redemption is drawing *"near."* Since "these things" include tribulational events, a pretribulational redemption would have already taken place! It is not correct to say that Jesus exhorts His followers to watch *after* the signs have all appeared.[4] On the contrary, Jesus tells the disciples to lift up their heads, not after the signs, but "when these things *begin* to take place."[5]

Some segregate the exhortations to watchfulness in the Olivet Discourse and those in the epistles: "The church is uniformly exhorted to look for the coming of the Lord, while believers in the tribulation are directed to look for signs."[6] But Jesus directs tribulational saints to look for His *Parousia*—and to do so *through* the signs. John 14:3; 1 Corinthians 15:51, 52; and 1 Thessalonians 4:13-18 are cited to show the absence of signs in exhortations to the Church.[7] However, in the first two passages cited there are no exhortations to watch, and in 1 Thessalonians the exhortation follows in chapter five in connection with the day of the Lord, which will be preceded by signs—viz., the apostasy and the man of lawlessness, or Antichrist (2 Thess. 2:2-4), Elijah (Mal. 4:5), and celestial phenomena (Joel 2:30, 31; cf. Luke 21:25).

In support of the thesis that God intends signs only for Israel, appeal is made to 1 Corinthians 1:22: "Jews ask for signs. . . ." The verse does not bear on our discussion here, however, because Paul has in mind *miracles* as divine authorization of the Gospel, not events preliminary to the posttribulational coming of Christ. Even had Paul included eschatological signs in his purview, the thesis would not gain support. For God *did* grant signs to be done before the Gentiles (see, for example, Gal. 3:5 and Acts, *passim*). The verse merely indicates that Jews *ask* for a sign before they are willing to believe (and even then most of them do not), not that God never gives signs to Gentiles. He did, and was doing it through Paul at the very time of the Corinthian correspondence (Acts 19:10ff.).

---

[4] *Pace* Walvoord, *RQ*, 82.

[5] The belief of Thiessen that the admonitions from Olivet "belong to the Church as well as to Israel" is puzzling, if not muddled, since he puts himself in the awkward position of inferring imminence for the Church but not for Israel (Thiessen, 47).

[6] Walvoord, *BibSac*, 113:197, and *RQ*, 196.

[7] Walvoord, *BibSac*, 113:303.

When Jesus tells His disciples that it is not for them to know the times or epochs (Acts 1:6, 7), He does not deny the relevance of signs. He rather indicates that fulfillment of the great commission (v. 8) commands greater attention than interest in the restoration of Israel. *Delay* for the fulfillment of that commission, not imminence, is taught here.

In the NT outside the gospels we do not confront so complete an absence of eschatological signs as is sometimes claimed, to say nothing of the fact that the writers of the epistles nowhere negate the relevance of the signs given by Jesus. Conditions of gross wickedness signal the last days (1 Tim. 4:1-3; 2 Tim. 3:1-7; Jude 17, 18; cf. Matt. 24:11; 2 Pet. 3:3, 4). The revelation of the man of lawlessness and the apostasy presage the day of the Lord (2 Thess. 2:1-5), for which the Church is to watch (1 Thess. 5:4-8). *Prima facie,* the tribulational events delineated in the major portion of Revelation are meant to be signs for the Church; otherwise Revelation loses most of its significance as a document addressed "to the seven churches that are in Asia" (1:4). Furthermore, even now OT prophecies are very possibly coming to pass, a broad hint that signs do have relevance to the Church. Outstanding are the rise of Russia (Ezek. 38, 39), the revived national consciousness of the Jews and their restoration to the land of Palestine as a reconstituted nation (cf. Jer. 23:7, 8; Ezek. 37; Joel 3:1; Zech. 10:9).

In turning outside the gospels to specific exhortations to watch, we may note two items. First, isolated verses or even clauses within verses make some of the exhortations (Gal. 5:5; Phil. 3:20; 1 Thess. 1:10; Tit. 2:13; Heb. 9:28; 1 Pet. 1:13; Jude 21). We can hardly view the omission of tribulational signs as decisive, then, for it may derive from the taking for granted of a knowledge of the signs (cf. 2 Thess. 2:5 with 1 Thess. 5:1) and from the inappropriateness of signs in those passages because of the uneschatological nature of the surrounding subject matter.

Second, prophetic passages which form the context of other exhortations to watch require considerable explaining away by any who would infer imminence from those exhortations. In Romans 8:18-25 the redemption of our bodies coincides with the deliverance of nature. But that deliverance will certainly not occur before the ravages of the tribulation. In 1 Thessalonians 5:4-8 Paul exhorts Christians to watchfulness for the day of the Lord, which "will not come unless the apostasy comes first, and the man of lawlessness is revealed" (2 Thess. 2:3). In 1 Corinthians 1:7; 2 Timothy 4:8; and Hebrews 10:25 the exhortations likewise relate to "the day," presumably the same day of the Lord for which Paul urges preparation and provides precursive events in his Thessalonian correspondence. Exhortations to watch have to do with "the end" (1 Cor. 1:7; 1 Pet. 4:7); yet, as we shall see, "the end" comes after the tribulation. Apart from the term "end," these verses also are eschatologically isolated, just as those discussed in the last paragraph. The exhortation in Revelation 16:15 comes before the last bowl of divine wrath, which immediately precedes the posttribulational advent, and is elicited by the mention in verses fourteen and sixteen of the Battle of Armageddon, the occasion of Jesus' return.[8]

The exhortations in the Olivet Discourse refer by context to the posttribulational Parousia and thus undermine the premise that expectancy presupposes imminence. Elsewhere the exhortations, shorter by comparison, appear either in uneschatological passages or in passages which tend toward posttribulationalism. In his presentation of proof-passages even so strong an advocate for imminence as Payne feels forced to rest his argument on the terms for expectancy[9] despite prior admission that those terms in themselves do not necessarily connote imminence.[10]

A NECESSARY DELAY

If the second coming could not have been imminent for those originally commanded to watch at the time they were so commanded, then the commanded expectancy could not have implied imminence of the event looked for. It then becomes unnecessary for us to regard Jesus' coming as imminent, for we have received no further and no different exhortations. In other words, if a delay in the Parousia of at least several years was compatible with expectancy in apostolic times, a delay for the several years of the tribulation is compatible with expectancy in current times.

Jesus clearly indicates to the early disciples that His coming will be delayed for some time. The express purpose of the parable concerning the nobleman who went to a "far country" is that the disciples should not think "the kingdom of God was going to

---

[8] The context is therefore not irrelevant, *pace* Payne, 101.
[9] Pp. 95-102.
[10] Pp. 86-88.

appear immediately" (Luke 19:11-27). "While the bridegroom was delaying" also intimates delay (Matt. 25:5). In the parable of the talents, Jesus likens His return to the lord who "after a long time" came back from a far country (Matt. 25:19).

Jesus bases the parable of the servants on the presupposition of a delay in His coming, for without the delay no interval would have provided opportunity for the servants to display their true colors (Luke 12:41-48; Matt. 24:45-51). And when Jesus has the wicked servant say, "My master will be a long time in coming," He tacitly admits that there will be a delay. As the wicked servant's eternal judgment "with the unbelievers (or hypocrites)" shows, *the contrast in servants distinguishes true disciples, whose characteristic it is to watch, from false disciples, whose characteristic it is not to watch.* The necessary delay made no difference to the expectant attitude of the true servant, but it revealed the falsity of the wicked servant. Jesus does not condemn recognition of delay, but the attitude which takes selfish advantage of the delay. Moreover, readiness denotes not so much tiptoe anticipation as faithful service day by day: "Who then is the faithful and sensible steward, whom his master will put in charge of his servants to give them their rations at the proper time? Blessed is that slave whom his master finds so doing when he comes" (Luke's version).

We might suppose that the long period of delay required in the parables would be satisfied by "a few years."[11] But a few years is all the delay posttribulationism requires. Jesus could not have given in good faith the great commission with its worldwide extent—"all the nations" and "the remotest part of the earth"— without providing a considerable lapse of time in order that the disciples might have opportunity to perform the task. The long-range missionary endeavors of Paul may not possess independent argumentative weight (Paul's journey to Rome was contingent on the Lord's will, Rom. 1:9, 10). Yet as the Lord's commission for him to go "far away to the Gentiles" (Acts 22:21) and to witness before "kings" (Acts 9:15) and as the promise in Jerusalem that he would "witness . . . at Rome" (Acts 23:11; cf. 27:24) link up with the great commission generally, they gain considerable weight.

---

[11] Walvoord, *BibSac*, 113:2.

It may be countered, with an appeal to Paul's statement "the gospel ... was proclaimed in all creation under heaven" (Col. 1:23), that "the extensive preaching of the gospel in the first century might ... satisfy the program of preaching to the ends of the earth."[12] However, Paul wrote his statement during his first Roman imprisonment, some thirty years after Jesus gave the great commission, an interval more than four times as long as the tribulation. And Paul had not fulfilled his intention of visiting Spain, where the Gospel had not yet been preached (Rom. 15:20, 24). Evidently he himself did not regard the great commission as fulfilled. Apparently, then, in Colossians 1:23 Paul is not affirming a fulfillment of the great commission, but is setting the universality of the Gospel (the good news is *for* all men, even though it has not reached all men) in opposition to the esotericism of the Colossian heresy.

Of corroborative value is the personal history of Peter (John 21:18, 19; 2 Pet. 1:14). Jesus foretold that Peter, then middle-aged ("when you were younger ..."), would die at an infirm old age ("when you grow old, you will stretch out your hands, and someone else will gird you ..."). If we try to save the imminence of the Parousia by saying that Peter could have been martyred at any time, we forget that his infirmity and old age were not imminent. And if we say that the prediction concerning Peter was not common knowledge among Christians until long after his death, we overlook the presence of other apostles on the occasion of the prediction. Furthermore, John writes of the incident in order to correct a misimpression which had arisen concerning his own death. The whole matter, then, must have received some publicity in the early Church.

To claim that these delays were general in nature, without specific length,[13] merely avoids the issue. Whether general or specific, long or short, the delays were delays and, by being stated, rendered the second coming nonimminent to the apostolic Church. Moreover, the delays were not entirely general in nature. The specificity of the great commission ("in Jerusalem, and in all Judea and Samaria, and even to the remotest part of the earth"), of the promise that Paul should bear witness at Rome, and of Peter's old age as a time of infirmity to the degree of in-

---

12 Walvoord, *BibSac*, 113:2.
13 Wood, 37.

ability to dress himself make the delays much more pointed than the doctrine of imminence can allow.

Again, to claim that the delays had been fulfilled by the time the exhortations to watch were written[14] runs afoul of historical facts. *At least* those exhortations to watch in the epistles appeared in writing before the disciples could have fulfilled the great commission, before Paul had completed his extensive missionary efforts, and before Peter had reached old age, become infirm, and died. From the very beginning, even before the written exhortations, Christians knew that they were to watch through the *oral* ministry of Jesus and the apostles and prophets. In one of his *earliest* epistles Paul already commends believers for their watchfulness (1 Thess. 1:9, 10). The point remains that if watching could not have connoted imminence in the apostolic age, it need not connote imminence now.

But should we not think that all else was contingent upon the second coming, that an "only if Christ does not return beforehand" qualified every other expectation? Possibly, but only possibly, in connection with the personal circumstances of Peter and Paul. It is very hard to think, however, that an imminent return of Christ might have taken away sufficient opportunity to fulfil the great commission. Moreover, when imminence becomes the ruling principle by which all else was and is rendered contingent, even the events of the tribulation do not have to take place; they might "die on the vine" just as the great commission and the predictions concerning Paul and Peter would have done had Jesus returned beforehand.

STIMULUS FOR HOLY LIVING

The purifying influence of the second coming does not lie in the fear of "getting caught" at the unexpected moment of the Parousia, but in the fact that our *whole* life will pass in review before the Lord. Jesus may not come today, but what we do today He will examine when He does come, and that is what incites us to holiness of life. The character and consequences of an event determine its motivating force much more than the time of its occurrence. Although we recognize the necessity of an intervening period, the delay does not lessen our anticipation. The cer-

---

[14] Wood, 39.

tainty, the character, and the blessedness of our Lord's return make for us a glorious prospect which no interval of time can dim.

Must we stop looking for Christ Himself, then, and begin to look for the intervening events?[15] Hardly, because looking for a preceding series of events does not exclude looking likewise for Jesus' personal return immediately following. Expectancy of the Parousia depends, not upon the temporal factor, but upon an eagerness to see our Lord face to face, an eagerness intervening events cannot diminish if our love for Him is genuine. Besides, the intervening events play a *positive* role in our looking for Jesus Himself. Rather than diverting our attention from the second coming, they direct our attention to it. For they are guideposts, warnings, confirmations of faith, incitements to readiness, encouragements for our anticipation. The return of Christ is the goal toward which they point. The coming to pass of definite signs that harbinger His return will intensify expectancy more than a vague "any moment" which has lain dormant for almost two thousand years.

In Titus 2:11-14, where we read of "the blessed hope," the incentive to holy living is "the grace of God." In 2 Peter 3:11-14, the incentive is the character of the new creation, in which no unrighteousness will dwell. In 1 Thessalonians 5:2-4, Paul writes that the day of the Lord will come as a thief in the night to those who are not watching, the unsaved; but those who are watching, the saved, need *not* be surprised. In 1 John 3:1-3, the incentive to self-purifying is the expectation of one day becoming just as pure as Christ is. In none of these passages does imminence form the crux of the exhortation to righteous living.[16]

PREDICTABILITY

The question arises whether posttribulationism would enable us to calculate the time of Jesus' return—say, by figuring seven

---

[15] Payne, 98; Linton, 35, 36.

[16] Wuest attempts to build a case for imminence on the subjunctive mood introduced by ἐάν in 1 John 2:28: "When he shall appear" (*BibSac*, 114:68, 69). But ἐάν with the subjunctive in the protasis of a conditional sentence by no means must denote uncertainty in the sense of imminence, and, in fact, usually does not. For example, Paul uses this very construction of his proposed journey to Spain, a journey he planned to make only after visiting Jerusalem and then Rome (Rom. 15:24). All that John's exhortation requires is the possibility of Jesus' appearance within a lifetime: "if He should appear" (NASB).

prophetic years (2,520 days) from the Antichrist's making a covenant with the Jews to the second advent, or at least by counting 1,260 days (three and a half years) from the easily recognizable breaking of the covenant ("when you *see* the abomination of desolation") to the Parousia. A negative answer to the question arises out of two considerations:

First, Jesus said that the days of the tribulation will be "cut short," or "shortened" (Matt. 24:22; Mark 13:20—not "short" or "limited" as sometimes understood). It has been suggested that the shortened days are individual days reduced in number of hours.[17] The more natural understanding, however, is to take "those days" collectively, for how would shortened individual days prevent "all flesh" from being destroyed? And we may balk at supposing that the earth will rotate faster than usual when a more natural understanding avoids such a supposition. If those days as a whole will be shortened, we may think that Daniel's seventieth week is, already, the shortened period. Apparent support for such an interpretation comes from the past tenses ("had been cut short," "had shortened," "shortened"). But the future tense ("shall be cut short") shows that the past tenses are to be treated as the common "prophetic perfect." The future is as certain as the past. And the fact that Jesus made His statement long after the revelation of the chronology of seventy weeks renders untenable the view that the seven years of the seventieth week are already the shortened period. Jesus hardly implies that God originally planned the seventieth week to run longer than seven years, or that He intended a period longer than the seventy weeks. The very symbolism of the number seven militates against the suggestion. To say that the cutting short refers to the already determined end of an already determined length of time renders Jesus' statement vapid. We do better to take it at face value. For the sake of the persecuted saints God will not allow the seventieth week to run its full course. So long as this interpretation is even credible, not to say convincing, no one will be able to calculate the end of the tribulation with certainty.

Second, that which positively proves the time of the posttribulational advent to be incalculable is Jesus' plain statement that no man, not even the angels or the Son of man, can know the day or hour of His coming—*and this He said in immediate con-*

---

[17] M. Coder, in *Understanding the Times*, 167.

nection with His coming after the tribulation (Matt. 24:36, 42, 43; Mark 13:32). The element of uncertainty is there,[18] but it is slight. Jesus' emphasis on "day," "hour," and "watch of the night" shows that we shall not know exactly. But the delineation of preceding signs, including especially if not exclusively tribulational events, shows that we will know approximately. The shortening of the tribulation thus enables us to resolve general predictability and specific unpredictability without rending the exhortations to watch from their posttribulational context and without minimizing the function of signalling events by resorting to the historical view[19] with its vagaries. We are to watch, both because we cannot know exactly and because we must be alert to the signs which will enable us to know approximately.[20]

The full force of the exhortations to watch for Jesus' return, then, does not require imminence of the Parousia. A tribulational interval no more destroys expectancy than did necessary delays during the apostolic age. A number of the exhortations to watch, including the fullest, appear in the immediate context of the posttribulational advent and include the observation of precursive signs during the tribulation. Such signs do not enervate expectancy, they stimulate it. Self-purification in the light of the second coming rests, not on the fear of sudden exposure, but on the certainty of the event and on the knowledge that the conduct of our whole Christian life will be revealed in the light of divine presence. Concerning NT exhortations to watch, we are led to the conclusion: until tribulational events have taken place, New Testament expectancy does not mean to look for the return of the Lord as a present possibility, but to look *forward* to His return after the events of the tribulation.

---

[18] As Payne emphasizes, 95, 96—cf. also Matt. 24:42.

[19] I.e., that the desecration and destruction of the temple in A.D. 70 exhausted the prophecy of the abomination of desolation.

[20] Cf. Walvoord, *BibSac*, 129:25, 27.

4

Wrath and Rapture

We now examine the argument that the tribulation will be a time of divine wrath and therefore the Church must first be removed from the earthly scene of judgment.

> Why should a child of God's grace—who is saved by grace, who is kept by grace, who has all the wonderful promises of God—be forced to go through a period which according to Scripture is expressly designed as a time of judgment upon a Christ-rejecting world?[1]

Sometimes the argument is so stated as to be marred by an appeal to fear.[2]

THE EXEMPTION OF ALL SAINTS FROM DIVINE WRATH

Pre- and posttribulationists agree that a host of saints, consisting of both Jews and Gentiles, will be present on earth during the tribulation. Therefore, whatever problems pretribulationists may turn up regarding the presence of the Church in a period of divine wrath are their own problems, too; for whether or not the tribulational saints belong to the Church or to another group of redeemed people, they also have escaped God's anger by virtue of

---

[1] Walvoord, *Thess*, 83.
[2] See, e.g., Linton, 6, 21, 34-37.

the blood of Christ, who underwent their judgment for them (Rev. 7:14). Will Jewish and Gentile saints suffer God's wrath during the tribulation, according to pretribulationism? If not, neither would the Church have to suffer God's wrath in the tribulation. If so, arguments against the suffering of wrath by the Church apply equally to tribulational saints of other sorts.

Or, if tribulational saints will receive shelter within the period of divine wrath, may not the same hold true if Christians enter that period, i.e., if Christians turn out to *be* the saints of the tribulation? "Romans 8:1 assures that there is no condemnation, or judgment, to them that are in Christ Jesus . . . does it not also include deliverance from that time of judgment . . . which is primarily characterized by the pouring out of the vials of the wrath of God?"[3] But would not tribulational saints not belonging to the Church nevertheless be in Christ? Would not His blood justify them (Rev. 7:14!)? If not, how would they be saved? If so, why would they be in the tribulation, if the pretribulational line of reasoning is correct?

We can hardly answer that endurance of the tribulation constitutes a penalty for failure to believe in Christ prior to the tribulation. Such an explanation would merely side-step the problem of the way in which any person saved by the blood of Christ could be subject to divine wrath. Tribulational saints might and should be individually raptured immediately upon conversion in order to escape divine wrath if it is true that earthly presence in the tribulation will necessarily entail the endurance of divine wrath. Many will be saved during the tribulation who had no previous opportunity to believe. Some even hold that *only* such people will be converted during the tribulation (cf. 2 Thess. 2:11, 12). Are we to think that those saints will have to endure God's wrath because the Church failed to preach the Gospel to them before the tribulation—while the guilty Church goes scot-free?

It is argued that "the character of the judgments which will fall is such that they will affect everyone. . . ."[4] But pretribulationists, too, see saved people throughout the world during the tribulation, including a group of 144,000 Jews scattered over the earth as evangelists—and the 144,000 are expressly said to be sealed for protection (Rev. 7:1-3). If the judgments cannot

---

[3] Stanton, 44.
[4] Walvoord, *RQ*, 69.

discriminate between saved and unsaved, sealed and unsealed, how are we to explain that the saints in general and the 144, 000 in particular must be exempt from divine wrath? For a pre-tribulationist the only recourse is to claim a special promise for the Church that she will escape not only the wrath, but also the *time* of wrath (see below on Revelation 3:10).

VARIETIES OF DISTRESS IN THE TRIBULATION

We can distinguish different kinds of distress during the tribulation: the wrath of God poured out directly upon the unregenerate in retribution for unjudged sin, ravages of Satanic and demonic forces let loose on earth within God's permissive will, evils and violence which stem directly from man's own wickedness, persecution of saints by the Antichrist, and the chastisement of Israel designed to lead the people to repentance at the second coming.

It is not a point of disagreement whether the Church will ever suffer God's retributive wrath. She will not (John 3:36; 5:24; Rom. 5:9; 8:1; Eph. 2:3; 5:6; 1 Thess. 1:10; 5:9). And there are clear indications in the book of Revelation that the bowls of divine wrath will not touch saints, indications in addition to the theological necessity that God's wrath not touch a saved person. Just as the three woes, which are the last three trumpets, will come upon the "earth-dwellers" (8:13) in contradistinction to the saints, so also the bowls will be poured only upon the wicked. The first bowl will be poured upon "the men who had the mark of the beast and who worshiped his image" (16:2). The turning of the sea into blood, in the second bowl, does not need to involve saints. The third bowl will be directed against those who "poured out the blood of saints and prophets, and Thou hast given them blood to drink" (16:6). The fourth bowl will fall on those who in response "blasphemed the name of God ... and they did not repent, so as to give Him glory" (16:9). The same will happen under the fifth bowl (16:11). The sixth bowl will concern the kings of the east and the armies which will gather to Armageddon. The seventh bowl will reach to the very end and have to do with Babylon (out of which God's people have been called "that you may not receive of her plagues," 18:4) and the cities of the nations. The recipients will again respond with blasphemy (16:17-21). It should be evident that the bowls of divine wrath will concern the wicked alone.

The remarkable parallel between some of the bowls and the plagues on Egypt—grievous sores, the turning of water to blood, gross darkness—further suggests that tribulational saints will be protected from divine wrath, in view of Israel's protection at the time of the plagues preceding the Exodus. This parallel gets support from the song of redemption composed by Moses and the Lamb: the song likens the second coming to the Exodus from Egypt under Moses and under the atoning blood of the Passover Lamb (Rev. 15:3).

It may be objected that the ill wind of divine wrath begins to blow long before the pouring out of the bowls in the finale of the tribulation. If true, that would not militate against posttribulationism, for the Church would receive protection throughout the whole time just as any other tribulational saints and the 144,000 will receive protection. But since the question is broached concerning the time at which God's retributive wrath will begin, we need to search for an answer.

All the distresses of the seals—militarism, war, famine, death, martyrdom—are common to our era and therefore do not preclude the presence of the Church. Under the sixth seal wrath is mentioned, but not as the contents of the seal. Rather, an ingressive or a dramatic aorist portrays the wrath as starting or about to strike. As we shall see in the chapter on Revelation, the sixth seal brings us to the end of the tribulation. Therefore the mention of wrath here does not prove that it begins before the pouring out of the bowls. Under the seventh seal there is no plague, but an ominous silence denoting that the end has come (8:1, 2).

The similarity of the first four trumpets to the Egyptian plagues at least allows that the saints will receive protection like that afforded the Israelites (8:6-12). The fifth and sixth trumpets are the first and second woes directed against the "earth-dwellers" as distinguished from saints (8:13-9:21). The plague of demonic locusts in the fifth trumpet and the demonic army from the Euphrates in the sixth trumpet suggest that the plagues of the trumpets have their origin, not in God's retributive wrath, but in the ragings of Satan and his demonic hosts. The "great mountain burning with fire" and "thrown into the sea" and the fallen star called "Wormwood" may well be fallen spirits who vent their wrath upon the earth. The seventh trumpet, like the seventh seal, again brings us to the end of the tribulation when "the mystery of God is finished" and "the kingdom of the world has become the kingdom of our Lord and of His Christ" (10:7; 11:15-19).

We miss the mark if we say that the reference to "the great tribulation" in Revelation 7:14, appearing as it does before the whole series of seven trumpets and even before the seventh seal, prevents denying the arrival of wrath prior to the seventh trumpet.[5] For the episodical vision in 7:9-17 leaps forward to a time *after* the tribulation, indeed, to the eternal state when the redeemed who have "come out of the great tribulation" "shall hunger no more, neither thirst any more" and "God shall wipe every tear from their eyes" so that they stand "before the throne and before the Lamb, clothed in white robes, and palm branches in their hands," and "serve Him [God] day and night in His temple" (cf. Rev. 21, 22). Furthermore, "the great tribulation" mentioned in 7:14 may allude to the intense *persecution* out of which the multitude of saints emerge rather than God's retributive wrath. Similarly, to deduce that in 15:1 the designation of the bowls as the "last" and as those which "fill up" (better, "finish") God's wrath implies previous retribution[6] overloads the words "last" and "fill up." The two expressions simply denote that the bowls will be poured out at the end of the tribulation and that they will contain a complete portion of divine wrath for that occasion.

In the Olivet Discourse Jesus speaks of persecution against the saints and of the nations' wrath against Israel throughout the seventieth week, or at least during the latter half of it. He cannot be referring to divine wrath, because the saints are to flee from it (Matt. 24:15ff.). Not until the final crisis at Armageddon, when Jesus descends (and the Church is caught up if posttribulationism be correct), will God pour out His wrath upon the unregenerate.

When we come to the terms which describe the distresses of the tribulation, we find further evidence that saints will be exempt from divine retribution. Θυμός, a violent outburst of anger, represents God's wrath in nine out of eighteen occurrences in the NT, all nine in Revelation. A survey of these occurrences shows that the divine θυμός strikes only the wicked (14:8—Babylon; 14:10—

[5] Stanton, 183.

[6] Harrison, *BibSac*, 114:322.

worshipers of the beast; 14:19—the armies at Armageddon; 15:1, 7; 16:1, 19—the earth-dwellers; 18:3—fornicators with Babylon; 19:15—the armies at Armageddon). 'Οργή, the settled state of wrath, stands for God's anger about twenty-seven times in the NT. Paul clearly states that believers are "saved from the wrath of God through Him [Christ]" (Rom. 5:9), "delivered . . . from the wrath to come" (1 Thess. 1:10 AV), "not destined . . . for wrath" (1 Thess. 5:9). The divine ὀργή falls only upon the wicked (Rev. 6:16, 17; 14:10; 16:19; 19:15).

In coming to "tribulation" (θλῖψις , and its verbal cognate θλίβω), we discover an entirely different situation. Out of fifty-five occurrences, about forty-seven refer to tribulation endured by saints. Only twice, neither time within the framework of Daniel's seventieth week, does the word refer to God's anger against sinners (Rom. 2:9; 2 Thess. 1:7). (The latter verse speaks of divine judgment on persecutors at Jesus' revelation "in flaming fire" but not of divine wrath during the previous period.) In the context of the seventieth week, "tribulation" refers to the persecution of the saints (Matt. 24:9, 21, 29; Mark 13:19, 24; Rev. 7:14). The tribulation of the seventieth week has to do, then, not with God's wrath against the sinners, but with the wrath of Satan, the Antichrist, and the wicked against the saints.

"In the world you have tribulation" (John 16:33). "Through many tribulations we must enter the kingdom of God" (Acts 14:22). "We also exult in our tribulations" (Rom. 5:3). "I, John, [am] your brother and fellow-partaker in the tribulation . . . in Jesus" (Rev. 1:9). "You will have tribulation" (Rev. 2:10). This is not to say that because the Church has tribulation now, she must enter the period of tribulation known as Daniel's seventieth week. We are not to ignore the distinction between tribulation in general and the time of unprecedented tribulation at the end of the age. But since the Church does have tribulation now, the tribulational character of the seventieth week does not militate against the presence of the Church. The facts that the Church has been destined to tribulations in general (1 Thess. 3:3) and that throughout this age the Church has been opposed by and has suffered from antichrists (1 John 2:18, 22; 4:3) constitute presumptive evidence that the Church will endure *the* tribulation and withstand *the* Antichrist. That the distresses of the seventieth week will be more intense and widespread than ever before does not prove the absence of the Church—there will be saints of one kind or another on earth, and God is no respecter of persons.

The blessedness of the blessed hope does not consist in exemption from persecution and trial, but in seeing the Savior face to face. If the general persecution predicted by Jesus did not take away that blessedness from the early disciples, neither should the specific persecution predicted for the seventieth week take away the blessedness of the hope for contemporary Christians. Church history testifies that the hope of Christ's return has burned more brightly for suffering believers than for the comfortable. "Why . . . should the last generation suffer that from which the vast host have been spared?"[7] The answer lies hidden in the perfect purpose and providence of God. Why should any saint or generation suffer more trial and persecution than another? Our doctrine should not be influenced by timorous feelings regarding entrance into the great distress. "Be strong." "Endure hardness." "To you it is graciously given to suffer in behalf of Christ." These scriptural admonitions do not refer specifically to the persecution of saints during Daniel's seventieth week, but they do dictate the proper Christian attitude toward suffering.

The claim that martyrdom will be universal and thus would leave no part of the Church alive for translation at the rapture rests on Revelation 13:7, 8, 14, 15.[8] But the power of the beast over the saints (vv. 7, 8) is readily satisfied by widespread persecution. To be sure, the false prophet will have authority to kill those who will not worship the beast's image (vv. 14, 15). However, it is practically inconceivable that he will demand every living human being to go to the temple in Jerusalem for worship of the image. We do better to restrict the application of the scriptural statement to Jews in Palestine after the Antichrist breaks his covenant with them and sets up the abomination of desolation, which is probably his image erected within the temple (see Dan. 9:27; Mark 13:14; Matt. 24:15; 2 Thess. 2:4; and Rev. 13:14, 15; cf. also Rev. 12:17). Furthermore, the false prophet's authority to kill those who refuse to worship the beast's image need not imply that he will actually exterminate them all. Pretribulationists can scarcely afford to assert universal martyrdom, because they, too, must preserve a host of saints throughout the tribulation, if not to be raptured,

---

[7] Chafer, *Theology*, IV, 366.
[8] R. T. Ketcham, *Pre, Mid, or Post-Tribulation Rapture?* 29, 30.

at least to become the "sheep" who pass into the millennium (see Matt. 25:31-46 according to the usual dispensational understanding).

Failure to distinguish between the wrath of God and other types of distress, such as persecution, has led to the charge that posttribulationists inconsistently say that the Church will be sheltered at the same time they expound the woes of the Church during the tribulation. The answer is simple: the Church will receive shelter from the penal judgments of God but will suffer persecution from other quarters.[9]

THE HERMENEUTICAL QUESTION

We sometimes hear that posttribulationism leads to excessive spiritualization in order to reduce the intensity of the tribulation for making the presence of the Church more palatable and in order to equate the Church with Israel for easier proof of the Church's presence in the tribulation. This process, it is said, undermines the foundation of premillennialism in literalistic interpretation of Biblical prophecy. But a toning down of the intensity of the tribulation is *not necessary* to a posttribulational position, because the Church will not suffer divine wrath regardless of its intensity. Neither is it a necessary procedure to equate Israel and the Church, for although the term "Church" does not appear in tribulational passages with an earthly setting, neither does the term appear in passages which describe heavenly scenes during the tribulation.

But let us test the claim that pretribulationism forms the bulwark of literalism in contrast to a spiritualizing tendency in posttribulationism. The surprising contradiction surfaces in several commentaries on Revelation by outstanding pretribulationists. For example, Walter Scott, A. C. Gaebelein, and H. A. Ironside together allegorize the sixth seal in Revelation 6 in the following manner: the earthquake stands for subversion of existing authority; the sun for supreme governing authority; the

---

[9] In no sense need we make the tribulation a purgatory in which the Church will pay for her sins. The real purgatorists are partial rapturists. In fact, pretribulationism comes closer than posttribulationism to a concept of purgatory. For if pretribulationists believe that presence in the tribulation entails suffering of God's wrath (and if not, they cannot argue for the absence of the Church from the wrathful nature of the period), then the tribulation becomes a purgatory—not for the Church, but a purgatory nevertheless for the saints whom pretribulationists do see in the tribulation.

moon for derivative authority in the moral realm; stars for all lesser authorities; blackness for the darkening power of Satan; blood for death; removal of the heavens for the disappearance of political, civil, and ecclesiastical systems; mountains for settled powers; and islands for centers of trade, commerce, and wealth. Gaebelein writes, "Most of it is symbolical. . . ."[10] On the hail and fire of the first trumpet, Scott comments, "These are not to be understood as literal destructive agencies. They are symbols."[11] Again, at Revelation 9:2 he, as well as Gaebelein, spiritualizes air into moral influence and smoke into satanic delusion.[12] Concerning the second trumpet, Gaebelein takes the mountain for a kingdom, the sea for nations, and the fire for revolution.[13] Scott, Gaebelein, and Armerding join in the opinion that the number "two" of the two witnesses in Revelation 11 is symbolic.[14] Scott also symbolizes the number 144,000.[15] Ironside writes, "As in the case of the seven trumpets and, in measure, of the seven seals, I do not profess to be able to tell you just how much we are to take as symbolic and how much as literal. . . ."[16] On the other hand, some posttribulational commentators on Revelation, such as Henry W. Frost[17] and Beasley-Murray,[18] for the most part exceed the foregoing pretribulationists in literalmindedness.

We dare not infer that all pretribulationists allegorize and all posttribulationists literalize or that the pretribulationists mentioned *always* allegorize and the posttribulationists always literalize. The issue is not so simple as to be settled by equating posttribulationism with a spiritualizing interpretation and pretribulationism with the literal method and hastily deducing the correctness of pretribulationism and a logical necessitation of amillennialism in posttribulationism. Some have turned from preto posttribulationism and finally to amillennialism. But that proves no more than does the entanglement of some pretribulationists in the labyrinth of hyperdispensationalism. The swing of the pendulum in the thinking of an individual may derive from reverse psychological reaction or from a number of other factors

---

[10] *The Revelation*, 56.
[11] *Exposition of the Revelation of Jesus Christ*, 183.
[12] *Ibid.*, 203.
[13] *The Revelation*, 61.
[14] Scott, 230; Gaebelein, 69, 70; Armerding, *BibSac*, 100:94.
[15] P. 66.
[16] *Lectures on the Revelation*, 275.
[17] *Matthew Twenty-Four and the Revelation*.
[18] In *NBC*.

quite unrelated to logical necessities inherent in one position or another.

METHOD AND SPHERE OF EXEMPTION

If we ask why the Church should remain on earth even though the purposes of the tribulation relate directly to Israel and the nations, the answer is identical to that which pretribulationists would have to give were we to ask the same question concerning the presence of other saints in the tribulation—viz., to be the objects and witnesses of God's saving grace. The discussion now resolves itself into two questions: What is the method by which God exempts the Church from divine wrath—removal or protection? Has God given the Church a special promise above that given to saints in general, a promise that she will escape the *time* of the seventieth week as well as the wrath? The answers to these questions revolve around the exegesis of certain verses.

"But keep on the alert at all times, praying in order that you may have strength to escape all these things that are about to take place, and to stand before the Son of Man" (Luke 21:36). To interpret the term "escape" in terms of a pretribulational rapture[19] leads us into partial rapturism—only those who watch and pray will escape by prior rapture—unless watching and praying characterize all true disciples. But is it necessary, or even preferable, to regard the escape as an evacuation to heaven?

The immediately preceding context indicates that the persons Jesus was addressing would live in the time of the Antichrist and tribulation. It would be a jarring reversal should the disciples represent a Jewish remnant separate from the Church throughout the Olivet Discourse but in this one verse suddenly turn into representatives of the Church. Moreover, the word for "escape" is ἐκφεύγω, *escape out of the midst of*, contrary to the belief that the Church will never find itself in the tribulation. Frost opines that Jesus does not refer to a physical escape, since the foregoing verses describe the affliction and martyrdom of many saints, but to the spiritual attitude of an overcoming steadfastness under persecution, as the verb "stand" may sometimes connote (Rom. 14:4; 1 Cor. 7:37; 2 Cor. 1:24; Eph. 6:11, 13, 14; Col. 4:12; 1 Pet. 5:12; Jude 24).[20] However, this suggestion seems to minimize the ex-

---

[19] Linton, 23.
[20] Frost, 37, 38.

pression "escape all these things," for courageous endurance is not the same as escaping. Ladd suggests that the phrase "all these things" does not refer to the extended period of the tribulation, but to the judgments clustered at the second coming itself, of which the foregoing verses have spoken.[21] It is probably better to take the verb ἐκφεύγω as an echo of verse twenty-one, where φεύγω is used of the flight from Jerusalem by the elect. Ἐκφεύγω then has special reference to the flight of the Palestinian remnant from the Antichrist (cf. Rev. 12:14-16), and the next phrase, "to stand before the Son of Man," refers to a standing in His presence *following* the preservation of the remnant by successful flight during the latter half of the tribulation.

"And to wait for His Son from heaven, whom He raised from the dead, that is Jesus, who delivers us from the wrath to come" (1 Thess. 1:10). "For God has not destined us for wrath, but for obtaining salvation through our Lord Jesus Christ" (1 Thess. 5:9). Neither of these verses states the method by which God will save believers from wrath. Therefore both offer inconclusive evidence either for prior removal from wrath or for protection in the midst of it. For that matter, neither of the verses places the wrath to come in Daniel's seventieth week. Perhaps Paul has in mind eternal wrath, or the wrath poured out right at the second coming—a view favored by the contextual discussion of the day of the Lord, which will begin not until the posttribulational advent (see 2 Thess. 2:1-4 and the chapter below, "The Day of the Lord"). Even if the wrath should begin to arrive already within the seventieth week (an interpretation which the context does not support), the method of exemption could still be preservation on earth; for the basis of exemption is "salvation through our Lord Jesus Christ," no less the possession of believers in Christ during the tribulation than of believers before the tribulation.

Probably the most debated verse in the whole discussion about the time of the Church's rapture is Revelation 3:10:

> Because you have kept the word of My perseverance, I also will keep you from the hour of testing, that hour which is about to come upon the whole world, to test those who dwell upon the earth.

In favor of pretribulationism appeal is made to J. Moffatt, who writes that "rabbinic piety (*Sanh.* 98b) expected exemption

---

[21] Ladd, 86, 87.

from the tribulation of the latter days only for those who were absorbed in good works and in sacred studies."[22] However, the appeal to rabbinic tradition leaves wholly unanswered the very point in question, which is whether the exemption will come by preservation or by prior removal. Also, the rabbinic tradition rests on the legalistic basis of law-keeping and study of the Torah for exemption and could lead us only to partial rapturism. That rabbinic tradition provides little support, then, for a pretribulational understanding of Revelation 3:10.

Our first major question concerns the exact force of the Greek preposition ἐκ, translated "from." Essentially, ἐκ, a preposition of motion concerning thought or physical direction, means *out from within*.[23] Ἐκ does not denote a stationary position outside its object, as some have mistakenly supposed in thinking that the ἐκ of Revelation 3:10 refers to a position *already* taken outside the earthly sphere of tribulation. Other prepositions— ἐκτός, ἔξω, ἔξωθεν, ἄνευ, and χωρίς—would have properly denoted a place apart from the hour of testing. But ἐκ was used in this sense only in exceptional cases in classical Greek, "chiefly in early writers."[24] The basic idea of emergence from within is illustrated by usages in other verses of similar expression. The large host of tribulational saints will be "the ones who come out of the great tribulation" (Rev. 7:14). "The Lord knoweth how to deliver the godly out of temptation" (2 Pet. 2:9 AV). The primary sense of emergence in ἐκ would therefore seem to thwart a pretribulational interpretation of the verse, for emergence from within could only mean that the Church had been within the hour of testing.

To defend the position that ἐκ may signify complete immunity, H. Alford and J. Moffatt are quoted to the effect that the grammar "permits" such an interpretation.[25] But there should be candor enough to admit that the grammar equally permits the posttribulational interpretation since it is the latter position which Alford and Moffatt themselves adopt. Alford is also cited as writing that it is hard to distinguish between τηρεῖν ἐκ (*keep out from*) and

[22] *EGT*, V, 368; cf. Barnhouse, *Eternity*, 9:31 (Nov., 1958).

[23] BAG and LSJ also list the meaning "away from," but the ensuing treatments show that emission is meant. BAG go on to say that ἐκ is used "of situations and circumstances out of which someone is brought" and cite Revelation 3:10 as an example.

[24] LSJ. Certain idioms such as ἐκ δεξιῶν ("on the right hand") and ἐκ βελέων ("out of shot") lingered on, but we are not dealing with a frozen expression in Revelation 3:10.

[25] Thiessen, 22, 23.

τηρεῖν ἀπό (*keep away from*) in John 17:15 and James 1:27. Buttman-Thayer are added for the view that ἐκ and ἀπό often denote the same relation.[26] Significantly, however, ἀπό (*away from*) does not deny the thought of emergence, but only does not affirm it.[27] Therefore, we are more accurate to say that ἀπό often includes the meaning of emission in ἐκ (in fact, ἀπό has usurped the place and meaning of ἐκ in modern Greek) than that ἐκ loses its primary sense of emergence in approaching ἀπό.

Abbott's doubt that in the LXX and in John ἐκ always implies previous existence within, "though it does commonly," has become yet another appeal to authority.[28] But Abbott is not to be followed here:

First, if ἐκ ever occurs without the thought of emergence, it does so very exceptionally. This fact incapacitates Revelation 3:10 as a *proof*-text for pretribulationism.

Second, the citation by Thiessen of Abbott's opinion comes through A. T. Robertson.[29] But Robertson gives that opinion *disapprovingly*. And what Robertson himself writes, when quoted more fully, damages the pretribulational position:

> Abbott doubts if in the LXX and John ἐκ always implies previous existence in the evils from which one is delivered when used with σώζω and τηρέω. Certainly in John 17 ἐκ occurs rather frequently, but τηρήσῃς ἐκ τοῦ πονηροῦ (17:15) may still imply that the evil once had power over them (cf. Jesus' prayer for Peter). Certainly in John 12:27, σῶσόν με ἐκ τῆς ὥρας ταύτης, Jesus had already entered into the hour. Cf. δυνάμενον σώζειν ἐκ θανάτου (Heb. 5:7) where ἐκ may accentuate the power of God (δυνάμενον), though he had not yet entered into death. In Rev. 3:10 τηρήσω ἐκ τῆς ὥρας τοῦ πειρασμοῦ we seem to have the picture of general temptation with the preservation of the saints.[30] The word means 'out of,' 'from within,' not like ἀπό or παρά .... In the N.T. ἐκ is still ahead of ἀπό.[31]

Third, Abbott's opinion that ἐκ does not need to imply previous existence within the object when used with τηρέω (the word for "keep" in Rev. 3:10) in the LXX and in John is totally meaningless. The two words never appear together in the LXX! And their

[26] *Ibid.*
[27] Robertson, 577.
[28] *Ibid.*
[29] *Ibid.*
[30] Robertson, 598.
[31] Robertson, 596.

only other partnership in Johannine literature comes in John 17:15, where preservation rather than evacuation is in view.[32]

Fourth, although ἐκ does not always imply the actual experience of the evil out of which one is delivered (John 12:27; 2 Cor. 1:10; 1 Thess. 1:10), it does imply the immediate and dangerous presence of the evil.

Fifth, the preposition ἐκ appears in John's writings approximately 336 times, far more often than in the writings of any other NT author. There is not a single instance where the primary thought of emergence, or origin, cannot fit, indeed, does not best fit the thought of the context. Surely the invariability of meaning in such a high number of occurrences establishes the Johannine usage.

Sixth, if we imagine that ἐκ denotes exit, but say that the Church will be caught out right after the *beginning* of the seventieth week, we render the word τηρέω (*keep* or *guard*) practically meaningless and sacrifice the dispensational stand that the Church can have no part in an Israelitish period such as the seventieth week. It would be sheer sophistry to say that the Church will be removed immediately upon entrance into the hour, for then the keeping will last only for an instant and the promise becomes devoid of real meaning.

It is sometimes asked why διά (*through*) or ἐν (*in*) does not appear if the last generation of the Church will indeed be present on earth during the hour of testing. The answer lies in a matter of emphasis. 'Εν would have placed all the emphasis on presence within. Διά would have distributed the emphasis between entrance, presence within, and emergence. As it is, ἐκ lays all the emphasis on emergence, in this verse on the final, victorious outcome of the keeping-guarding. The same emphasis crops up in Revelation 7:14, where the saints come "out of the great tribulation." The elder might have said that they had come "through" the great tribulation. But, though not denying the notion which the preposition "through" would have conveyed, he stresses the thought of emergence. On the other hand, we may ask why ἀπό (*away from*, without a *necessary* implication of previous presence within) does not appear in Revelation 3:10 and thus at least *permit* a pretribulational interpretation. Or, why was not a preposition used which

---

[32] See below.

would have *required* the interpretation of previous removal—ἐκτός, ἔξω, ἔξωθεν, ἄνευ, and χωρίς?

In seeking to harmonize the meaning of ἐκ with pretribulationism, appeal is made to a quotation from MM: "The clause in the early manuscript [cited by MM] reads, 'has removed it [the donkey] from my reach.' The donkey was placed out of the reach of the person spoken of. God promises to guard this Church out of the reach of the great tribulation."[33] But does God promise that? The citation from MM states *removal;* whereas Revelation 3:10 states *keeping,* or *protection.* In the phrases "out of the reach of the great tribulation" we have an unwarranted interpolation of the words "reach of," which are expressed in the secular manuscript (ἐκ μέσου—MM; cf. 2 Thess. 2:7), but not in Revelation 3:10. The fact that the donkey was removed out of reach shows that it had been within reach and proves that even here ἐκ denotes emergence from within the sphere of the preposition's object.

Τηρέω (*keep*) also bears importantly on the meaning of Revelation 3:10. Where a situation of danger is in view, τηρέω means to *guard.* The presence of danger is implicit in the idea of guarding. But if the Church will be in heaven during the hour of testing, where will be the danger which would require God's protecting hand upon her? Throughout the LXX and the NT τηρέω always occurs for protection within the sphere of danger (as also the Hebrew words translated by τηρέω in the LXX). In our Lord's prayer for His own we find a striking confirmation that keeping necessarily implies the presence of danger: "I am no more in the world; and yet they themselves are in the world. . . . keep them" (John 17:11, 12). Jesus contrasts His absence from this earthly scene with the presence of His disciples here. The keeping is required by their presence in the sphere of danger. The plain implication is that were they absent from the world with the Lord, the keeping would not be necessary. Similarly, were the Church absent from the hour of testing, keeping would not be necessary.

There is but one other place in Biblical Greek (LXX and NT) where τηρέω and ἐκ occur together, John 17:15: "I do not ask Thee to take them out of the world, but to keep them from the evil one." The parallels between John 17:15 and Revelation 3:10 are very impressive. Both verses appear in Johannine literature. Both come from the lips of Jesus. A probability arises, therefore, of similar usage and meaning. In John 17:15 the words "take out of"

---

[33] Wuest, *BibSac,* 114:68.

(ἄρῃς . . . ἐκ) mean to *lift* or *raise up* and *remove*.[34] The expression gives an exact description of what the rapture will be, a lifting up and removal. Yet it is this expression against which Jesus throws τηρέω ἐκ in full contrast and opposition. How then can τηρέω ἐκ refer to the rapture or to the result of the rapture when in its only other occurrence the phrase opposes an expression which would perfectly describe the rapture?

We cannot eliminate the parallel between the two verses by distinguishing a moral realm in John 17:15 and a physical realm in Revelation 3:10. For it is the physical presence of the disciples in the world which places them in the moral sphere of the evil one. Besides, purely moral protection from the evil one would seem to be more difficult than simple physical protection during the tribulation (cf. Eph. 6:12). But Paul recognizes no separation between moral and physical realms in praying for the preservation (τηρέω) of spirit, soul, and body (1 Thess. 5:23). We must therefore conclude that Thayer is correct in his discussion of τηρέω when he writes, "*To keep*: . . . by guarding to cause one to escape in safety out of," and cites John 17:15 and Revelation 3:10.[35]

It is reasoned from the word "hour" that "the point is not that the church will escape the wrath of God, but that it will escape the *time* of the wrath of God. . . ."[36] There is no difficulty for posttribulationism, however, when we properly understand τηρέω ἐκ as protection issuing in emission. Rather, presence within the period is directly implied. Further considerations undercut stress on the term "hour":

Even in the air or in heaven, as a result of rapture, the Church would not have escaped the period of time which is Daniel's seventieth week. That period will elapse in heaven as well as on earth, as is evidenced by the many shifts between heaven and earth in the visions of the Apocalypse.

The word "hour" appears many times in the gospels with reference to the passion of Jesus (Matt. 26:45; Mark 14:35, 41;

---

[34] BAG, Thayer.

[35] We have already discussed the charge of inconsistency in understanding passages such as Revelation 3:10 in terms of protection for the Church while admitting that other passages teach the suffering of tribulational saints. The Church will suffer the wrath of Satan and the Antichrist in the form of persecution. In Revelation 3:10 Jesus promises protection from that which comes upon the wicked earth-dwellers. Persecution, then, cannot possibly be in view.

[36] Walvoord, *BibSac*, 113:303; cf. Walvoord, *RQ*, 70.

John 2:4; 7:30; 8:20; 12:23, 27; 13:1; 17:1). The emphasis falls on the *experience* within the time, not the period as such. In the request, "Father, save Me from this hour," Jesus would not have been praying for deliverance from the period of time, through which He would have gone even had He not died. Rather, He contemplates asking for deliverance from the *events* within the period of time (John 12:27). This is a common way of speaking. To pray, say, for deliverance from a time of illness is not to ask that one should be taken out of the world before he becomes ill—he is already ill—but that the Lord should preserve and bring him safely out of the period of illness. Stress does not lie on the period of time *per se,* but upon the prominent characteristics of the period. Even more is this true in the language of predictive prophecy. Because God preordains and foreknows the course of history, certain critical events are allied to the time in which they will happen. The correspondence makes it possible to refer to the period, not as mere passage of time, but as a set of distinctive events. Therefore, to demand that the expression have been turned around into the awkward form "testing of the hour" (what hour?) fails to catch the idiom.

A promise similar to Revelation 3:10 was given to Israel in relation to the Babylonian exile and/or the tribulation (in either instance Israel was or will be present): "Alas! for that day is great, there is none like it; and it is the time of Jacob's distress, but he will be saved from it" (Jer. 30:7). The similarities to Revelation 3:10 are noteworthy: the hour of testing vis-à-vis the time of Jacob's distress (both being periods of time); "keep" vis-à-vis "save" (יָשַׁע bearing an even stronger meaning than τηρέω); ἐκ vis-à-vis מִן (both meaning *from, out from*). In its original Hebrew form and also in its Septuagintal form (σώζω with ἀπό, numbered 37:7 in the LXX), the expression would favor prior removal far more than does Revelation 3:10. Yet of course it does not, since Israel endured the Babylonian exile and will yet endure the tribulation. If a pretribulational rapture was not or will not be required for deliverance from the time of Jacob's distress, neither will a pretribulational rapture be required for preservation from the hour of testing.

The objects of the hour of testing are "those who dwell upon the earth," a term which in Revelation acquires a moral connotation in describing those who, in contrast to the saints, derive their citizenship from the earth (see the concordance). Some have therefore reasoned that the Church will not be present on

earth during a time of testing intended for earth-dwellers. However, the argument backfires, because all recognize that saints of
one kind or another will be present on earth during the tribulation. Therefore, mere presence on earth will not necessarily bring
one into the experience of the hour of testing. And it is not certain that the "hour of testing" includes the whole seventieth
week, or even the latter half of the week. Of course, the term
"hour" may refer to a longer period than sixty minutes, but in
the Olivet Discourse and elsewhere in Revelation "hour" frequently refers to the events clustered around Armageddon and
the second coming. Hence, the hour of testing may refer only to
the very last crisis at the close of the tribulation.

Jesus' statement "I am coming quickly" (v. 11) follows the
promise in Revelation 3:10. It is argued that the immediacy of
the reference to the second coming shows the method of preservation to be a pretribulational advent of Christ. But the ensuing
exhortation to "hold fast" provides an alternative connection for
the reference to the second coming. Or, granting a link with
verse ten, we may well understand that preservation will culminate in the Parousia at the close of the hour of testing. The context of Revelation offers description only of Jesus' return at the
close of the tribulation (19:11ff.). It would therefore seem more
appropriate to take 3:11 as a reference to that advent rather than
to a pretribulational advent lacking identification and description
elsewhere in the book.

OT TYPOLOGY OR PRECEDENT

Some have cited the translation of Enoch and the deliverances
of Noah, Lot, and Rahab as typological support for pretribulationism. But although the NT compares the Flood and the judgment on Sodom and Gomorrah to the destruction which will
take place at Jesus' coming, nowhere do the deliverances of
Noah and Lot stand for the rapture. Realizing that they should
not base NT doctrine on undelineated OT typology, others call
the aforementioned incidents illustrations of the principle of deliverance from wrath. How well do they serve as such illustrations
(or types)?

The translation of Enoch occurred at least 669 years before
the Flood (according to the Hebrew text without allowance for
gaps—variants in the LXX and the Samaritan text do not affect
the point of the argument). The long interval precludes any con-

nection between Enoch's translation and the judgment of the Flood. Noah has done double duty for Israel and the Church. But representing the Church, he fails to support a pretribulational rapture because he went through and emerged from the Flood. He likewise fails to represent Israel in that he was untouched by the Deluge, whereas the tribulation will be the time of "Jacob's trouble." Also, the righteousness which caused God to preserve Noah and his family will hardly characterize Israel prior to the tribulation.

Lot left Sodom before the fire and brimstone fell. But Lot, drawn reluctantly out of Sodom, makes a poor picture of the rapture. Furthermore, he remained within the sphere of judgment in the cities of the plain while the fire and brimstone fell (Gen. 19:18-25). That was not removal, but sheltered protection. Rahab still resided in Jericho when the city fell (Josh. 6:22, 23). Although she moved out before the Israelites burned the city, the divine stroke of judgment preceded her removal. If anything, these OT incidents support the posttribulational concept of protection within the sphere of danger.

We even read that the marriage of Joseph (Christ) to a Gentile bride (the Church) before the famine (the tribulation) and before Joseph was revealed to his brothers (the posttribulational advent) corroborates pretribulationism.[37] But the NT makes none of these typological identifications. Are we to identify Egypt, where Joseph is, with heaven, where Jesus is? Where do the two journeys to Egypt by Joseph's brothers and finally that of the whole family fit? Why does not Joseph go to Canaan with his Gentile wife rather than his brothers come to him in Egypt, since Jesus comes with the Church to the nation of Israel rather than Israel goes to Him in heaven? This typological interpretation would seem to teach a rapture of Israel to heaven as much as a pretribulational marriage of Christ and the Church. Also, Joseph apparently takes his bride soon after his exaltation, at the beginning of the seven plenteous years and long before the years of famine, which supposedly represent the tribulation (Gen. 41:44, 45). And the famine strikes Egypt, where Joseph and his wife are. Will the tribulation strike heaven, where Jesus and the Church will be?

As now, the Church will suffer persecution during the tribulation, but no saint can suffer divine wrath. Supposed special prom-

---

[37] Linton, 40.

ises to the Church and illustrative or typological incidents in the OT fail to support removal of the Church prior to the tribulation. But they do favor protection. Divine wrath does not blanket the entire seventieth week, probably not even the latter half of it, but concentrates at the close.

5

Pertinent Points in the Revelation

As the major book of prophecy in the NT, Revelation has great pertinence to discussion of the rapture. Here we selectively consider both pre- and posttribulational arguments drawn from that book.

"AFTER THESE THINGS"

The over-all scheme of Revelation first commands our attention. The various futuristic views revolve around the meaning of 1:19: "Write therefore the things which you have seen, and the things which are, and the things which shall take place after these things ($\mu\epsilon\tau\grave{a}$ $\tau a\hat{v}\tau a$)." The things past, present, and future are frequently taken from a symbolic standpoint and as an outline of the book: the things past, which John had seen, are the vision of Christ (1:10-20); the things present are the seven churches, representative of the Church age; at 4:1 or thereabout, John, representative of the Church, is caught up to heaven and the things future have to do with the tribulational period. The line of reasoning proceeds, if the future things (the tribulation) will follow the present things (the Church age), the Church age will have to terminate before the tribulation. But that line of reasoning is fraught with serious weaknesses:

Even under an interpretation of chapters two and three as representative of eras of church history, it is quite possible to hold that the application of these chapters to the Church age is not in view *in 1:19*. "These things" would then refer solely to the contemporary situation of the seven Asian churches in the first century.

John mentions neither the seals, the trumpets, nor the bowls after their introduction and description. Yet, as we shall see, the last of each of these reaches to the end of the tribulation. So also chapters two and three may reach to the end of the tribulation, with a stepping back at 4:1 in order to describe final events in greater detail.

The birth of the male child in chapter twelve, though in the futuristic section of the book, reaches back to the incarnation of Christ. If the futuristic section (4-19) may reach back to the incarnation, the present section (2, 3) may reach forward through the tribulation.

Μετὰ ταῦτα appears "quite generally" in the sense of "afterward."[1] Indeed, that is the rendering adopted in most translations of 1:19 (cf. John 13:7; Acts 7:7; 1 Pet. 1:11). Given the possibility of the general sense, we should not press the phrase for proof of a dispensational cleavage between chapters three and four.

More crucially, does the phrase "after these things" denote a chronological progression from the *historical fulfillment* of a vision's contents, or a progression of time from the *seeing* of a vision by John? The pretribulational argument rests on assumption of the former. Usage throughout the remainder of the book favors the latter, for the phrase signifies passage from one vision to another in 7:9; 15:5; 18:1; 19:1; and in 9:12 and 20:3, transition within a single vision. Since the phrase indicates merely a progression from or within the time a vision was *received,* we have no warrant for assuming that it indicates passage from one period of time to another in the fulfillment of the contents.

We may think at first that 4:1b, "what must take place after these things," denotes a transition from the Church age to the tribulation. But in 4:1a John writes, "After these things I looked, and behold. . . ." Clearly John means that after receiving the vision of Christ and the dictation of the letters, he saw another vision. The phrase expresses, not transition from the Church age to the tribulation, but sequence in the personal experience of John. It is only natural that the second occurrence should conform to

---

[1] BAG, 511.

this meaning. Accordingly, "what must take place after these things" takes place after John's experience in chapters 1-3, not after the prophetic fulfillment of those chapters (if they are predictive—granted here only for the sake of argument). All that 4:1 means is that after receiving his first vision on earth, John was caught up to see another vision in heaven. "What must take place" does so after the *reception* of the previous vision, *for* μετὰ ταῦτα, *as used in Revelation, refers to time after the giving of a vision, not to time after the fulfillment of a vision.*

Since the transition from past to present was not a dispensational change, but purely John's experience, it is not likely that the transition from present to future is dispensational in character. Unless we can show that μετὰ ταῦτα technically denotes a dispensational change, we have proved nothing in favor of pretribulationism. But to establish the phrase as a *terminus technicus* is to prove too much, for it results in six or seven dispensational changes during the tribulation, every time the phrase appears in Revelation—and that is a *reductio ad absurdum*. If the other occurrences of μετὰ ταῦτα refer to John's personal experiences, so also may 1:19 and 4:1. We therefore conclude that the boundary between present and future will not be crossed at the end of the Church age, but that John has long since crossed that boundary in his receiving of visions.

1:19 and 4:1b are also subject to different punctuation and translations which erode a pretribulational argument based on distinctions between past, present, and future in terms of fulfillment. Possibly μετὰ ταῦτα in 4:1b goes with the *following* verse, as in some codices of the Vulgate, Ambrosius, Hieronymus, and the ASV margin: "After these things I immediately was in the Spirit: and behold. . . ." Bullinger translates 1:19, "Write therefore what things thou sawest and what they are, even what things are about to happen hereafter."[2] Alford gives another possible translation which in rendering εἰσίν takes account of the meaning *signify* for the double εἰσίν in the next verse: "Write therefore the things which thou sawest and what things they signify and the things which are about to happen after these."[3] The advantage of Alford's translation is its uniting of John's vision of Christ with the dictation of the messages to the seven churches, *for both took place in a single episode.*

---

[2] *The Apocalypse*, 159.
[3] IV, 559.

The Scope of Chapters Two and Three

There are many applications of the messages to the seven churches. Nearly all commentators agree that they apply primarily to then existent churches, the individuals in those churches, and perhaps especially the ecclesiastical leaders (maybe the "angels" in the sense of "messengers"). The messages also apply indirectly to all churches and Christians. Finally, some put forward the claim, disputed by others, that the seven churches represent seven distinctive types of churches which were to arise in seven roughly distinct and successive eras of church history and which in some instances have continued to exist throughout later eras. Even were the last interpretation embraced, however, pretribulationism would not follow.

For example, in order to have 3:10 teach a pretribulational rapture for the Philadelphian church, we may make Laodicea represent apostate Christendom, which will go through the tribulation.[4] But what becomes of the supposed contrast between lukewarm Christians and hotly fervent tribulational saints, a contrast in which Laodicea represents the presently lukewarm but true Church which will be raptured before the tribulation?[5] Obviously, Laodicea cannot be both present in the tribulation and raptured before it, cannot represent both apostate Christendom and the true Church.

Concerning the contrast between lukewarmness and heat, "the Laodicean church, being last, could never go through the tribulation and still be called 'lukewarm.' For tribulation, as history has shown, has generally resulted in an ice cold or a red hot church."[6] But there are a number of plausible explanations for the coexistence of both fervent and lukewarm Christians in the tribulation. Jesus said that in the tribulation "most people's love will grow cold" (Matt. 24:12). The Laodicean church contains both the lukewarm and the overcomers (Rev. 3:21). Believers of the Philadelphian kind might continue to live in the Laodicean era if that be considered the tribulation. A concurrent existence in the tribulation would provide a basis for the presence of both the persecuted (Philadelphians) and the lukewarm (Laodiceans). Lukewarm Laodiceans might obey Christ's call to repent

---

[4] Stanton, 48.
[5] Stanton, 265.
[6] Ludwigson, 127, not necessarily his own argumentation (here or elsewhere).

(3:18-20). (When Jesus wishes the Laodiceans were hot or cold rather than lukewarm, he may be alluding to the healing hot springs and to the refreshingly cool mountain streams around Laodicea. In this sense coldness would be commendable. It does seem incomprehensible that the Lord would prefer complete apostasy—if that be indicated by coldness—to mere lukewarmness.)

Perhaps containing apostates, Laodicea cannot be wholly apostate, because within her are overcomers (3:21) and because she is one of the seven lampstands among which Christ performs His royal, priestly ministry (1:10-20). Like the other churches, the Laodicean church contains both true and false professors of Christianity. If she will enter the tribulation, therefore, saints of the Church will be present in the tribulation. However, if the Laodicean church will not enter the tribulation but will be raptured beforehand, the alleged promise of rapture in 3:10 should have been given, not to the church in Philadelphia, but to the church in Laodicea as representing the last type and era of the Church at large.

THE QUESTION OF THE RAPTURE IN 4:1, 2

It is often thought that John's experience in hearing a trumpet-like voice and being caught up to heaven (4:1, 2) constitutes a symbolic description of the rapture. John then becomes representative of the Church—he was one of the twelve apostles, one of the special three, the one whom Jesus loved, and the one whose name means, "Jehovah hath been gracious."[7] However, in Revelation 4:1ff. John lays no stress on his apostolic or official capacities, nor does he hint at symbolism. The passage reads like a straightforward narrative describing what happened to John as an individual. Still other weaknesses appear in taking John's catching up as indicative of the rapture:

Those who believe that Jesus will descend for the Church and remain in *mid-air* for the duration of the seventieth week (so Strombeck) cannot hold that John's going *to heaven* is a picture of the rapture. According to their own view the Church will not go to heaven. "Come up here" is spoken to the two witnesses in 11:12, where midtribulationists appeal to the statement. But if we deny that "Come up here" in 11:12 refers to the Church's rapture, we should have the candor to admit that the

---

7 Strombeck, 186.

same phrase need not refer to the rapture in 4:1. More seriously, John does not maintain his heavenly viewpoint throughout Revelation, as we see from 10:1; 11:1ff.; 13:1; 14:1; 18:1. He was transported back and forth between heavenly and earthly settings. Has John suddenly lost his symbolic value as representative of the Church? Or will the Church be raptured only to commute between heaven and earth during the tribulation? "There is no convincing reason why the seer's being 'in the Spirit' and being called into heaven typifies the rapture of the church any more than his being taken into the wilderness to view Babylon indicates that the church is there in exile."[8]

John addresses the Apocalypse "to the seven *churches* that are in Asia" (1:4). See also 22:16: "for the churches." The book of Revelation treats final events in fuller detail than does any other portion of the NT. Yet not a single verse in Revelation straightforwardly describes a pretribulational rapture of the Church or advent of Christ. Rather, the book begins with a terse description of Christ's return (1:7), acknowledged by all to be posttribulational, and climaxes with a detailed description of that same advent (19:11-16). Furthermore, the purpose of the Apocalypse is "to show to His bond-servants, the things which must shortly take place" (1:1). For the Church, *by far* the most important event shortly to take place is the pretribulational return of Christ if there be such. Yet though John provides minute delineations of tribulational events and of the posttribulational advent and addresses and relates his book to churches, not a syllable depicts a pretribulational return of Christ. For the most part the book of Revelation becomes an anachronism under pretribulationism. It is incongruous that the major book of prophecy in the NT, written to churches for the express purpose of instructing them regarding final events, should not contain a full description of the hope of the Church and yet in its major portion painstakingly chronicle events which according to pretribulationism have no direct bearing upon the Church.[9]

---

[8] Tenney, *Interpreting Revelation*, 141.

[9] It will not do to say that a pretribulational rapture was made so clear in previous NT writings and was so universally believed among Christians that in the Apocalypse John (or Jesus) takes the matter for granted. We shall see, as we already have in part, that previous NT writings did not make clear a pretribulational rapture. Moreover, patristic writings do not evince pretribulationism in the early Church.

THE TWENTY-FOUR ELDERS

In lieu of an account in Revelation of a pretribulational advent and under the assumption that John was in a kind of prophetic future, the presence of the twenty-four elders in heaven often becomes an argument that the Church had just been raptured when John saw them (4:1ff.). However, do the twenty-four elders represent the Church? As used elsewhere, the term "elder" may carry one or more of several connotations: age, dignity, rulership or some other official capacity.[10] Possibly the twenty-four elders stand for the Church. But then, "elders" may merely denote twenty-four beings, human or celestial, who, quite apart from representation of the whole Church as present, have official responsibility for leading the heavenly worship of God, a function we know they perform (4:9-11; 5:8-12).

It is argued that elders stand in a representative capacity elsewhere in the Bible.[11] Perhaps, but it is very difficult, if not impossible, to prove. A close examination of the term "elder" reveals that the prominent idea is rulership, or leadership, rather than representation. We tend to read representation into the term from our democratic heritage. But the elders of Israel were not their representatives; they were "officers over them." The elders of the churches are those who "rule," the "overseers." See Numbers 11:16; Isaiah 3:2-4; Acts 4:5, 8; 1 Timothy 5:17; 1 Peter 5:1, 2.

It is argued further that "elders" in the Bible are always men and in Revelation are distinguished from celestial beings.[12] John distinguishes the twenty-four elders from the four living creatures and from myriads of angels, it is true, but that does not rule out the possibility that the elders are *another* order of celestial beings. The four living creatures, though celestial, are described in terms of earthly creatures (Ezek. 1:10). Therefore the designation of the elders by an anthropomorphic term fails to preclude their being celestial. The close association of the elders with the four living creatures and the elders' task of interpretation (7:13, 14), elsewhere performed by angels (17:1), give plausibility to the view that the elders, too, are a celestial order of beings neither belonging to nor representing humankind.

---

[10] See BAG.
[11] English, 93.
[12] *Ibid.*

Again, although the elders speak of the redeemed, they do so in the third person without specifically including themselves:

> Worthy art Thou to take the book, and to break its seals; for Thou wast slain, and didst purchase for God with Thy blood men [supplied] from every tribe and tongue and people and nation. And Thou has made them to be a kingdom and priests to our God; and they will reign upon the earth (5:9, 10):

The Textus Receptus reads the first person, but in the Apocalypse the TR is in an "exceptionally corrupt state."[13] Although it supports the first personal pronoun, Sinaiticus (א) is eccentric in Revelation.[14] Alexandrinus (A), our best manuscript at this point, reads the third person and is followed by critical editors. The third personal pronoun does not necessarily exclude the elders from the redeemed (cf. Exod. 15:1, 13, 17), but it does produce the possibility, even the probability, that the elders do not include themselves. Furthermore, the twenty-four elders are set off from redeemed men in 11:16-18 and 14:3. And the four living creatures join in the song of redemption (Rev. 5:8-10). Yet those creatures were seen in heaven in the OT—and obviously no rapture was implied *then*. If therefore the presence in heaven of the living creatures and *their* participation in the song of redemption does not represent a raptured Church, why must that of the twenty-four elders? Thus is lost the force of the argument that the twenty-four elders are, or stand for, all the redeemed of the Church already in heaven at the beginning of the tribulation.

Even were it possible to prove that the elders represent the Church, it does not of necessity follow that the *entire* Church has arrived in heaven. A representative capacity might equally suggest that all those represented are not present, just as in a republican form of government elected representatives gather for legislative purposes precisely because the whole populace *cannot* do so.

Granted again for the sake of argument that the twenty-four elders represent the Church, do they represent *only* the Church? Two avenues are open to those who infer pretribulationism. First, the elders represent the redeemed solely of the Church. If so, it is very strange that the redeemed of Israel and of the na-

---

[13] Moffatt, *EGT*, V, 281.
[14] *Ibid.*

tions are not represented before the throne of God. To confine a representative capacity of the elders to the Church overlooks their singing of the redeemed in the very same terms which elsewhere apply to *all* the saints of the first resurrection (compare 5:10 with 20:6). Probably the closest parallel to the twenty-four elders is found in the names of the twelve tribes of Israel and of the twelve apostles of the Church inscribed on the gates and the foundations of the New Jerusalem. Twelve elders ought then to represent the saints of Israel.

Second, if twelve elders represent Israel and twelve the Church and if the presence of the elders implies the presence of all those represented, we can make several deductions. There must be a pretribulational resurrection and rapture of Israel. But this view most pretribulationists have discarded because the OT rather clearly places the resurrection of Israel at the end of the tribulation (Dan. 12:1, 2). If, on the other hand, the twelve elders representing Israel do not symbolize a resurrected and raptured Israel, neither need the twelve elders representing the Church symbolize a resurrected and raptured Church. Finally, it is clear that all the saints of Israel cannot be present in heaven at the beginning of the tribulation, for Israelitish saints will be on earth throughout the tribulation and the millennium. No problem exists, then, if all the Church is not in heaven during John's second vision.

If they represent the Church at all, do the twenty-four elders represent a *raptured* Church? Several elements in the passage have been held to imply an affirmative answer. First, this is the first occasion on which the elders are seen in heaven. Neither Isaiah (Isa. 6:1ff.), Ezekiel (Ezek. 1:4ff.), nor Daniel (Dan. 7:9-14) records having seen the twenty-four elders in his vision of God's throne.[15] Hence, when John saw them, the twenty-four elders must have just taken positions around the throne by virtue of their immediately preceding rapture. But the fact that Isaiah, Ezekiel, and Daniel do not record having seen the twenty-four elders does not justify our saying that they were not present. Neither Daniel, Ezekiel, nor John records seeing the seraphim whom Isaiah beheld. Yet Isaiah's was the first vision!

---

[15] Some also include John's vision in Revelation 1:9ff. This should be discounted, however, because John saw the vision on earth before being caught up to heaven. It was not a heavenly vision.

Neither Daniel nor Isaiah records seeing the four living creatures which Ezekiel and John saw. Neither Isaiah nor Ezekiel records seeing the angelic multitude which Daniel and John beheld. Neither Isaiah, Ezekiel, nor Daniel records seeing the seven lamps which are the seven Spirits of God (Rev. 4:5). Just as in the gospels differences appear among narratives of the same incident, so differences appear in the visions of God's throne. That the prophets did not all see alike does not carry any weight concerning the rapture or the time when the elders first took their places around the throne.

Second, it is also inferred that the elders represent a raptured Church from the crowns which the elders wear. The casting of the crowns before the throne suggests that the elders have just received them. Hence, the elders' crowns imply a prior resurrection, rapture, and judgment, since no one is crowned before resurrection, glorification, and judgment.[16]

The foregoing argument wholly assumes that the elders represent the Church, an assumption which, we have seen, lacks foundation. Moreover, crowns symbolize rulership, authority, and high position as well as reward (see Rev. 6:2; 9:7; 14:14). And beings other than human wear crowns without implication of reward (see again Rev. 9:7; 12:1; cf. 6:2; 14:14). Since the term "elder" connotes primarily official dignity, the crowns of the twenty-four elders probably call attention to high position rather than point to judgment and reward.

It is further difficult to conceive that the crowns imply an already judged Church, for the elders were already wearing them when John arrived in heaven. If the crowns imply rapture and reward, the rapture and reward must have taken place *before* John's being caught up into heaven. Then John's being caught up cannot symbolize the rapture. And since the text does not tell us at what time the elders received their crowns, the whole argument rests on conjecture. John clearly indicates that the casting of the crowns before the throne was an act continually repeated in conjunction with the incessant chant of the four living creatures (4:8-10). How long the creatures and the elders had been thus engaged in leading the heavenly worship of God we do not know, but there is no reason to believe that they had just begun.

Third, a resurrected, raptured, and judged Church is also in-

---

16 English, 97.

ferred from the wearing of white robes by the twenty-four elders. Even were a representative capacity for the elders demonstrable, the wearing of white robes by a special group like them need not mean that the whole Church is likewise robed. White robes portray holiness. But rapture, resurrection, and judgment of works are not prerequisite to holiness, as is easily verified. Jesus appeared in dazzling white raiment before His death and resurrection (Matt. 17:2; Mark 9:3; Luke 9:29). The Lord counsels the Laodiceans to buy and clothe themselves with white raiment *while they are yet on earth* (3:18; cf. 16:15). And the martyrs under the altar, *disembodied souls,* receive white robes (6:11). They have been neither resurrected, raptured, nor judged. White robes, then, do not necessitate a prior resurrection, rapture, and judgment of the Church. (These observations also militate against the same pretribulational inference from the white raiment of the army which returns with Christ— 19:14.)

After citing an impressive array of scholars who believe that the twenty-four elders represent the Church, A. J. McClain writes concerning those commentators, "Neither were they avowed supporters of Pretribulationism, a term which probably never occurs anywhere in their writings. ... [This] symbol [of the elders] ... to the pretribulationist, establishes his position beyond dispute."[17] "To the pretribulationist"—yes, for he already holds a pretribulational rapture as a premise when he approaches Revelation 4. But it is passing strange that a pretribulational rapture suggested itself to none of the thirty commentators cited, who did not approach the matter with the preconception that something in the passage ought to portray the rapture since here is its proper place in the chronology of Revelation. If not a single one of those erudite scholars suggested, much less held to, a pretribulational rapture despite their opinion that the twenty-four elders represent the Church, we might reflect long before drawing a pretribulational conclusion ourselves.

THE CHRONOLOGICAL STRUCTURE OF THE SEALS, TRUMPETS, AND BOWLS

Our view of the chronological structure of the seals, trumpets, and bowls largely determines whether we believe that divine

---

[17] William Culbertson and Herman B. Centz, eds., *Understanding the Times,* 206, 207.

wrath will begin to strike at the beginning of the seventieth week or during its latter half, or whether God will reserve it for the cataclysmic blast of judgment at Armageddon, when Jesus returns. The two most acceptable arrangements of seals, trumpets, and bowls may be schematized in the following manner:

```
Seals 1 2 3 4 5 6 7                    Second
      Trumpets 1 2 3 4 5 6 7           Coming
              Bowls 1 2 3 4 5 6 7
```

According to the above scheme the events under the seals, trumpets, and bowls will happen consecutively. The trumpets develop out of and constitute the seventh seal; the bowls develop out of and constitute the seventh trumpet.

According to another view, held also in whole or in part by some pretribulationists,[18] we are to regard each seventh in the seals and trumpets as reaching to Christ's return and the bowls as being poured out at the final crisis. Thus, there is a stepping back between seals and trumpets and between trumpets and bowls:

```
                          Second
                          Coming
Seals   1   2   3   4   5   6   7
        Trumpets 1 2 3 4 5 6 7
        Bowls 1234567
```

The universally acknowledged Semitic style of Revelation favors the second view, according to which the seals, trumpets, and bowls will find somewhat concurrent fulfillment. For the sweeping summary of a complex of events with later regressions to add more detail is a well-recognized feature of narratival style in Semitic literature. Chronologically, the apocalyptic visions dart back and forth with a swiftness that sometimes bewilders our Western minds. In 6:9-11 John briefly touches upon martyrdom. But in 12:13-17; 13:7, 8, 15; 14:13 he expands the same subject in greater detail. The episodical vision of the large multitude of

---

18 James M. Gray, *Synthetic Bible Studies,* 334; Wilbur M. Smith, *Moody Monthly,* 58:49; W. K. Harrison, *BibSac,* 115:203. Payne holds that the events under the seventh seal, the last three trumpets, and the last three bowls will take place after Jesus' descent onto the earth. Thus time is allowed for the gathering of the nations against Christ, who will already be in Jerusalem (Payne, 140). But Revelation 19:11-21 indicates that armies will have already gathered at Armaggedon when Jesus descends.

saints who have come out of the great tribulation (7:9-17) leaps to the end of the tribulation (cf. 7:15-17 with 21:3, 4). Chapter eleven likewise brings us to the end of the tribulation. The vision of chapter twelve takes us back to the birth of Christ and extends to the end of the tribulation (v. 14). In 13:5 the forty-two months again bring us to the end of the tribulation. The vision of the 144,000 standing with the Lamb on Mount Zion (14:1-5) can have its fulfillment only after Christ comes to earth (or the 144,000 have gone to the heavenly Zion following their preservation during the tribulation). In 14:17-20 we arrive at Armageddon, and again at 16:16. Finally, the full, detailed description comes in 19:11-21. The Semitic and apocalyptic character of Revelation forbids, then, our assuming that the seals, trumpets, and bowls follow one another in smooth succession.

Several specific considerations positively require us to believe that the seventh seal and the seventh trumpet bring us to the end of the tribulation and that the seven bowls are clustered at the end. The sixth seal leads us to the final catastrophe of judgment when Christ returns, for the wrath of the Lamb is just about to strike the wicked, who are calling upon the rocks and mountains to hide them (6:12-17). At first glance we might think that the divine wrath is placed in the past by a historical aorist.[19] But if the wrath has already fallen, how could the wicked be yet fleeing for refuge? Rather, the wrath is at the inception of its breaking forth (ingressive aorist) or on the verge of doing so (dramatic aorist)—"has just arrived" or "is here."[20] The celestial phenomena under the sixth seal are those which Jesus said would occur immediately after the tribulation and just prior to His return (Matt. 24:29, 30). If, then, the sixth seal brings us to a point of time between the tribulation and the second coming, the seventh seal must deal with the second coming itself.

The statements uttered under the seventh trumpet cannot have their fulfillment until the posttribulational advent (11:15-19). For the kingdom of the world will not become Christ's and He will not begin to reign over it until that advent (v. 15). Significantly, the phrase "is to come" is missing in the ascription to the Lord (v. 17). The time of the nations' wrath,

---

[19] Pentecost, 184.
[20] BAG, 311.

answered by God's wrath, will be Armageddon (v. 18). The judgment of the dead and the reward of the saints will come after the tribulation (v. 18). The opening of the temple and the revealing of the ark denote that the goal of the covenant has been reached; the kingdom in its full manifestation is now realized (v. 19). The mystery of God is finished; there will be no more delay (10:5-7). It is clear therefore that both the seventh seal and the seventh trumpet have to do with the advent of Christ at the close of the tribulation.

All seven bowls are clustered at the end and poured out immediately before and as Jesus returns. They are "the last," not merely because they reach to the end, but because they are all poured out *at* the very last (15:1). Notably, Armageddon is mentioned by name in the sixth bowl (16:16), and the fleeing away of the islands and the mountains (16:20) corresponds to the sixth seal (6:12-17).

The similarities between the seventh in each series also favor the view that they all relate to the end. In each we read of thunder, voices, lightnings, earthquake, and divine wrath (8:5; 11:19; 16:17, 18). And before each we detect indications that God's dealings for the age have drawn to a close: 7:14ff., "the ones who come out of the great tribulation," immediately followed by the seventh seal; 10:7, "then the mystery of God is finished" "in the days of the voice of the seventh angel, when he is about to sound"; and 16:17, "It is done," when the seventh bowl is poured out. The seventh seal, the seventh trumpet, and the seventh bowl must not be wrested apart, because their identical content and consummative character cannot have three successive and separate fulfillments.

Thus, God's wrath will not stretch throughout the whole tribulation. Those passages in Revelation which speak of divine wrath deal, rather, with the close of the tribulation.

The Church in Revelation 4-18

In Revelation 4-18 John does not mention the Church once by that name or by any other term distinctive to the believers of the present age. This, it is argued, implies the absence of the Church from the earth during the tribulation described in those chapters.

But in Revelation 4-18 the absence of the term "church" cannot carry very much weight unless the phrase "after these things" in 1:19 and 4:1 means "after the Church age." We have seen to the contrary that that phrase refers only to the visionary experiences of John in the first century. And to think that whatever prophetic sweep chapters two and three may contain stops short of the tribulation is to assume pretribulationism in the first place. If the Laodicean era of the Church includes Daniel's seventieth week, chapters two and three sweep the entire Church age to the posttribulational advent. The same· can be true if chapters two and three simply characterize types of churches which appear throughout the age. Then in the seais there is a stepping back for further detail on the closing period of the Church age, in the trumpets another, shorter stepping back for greater detail on the latter part of the tribulation, in the bowls a very short stepping back for details concerning the divine wrath to be poured out at Armageddon, and in chapters 17-19 a full account of the fall of Babylon and of the Parousia itself.

Although in chapters 4-18 John does not mention the Church as on earth by means of distinctive terminology, neither does he mention the Church as being in heaven or in the air by means of distinctive terminology. Yet the setting of most of these chapters and visions is in heaven. Thus, the omission of the Church as in heaven cancels out the omission of the Church as on earth. It may do even more, viz., create the presumption that the last generation of the Church is still on earth in these chapters since John has described no rapture.

An emphasis on the universal meaning of the term "Church" does not conform to the most frequent usage in the NT. Out of 114 occurrences, only 15 to 20 refer to the Church in the universal or generic sense. To demand, therefore, that the term appear with this sense in Revelation 4-18 is demanding more than is reasonable, especially since "church" bears only the local sense in chapters 1 to 3. And we should hardly require references to particular local churches in a general description of the tribulation.

The Church is not mentioned as such in Mark, Luke, John, 2 Timothy, Titus, 1 Peter, 2 Peter, 1 John, 2 John, or Jude, and not until chapter 16 of Romans. Unless we are prepared to relegate large chunks of the NT to a limbo of irrelevance to the Church, we cannot make the mention or omission of the term "church" a criterion for determining the applicability of a passage to saints of the present age. Perhaps it is forgivable to wonder whether an appearance of the term "church" in an indisputably tribulational passage would not be passed off as a reference to the congregation of Israel. The word does carry that sense in Acts 7:38 and in the LXX. It would be easy to say that the Israelitish character of the tribulation requires such an understanding. In other words, in demanding that the term "church" appear in a tribulational passage we forget that except by context that word no more distinguishes saints of the present age than do other terms which do designate tribulational saints throughout Revelation 4-18.

There is a dramatic style in Revelation. Once introduced onto the stage, the actors and elements which figure throughout the tribulation usually are not mentioned again. We encounter no problem, then, in that churches, once introduced in chapters two and three, do not appear as such in subsequent chapters. On the other hand, we read in the message to the church in Thyatira that overcoming believers will continue until the coming of Christ at "the end," when He will give them "authority over the nations" (2:25, 26). The ruling of the saints over the nations will begin at the setting up of Christ's earthly kingdom after the tribulation. And in the entire book of Revelation we read description of only one return of Christ, the posttribulational. We shall later see that "the end" will come at the close of the tribulation, in accordance with the Olivet Discourse. Both that discourse and the letter to Thyatira come from the lips of Jesus. We would expect Him to be consistent in His terminology. All evidence which can be gleaned from these verses points to the holding fast of Christians throughout the tribulation to the millennial kingdom.

Although in his description of the tribulation John uses no distinctive terminology for Christians, neither does he differentiate tribulational saints from Christians or vice versa. Coupled with the absence of a pretribulational rapture, resurrection, and Parousia in Revelation, the lack of differentiation appears to be more significant than lack of distinctive terminology for the Church. We have to interpolate a pretribulational rapture into Revelation before we can say that tribulational saints do not belong to the Church. But there is no validity in arguing a pretribulational conclusion from a pretribulational premise.

We need further examination of the terms which designate the saints whose presence in the tribulation all parties acknowledge. Of special interest is the reference to those who "die in the

Lord" (14:13). The term "Lord" refers to Christ, as it usually does in the NT after the gospels (see especially Acts 2:36; Phil. 2:9-11). Hence, to "die in the Lord" is equivalent to dying in Christ. Yet "the dead in Christ" shall rise at the rapture of the Church (1 Thess. 4:16-18). Walvoord even writes that the phrase "the dead in Christ" is a technical term for deceased members of the Church.[21] The resemblance between "the dead in Christ" and "the dead who die in the Lord" strikingly points toward the conclusion that those who "die in the Lord" during the tribulation are among the "dead in Christ" who will rise at the rapture (cf. also 1 Cor. 15:18). If so, the rapture must follow the tribulation, during which those saints "die in the Lord."

In 6:9; 12:17; 14:12; 20:4, tribulational saints are designated as those who keep the commandments of God and the testimony, or faith, of Jesus, just as John, who said he was in Patmos "because of the word of God and the testimony of Jesus" (1:9). It would seem that John, a member of the Church, groups himself with tribulational saints. And later John is classed with his "brethren that hold the testimony of Jesus" (19:10). The remaining appellations of tribulational saints are general terms which might be applied with equal propriety either to members of the Church or to Israelites. But in view of the address of Revelation "to the seven churches" (1:4) and in view of the glaring omission of even a short description of a pretribulational resurrection, rapture, or Parousia, we use better logic to regard tribulational saints as belonging to the Church.

In posttribulationism, the redeemed multitude who come out of the great tribulation constitute the last generation of the Church (7:9-17). To that it is objected, "The saints that will come out of the tribulation cannot be the wife of the Lamb because they will 'serve the Lamb day and night in his temple.' "[22] But Christians receive the designation "servants" many times in the NT. Is Jesus not the Lamb because He is the Shepherd? Why should not Christians be both bride and servants? It is further argued that the redeemed multitude cannot belong to the Church because previous generations of the Church would remain unaccounted for.[23] But especially in the context of the tribulation, why should not the last generation of the Church, the one hav-

---

[21] *RQ*, 39; cf. Col. 1:27.
[22] Strombeck, 129.
[23] *Ibid.*, 178.

ing come off victorious from the Antichrist, be singled out for special mention, just as the martyrs are given special mention in the first resurrection (Rev. 20:4-6)? In another vein it is argued that the redeemed multitude cannot belong to the Church because, contrary to Revelation 7:15, 17, during the tribulation there will be no divine throne on earth and no temple inhabited by God, nor will the Lamb be in the midst on earth.[24] But these considerations merely set the scene *after* the tribulation: the redeemed multitude have come out of the tribulation to enjoy the millennial earth.

THE 144,000 (7:1-8; 14:1-5)

Some have held that the 144,000 represent the Church (spiritual Israel) in the tribulation and that we are to identify them with the redeemed multitude in 7:9-17. The view is unlikely, however, because of apparently deliberate contrasts. John enumerates the 144,000 but characterizes the redeemed multitude as innumerable (7:9). He lists the twelve tribes of Israel from which the 144,000 come but states that the redeemed multitude derive "from every nation and all tribes and peoples and tongues" (7:9).

Most pretribulationists hold that the 144,000 compose a Jewish remnant who, in the absence of the Church, will evangelize the world during the tribulation. Now it is true that an angel calls the 144,000 "bond-servants" (7:3). But the designation may relate to a function other than preaching of the Gospel. The vision of the redeemed multitude immediately follows that of the 144,000 in chapter seven, and the vision of the angel with the eternal Gospel follows in chapter fourteen. However, the mere sequence of visions does not necessitate a causal connection in which the redeemed multitude will come into being as a consequence of the preaching of the eternal Gospel by the 144,000. In chapter fourteen the 144,000 are with the Lamb on Mount Zion—hence probably a millennial scene—so that in the next vision the preaching of the eternal Gospel during the tribulation has no connection. Besides, it is an *angel* who has the eternal Gospel. We are to associate him and his Gospel, not with the 144,000, but with the series of angels who appear in the remainder of the chapter and in the next two chapters. (It is difficult to equate

---

[24] English, 103.

Mount Zion in 14:1 with the heavenly Zion, because the 144,
000 will be preserved *on earth* throughout the tribulation
[7:14]. For the same reason, however, the scene is posttribulational even though Zion here be taken as heavenly.)

Since John does not reveal the function of the 144,000, the
usual view among pretribulationists remains conjectural. We may
construct other plausible roles for the 144,000. For example,
they may constitute a Jewish remnant—not members of the
Church and therefore not to be raptured—physically preserved
through the tribulation, converted immediately after the rapture as they see their Messiah descending onto the earth (Zech.
3:8, 9; 12:9-13:1; Mal. 3:1-5; Rom. 11:26, 27), and entering the millennium in their natural bodies to form the nucleus
of the reestablished Davidic kingdom. They would be "orthodox"
(though unconverted) Jews who will resist the seductions of the
Antichrist. The designation "bond-servants" (7:3), then, antici-
pates their role in the reestablishment of the Davidic kingdom.
Isaiah calls unregenerate Israel the "servant" of the Lord
(42:18-25) in anticipation of the nation's restoration (43:1ff.)—
exactly the interpretation here given for the 144,000. There are
similar anticipations of future work for God in the consecration
of Jeremiah before his birth (Jer. 1:5) and the filling of John
the Baptist with the Holy Spirit from his mother's womb (Luke
1:15) long before either could have been regenerate.

The 144,000 will be "first fruits" (14:4) in that they will
constitute the pledge of an abundant harvest of blessing when
the Messiah returns. They will be undefiled virgins (14:4) in the
religious sense that they will have resisted the seductions of pa-
gan beliefs and associated immoralities, particularly in the pres-
sure to worship "the image of the beast" (13:11-18; cf. 14:8;
2 Cor. 11:2; Jas. 4:4; and many OT passages where the contrasting figures of fornication and virginity bear a religious sense, especially in connection with cultic prostitution at
heathen sanctuaries). Against regarding the virginity of the
144,000 as celibacy is the teaching that lawful sexual inter-
course does not defile (Heb. 13:4; contrast Rev. 14:4, where
the "women" may be cultic prostitutes). Thus, the 144,000 will
include both men and women who will populate and replenish
the millennial kingdom of Israel. If they will resist the Antichrist
but remain unbelievers in Christ until the second coming, the
reason for their sealing at once becomes apparent: their unconvert-

ed state will require special protection from the wrath of God and the persecution of the Antichrist.

Three passages in the OT support the above view. In a context which concerns Armageddon and immediately after mention of the celestial phenomena which will come between the tribulation and the Parousia (Matt. 24:29, 30), Joel prophesies the salvation of a Jewish remnant (2:32). Likewise, Zephaniah prophesies that following the battle of Armageddon the Lord will convert the remnant of Israel, who are described in terminology *which John allusively quotes to describe the 144,000* (3:8-13; cf. Rev. 14:5). Zechariah foretells that the surviving Jews will repent when they look on Him whom they have pierced as He comes to deliver them from their surrounding enemies (12:2-13:1, especially 12:10-14, quoted in Matt. 24:30 concerning the posttribulational advent). What is more natural than to regard the 144,000 as forming that Jewish remnant, divinely preserved through the tribulation and converted at the end?[25]

A VISION OF THE RAPTURE

In 14:14-20 two harvests are reaped, the first by one like a son of man on whose head rests a golden crown, the second by an angel who casts his harvest into the winepress of God's wrath. The first harvest (vv. 14-16) is best taken as symbolic of the rapture. For the phrase "one like a son of man" identifies both the reaper of the first harvest and, in John's first vision, Christ Himself (1:13; cf. John 5:27). Immediately we think of "the Son of Man coming on the clouds of the sky" (Matt. 24:30) and Paul's comparison of the resurrection and translation of Christians to a harvest (1 Corinthians 15:23, 35ff.). The "white cloud" on which sits the reaper in John's vision corresponds to the clouds associated with the Parousia in Matthew 24:30; Acts 1:9-11; and 1 Thessalonians 4:17. The special dignity indi-

---

[25] We might think of two other possibilities predicated on the doubtful assumption that the 144,000 will be converted toward the beginning of the tribulation. The first is that they will belong to the Church but require special sealing because of the intensity of persecution in Palestine. The second is that the 144,000 will constitute a group of redeemed Jews set apart from the Church for natural-bodied entrance into the Davidic kingdom. The term "first fruits" regularly denotes a sacrifice in the OT and might allow the view that the 144,000 will be such a special portion for God in anticipation of what will come on a grander scale during the millennium.

cated by the golden crown also points to the Lord. The second harvest in Revelation 14:14-20 lands the wicked in "the great winepress of the wrath of God" (vv. 19, 20, Armageddon; cf. Joel 3:13). But in the first there is only the reaping as though the Son of Man gathers the harvest to Himself. The two harvests, then, seem to be distinct. The one terminates before the other begins. The Son of Man reaps the first, an angel the second. The first lacks the element of wrath. The second exhibits it prominently. The first reaping immediately follows the beatitude upon "the dead who die in the Lord" (14:13). Consequently, a description of the rapture in which "the dead in Christ shall rise first" (1 Thess. 4:16) follows very fittingly. The conjunction with Armageddon (see v. 20: "blood ... up to the horses' bridles, for a distance of two hundred miles" puts the rapture, figuratively described in the first harvest, at the close of the tribulation.

Whereas we have in the whole of Revelation no description of a pretribulational return of Christ, rapture, or first resurrection—an absence incredible from the standpoint of the book's being addressed to the churches and its purporting to reveal in detail final events—we do have the first harvest in 14:14-20, the return of Christ in 19:11ff., and the first resurrection in 20:4-6—all posttribulational.

It might be objected that the above interpretation of 14:14-20 violates the order of harvests in Matthew 13:36ff., where the wicked are reaped before the righteous. But this poses an equal problem in pretribulationism, where the rapture is thought to take place before the judgments of God on the wicked. In Matthew 13 the kingdom of heaven is in view, in Revelation 14 the armies assembled at Armageddon. This difference between spheres of judgment explains how the false professors within the kingdom may be purged before the rapture, while the rapture may be followed by a judgmental harvest at Armageddon of those who make no claim to belong to the kingdom of heaven. It has also been objected that the reaper on the cloud could not be Christ because an angel commands him to thrust in his sickle. But the angel merely relays the Father's will in a fashion which makes possible John's hearing and recording it (cf. Matt. 24:36; Mark 13:32).

The Marriage Supper of the Lamb

In 19:7-9 John records a hymn concerning the marriage supper of the Lamb. Three pretribulational lines of argument stem from these verses. First, the fine, white linen of the bride implies that the judgment of the Church's works will have already occurred. That in turn implies a preceding rapture. The argument has already received consideration in the section on the twenty-four elders. Additional proof that the bride's raiment does not require a preceding rapture and judgment comes from the Oriental custom of arraying the bride *before* the groom came to receive her.

Second and third, the marriage supper is spoken of as having taken place in the past and in heaven; hence Jesus must have previously come for His bride (the Church as distinct from Israel the wife of Jehovah) and taken her to heaven. But is the bride to be equated with the Church? Israel, too, is likened to a bride (Isa. 49:18; 61:10; 62:5; Jer. 2:32; Hosea 2:19, 20) and the Church is likened to a wife (Eph. 5:22-33). We should not expect to find rigid consistency in the biblical use of metaphors. To press woodenly the marital relationship of both Israel and the Church to the Lord would be to say that God is a bigamist. Mixed metaphors abound in the Scriptures: Christ is shepherd and lamb, king and slave, priest and sacrifice. The Church is priesthood and temple, body and bride. Spiritual relationships are so multiform and transcendent that they require seemingly contradictory, but really complementary, metaphors. Thus, since Israel as well as the Church is both bride and wife, we should not jump to the conclusion that the Lamb's bride and wife consists of the Church alone.

On the contrary, the context indicates that at the marriage supper of the Lamb the bride includes Israel: "Come here, I shall show you *the bride, the wife* of the Lamb. And he . . . showed me *the holy city, Jerusalem,* . . . with twelve gates, . . . and names were written on them, which are those *of the twelve tribes of the sons of Israel"* (21:9; 10, 12). If, therefore, the marriage supper does not require a pretribulational resurrection and rapture of the Israelitish segment of the bride, neither does it require a pretribulational resurrection and rapture of the Church. (In accordance with Daniel 12:1, 2, most pretribulationists acknowledge that Israel's resurrection will follow the tribulation.)

Nor is the marriage supper necessarily spoken of as in the past. The action in the aorist ($\hat{\eta}\lambda\theta\epsilon\nu$) may be ingressive or dramatic, denoting the inauguration or immediacy of the event. If this is the meaning, the marriage supper will occur immediately upon Christ's descent. Mathematical calculations whether the judgment of Christians and the marriage supper could take place *during* Christ's descent are altogether unnecessary, if not ludicrous.[26]

"THE ARMIES WHICH ARE IN HEAVEN"

"The armies . . . in heaven" will follow Christ as He descends (19:14). Some have identified these armies with angelic hosts. However, the white linen worn by the armies has been ascribed to the saints a few verses earlier. It is more natural, then, to assume that the saints are in view here, too. Identifying the armies with the Church, we might reason that the rapture must already have taken place, since the armies are in heaven. But the weakness in such reasoning lies in the equation of the armies with the *totality* of the Church. Are we to think that the OT saints, not yet resurrected, will be excluded from these armies? Where are most of the saints, where is most of the Church, *now*? In heaven. Either John does not distinguish living Christians because of the preponderating number of deceased saints, or he sees Jesus descending with the disembodied saints just before those on earth have been raptured. In the latter case he means the designation "in heaven" to distinguish the deceased in heaven from saints on earth who have not yet joined the heavenly train.

THE MARTYRS ONLY?

Some have thought that in the first resurrection mentioned in Revelation 20:4-6 only the tribulational martyrs will be raised. From this they infer that there must have been a separate, pretribulational phase of the first resurrection for the inclusion of other saints. Yet according to Daniel 12:1, 2 the resurrection

---

[26] Though recognizing the earthly setting of the marriage banquet, Walvoord nonetheless maintains that the bridegroom must have come for the bride before the marriage supper (*BibSac*, 123:102, 103). That is true, but the posttribulational advent itself may be the coming of Christ for His bride. A pretribulational argument has to rest on two premises, occurrence of the banquet during the tribulation and a setting in heaven. Both premises are bad.

of OT saints will occur after the tribulation, i.e., at the time of the first resurrection in Revelation 20:4-6. Therefore John's mention of the tribulational martyrs should not be taken to exclude the raising of other saints, or of the Church, at the same time. Limiting the first resurrection in Revelation 20:4-6 to martyrs requires one of two very unlikely assumptions: that no tribulational saints will die naturally, or that if some die naturally, they will not be raised at the second coming. It is true that in 20:4-6 John shines a spotlight on the tribulational martyrs just as he does elsewhere (6:9-11; 14:13; 16:6). But the special mention of their living and reigning with Christ is intended to encourage steadfastness in persecution. At the same time, the general term "first resurrection" and the co-reigning with Christ of those who will rise then leave room for all the saints to be included (cf. Matt. 19:28; 1 Cor. 6:2, 3; Rev. 2:26; 3:21; 5:10).

THE STAR AND SUN

Some have contrasted Christ's coming as "the bright, the morning star" (Rev. 22:16; cf. 2 Pet. 1:19), regarded as pretribulational, and His coming as "the sun of righteousness" (Mal. 4:2) at the beginning of the millennium. But the morning star appears immediately before dawn in the dark of night. If gross darkness will characterize the tribulation, the appearance of the morning star should occur during the dark, closing hours of the tribulation. So far as the previous tribulation is in view, then, the return of Jesus at the close of the tribulation will be the "morning star" which will signal the end of the night. So far as the millennium is in view, that return, like the rays of the dawning sun, will introduce the glorious Messianic reign

The Apocalypse is addressed to churches for their heartening by means of information concerning final events which will spell believers' victory and vindication. Yet nowhere does John describe, straightforwardly or figuratively, a pretribulational return of Christ, resurrection, or rapture of the Church. On the other hand, the descriptions of the reaping done by Christ immediately prior to and in connection with Armageddon, of the posttribulational advent, and of the first resurrection between the tribulation and the millennium perfectly fit and strongly support posttribulationism. As required by the address, scope, and purpose of the book, they provide a complete picture of the blessed hope of the Church—advent, resurrection, and gathering in rapture.

6

The Day of the Lord

The "day of the Lord," with its corollary the "day of Christ," figures prominently in discussion of the rapture. In these phrases the term "day" does not refer to twenty-four hours, but to a longer period of time, a period which includes the millennium and the final judgment. With reference to the time of the rapture, the crux of the argument lies in the *terminus a quo,* the beginning point, of the day of the Lord, not in its millennial extension. Most contemporary pretribulationists feel that the day of the Lord will begin immediately upon the rapture of the Church and will thereby include the tribulation. In this they depart from older pretribulationists.[1]

We need then to consider evidence which might lead us to identify the first part of the day of the Lord with the tribulation. Stanton amasses lengthy OT quotations describing the day of the Lord and parallels them with passages in Revelation.[2] However, the passages in Revelation concern the battle of Armageddon at the close of the tribulation. Therefore, the comparison rather favors the view that the day will begin at the posttribulational advent rather than earlier. Wood draws a parallel between phraseology in Joel 2:1, 2 ("the day of the Lord . . . there has never been anything like it") and Jeremiah 30:7;

---

[1] E.g., Scofield, *SRB*, Rev. 19:19, note; Gaebelein, *Harmony of the Prophetic Word,* 41; Anderson, *The Coming Prince,* 184; Thiessen, 39.

[2] Stanton, 75ff.

Daniel 12:1; and Matthew 24:21 ("great tribulation, such as has not occurred since the beginning of the world until now").[3] But in Joel 2:2 the clauses "there has never been anything like it, nor will there be again after it" do not refer to the day of the Lord, but to "a great and mighty people" who are an invading army of locusts in Joel's own time. Thus Joel is not talking about the tribulation or any other event in the future.

In a strenuous effort to include the tribulation in the day of the Lord, Strombeck compares the first and second seals of Revelation 6:2-4 with Paul's statement that "the day of the Lord will come just like a thief in the night. While they are saying, 'Peace and safety!' then destruction will come upon them suddenly . . ." (1 Thess. 5:2, 3).[4] But it is doubtful that the rider on the white horse in Revelation stands for the "peace and safety" of Paul's statement (so Strombeck), for the rider has a "bow" and goes out "conquering, and to conquer." And there is no necessity to identify (as Strombeck does) the sudden destruction in 1 Thessalonians 5:2, 3 with the taking of peace from the earth under the second seal, for the destruction when Christ returns at Armageddon will strike with even greater suddenness. Strombeck goes on to identify the third horseman of famine (Rev. 6:5, 6) with the famine in Joel 1:16-18, where the day of the Lord is mentioned. But, as just noted, the context in Joel centers around a plague of locusts in Joel's own time and only later leaps into the far future, and then not to the tribulation but to Armageddon at its close (2:4-10, 20, 30, 31; 3:12-17). Therefore, the condition of famine in Joel 1:16-18 describes the extremity to which the people in Judea were reduced long ago. Strombeck next compares death under the fourth seal with Isaiah 66:16: "Those slain by the Lord will be many." But in the Isaianic passage the prophet does not use the expression "the day of the Lord." An identification of that passage with the one in Revelation would therefore prove nothing. Furthermore, Isaiah 66:15, 16 probably refers to the Lord's coming in judgment at Armageddon (compare v. 15 with 2 Thess. 1:7-9), i.e., at the close of the tribulation.

Strombeck's last set of parallels draws upon the similarities of the sixth seal (Rev. 6:12-17) with Isaiah 2:19; 13:9-13; 34:4; Joel 2:30, 31; 3:16; and Zephaniah 1:15. However, we

---

[3] Wood, 13, 14.
[4] Strombeck, 46ff.

have already seen that the sixth seal brings us to the posttribulational advent.[5] Thus the parallel does not prove that the day
of the Lord includes the preceding seven years. Even were the
sixth seal to take place toward the beginning of the tribulation,
the same events will occur "immediately after the tribulation of
those days" (Matt. 24:29, 30). Hence, the OT passages about
the day of the Lord might parallel Matthew 24:29, 30 rather
than Revelation 6:12-17, with resultant loss of evidence for
the inclusion of the tribulation in the day of the Lord.

The effort to include Daniel's seventieth week in the day of
the Lord by paralleling passages about the day of the Lord and
passages in Revelation fails. Sometimes the parallels are more apparent than real. The contexts in those OT passages which mention the day of the Lord point to the crisis of Armageddon and
the Parousia, which will come immediately after the tribulation.
Some of the passages in Revelation likewise refer to that crisis,
which will bring judgment upon the wicked and deliverance for
the godly (cf. these very same aspects of the day of the Lord in
Joel 2:32-3:1, 16b-21; Amos 5:15, 18-20; Obad. 15, 17;
Zeph. 2:3; 3:11, 16; Zech. 14).

It is suggested that passages describing the tribulation and
using the phrase "in that day" (without the qualifying phrase
"of the Lord") demonstrate that the day of the Lord will begin
with the tribulation. But although "that day" many times refers
to the day of the Lord, we may doubt that such an indistinctive
phrase gained a stereotyped, technical meaning. In fact, the same
phrase appears many times in the OT historical books without
reference to the day of the Lord.[6] Even in the prophetical books
the phrase appears without reference to the day of the Lord.[7]
The very nature of the pronoun "that" requires a contextual antecedent. Hence, the context alone determines whether "that
day" refers to the day of the Lord. To demonstrate such a reference, we need in the passage either an express mention of the day
of the Lord or an identifiability of the events in the passage with
those which elsewhere are expressly associated with the day of
the Lord. And again, we shall have to deduct the many passages
containing the phrase "in that day" which describe only the final

---

[5] See above on Revelation.
[6] See a concordance.
[7] E.g., in Isa. 20:6; 22:12, 20; 23:15; Jer. 4:9; 39:16, 17; 48:41; 49:22,
26; Ezek. 24:26, 27; 45:22; Hos. 1:5; Haggai 2:23; Zech. 11:11.

crisis at Armageddon without inclusion of anterior distresses during the tribulation. When these factors are taken into account, the evidence for making the tribulation the first part of the day of the Lord disappears.

Several have reasoned from 1 Thessalonians 5:2, 3 that since the day of the Lord will come at a time of seeming peace and safety, it will have to begin before the catastrophic events of the tribulational period. However, Paul did not write, "When there shall *be* peace and safety," but rather, "While they are *saying* . . . ." The very form of the statement suggests that peace and safety will not be the actual condition of the world preceding the day of the Lord, but the expressed *wish* and/or *expectation* of men, which God will answer with a blow of judgment. Cf. " 'Peace, peace,' but there is no peace" (Jer. 6:14; 8:11; Ezek. 13:10). Perhaps just before Armageddon there will be a lull, a seeming end of world upheavals, which will excite men's hopes for the peace which has so long eluded them (as suggested by the three-and-a-half days' merriment in Rev. 11:7-11). Paul's statement does not require that peace and safety be a condition of fact. If peace and safety must exist as actualities when the day of the Lord begins, that day could not begin and the rapture could not occur at the present time. For the current condition of the world is neither peaceful nor safe.

A final argument that the day of the Lord begins with the tribulation rests on Revelation 1:10: "I [John] was in the Spirit on the Lord's day. . . ." According to the argument, "the Lord's day" is equivalent to the day of the Lord. Since John's visions deal largely with the tribulational period, the day of the Lord will cover that period.

The argument turns on the meaning of the phrase "on the Lord's day" (ἐν τῇ κυριακῇ ἡμέρᾳ), in which the adjectival form translated "Lord's" is notable. In some contrast, "the day of the Lord" regularly takes the form ἡ ἡμέρα τοῦ κυρίου , not with an adjective but with a noun in the genitive for the qualifier "of the Lord." The latter form appears frequently throughout the LXX and the NT. Those who endeavor to equate the two expressions argue that "the Lord's day" could have no other meaning in the NT because it did not apply to the first day of the week until one hundred years after the writing of the Apocalypse. That, however, is an overstatement, for very early in the second century, possibly even in the latter half of the first century, the term carries the meaning "Sunday" (*Didache* 14:1; Ignatius, *To the Mag-*

nesians 9:1). They further argue that the adjectival form "Lord's" legitimately translates the Hebrew "(day) of the Lord." That may be. But nowhere in the LXX does an adjectival rendering appear. A parallel is claimed in the comparison between Luke 17:22, "days of the Son of Man" (noun in the genitive), and 1 Corinthians 4:3, "man's day" (adjective). But those are not synonymous expressions, as a mere glance at the contexts will show. Nor are they the stereotyped kind of expression that "the day of the Lord" had come to be.

"The Lord's day" early became the technical expression for the first day of the week.[8] Deissmann thinks it possible that "the Lord's day" was a defiant Christian replacement of "Emperor's Day," celebrated at least monthly in Egypt and in Asia Minor, where the seven churches of Revelation were located.[9] The adjectival usage of κυριακός in "the Lord's supper" (1 Cor. 11:20), celebrated on Sunday, favors the idea that "the Lord's day" is Sunday. Perhaps the designation of one by κυριακός was the basis for like designation of the other. The natural reading of the context in Revelation 1:10 suggests nothing more than the first day of the week. John describes his experience according to place—Patmos; time—Sunday; and event—coming to be in the Spirit. Surely, then, the appeal to "the Lord's day" falls far short of showing that the tribulation comes within the day of the Lord.

Older pretribulationists had good reason to place the *terminus a quo* of the day of the Lord after the tribulation:

Paul writes that the day of the Lord cannot have come already because two outstanding events, which have not yet taken place, must take place *before* that day (2 Thess. 2:1-4). These events, the revelation of the man of lawlessness and the apostasy, which will culminate in his self-deification, will fall within the tribulation. It is self-evident that since these two events will occur *before* the day of the Lord, the day of the Lord cannot include the tribulational period during which they occur.

Malachi prophesies that Elijah will reappear "before the coming of the great and terrible day of the Lord" (Mal. 4:5). (The alternatives, personal Elijah or virtual Elijah, do not affect the argument.) Hence, the day of the Lord cannot include the tribulational period during which Elijah will minister—unless Malachi's

---

[8] See Alford's extended note, IV, 554, BAG, MM, Kittel, Thayer, Cremer.
[9] Deissmann, LAE, 357ff.

prediction has already been fulfilled or Elijah will reappear to minister before the tribulation.

Largely on the assumption that if Elijah were yet to come he would have to come before the tribulation, Armerding contends that John the Baptist completely fulfilled Malachi's prophecy.[10] This fails even to consider the possibility that the day of the Lord may not begin until after the tribulation. The nonmention of Elijah in Jesus' description of the tribulation in Matthew 24—an argument from silence in support of the Baptist's exhaustion of Malachi's prophecy—proves nothing, for neither is the Antichrist individually named in that description even though he predominates the human scene during that time. The gracious ministry of Elijah according to Malachi and the judgmental ministry of the two witnesses during part of the tribulation (Rev. 11:1-13)—an argument from contrast in support of the Baptist's exhaustion of Malachi's prophecy—need not contradict. In the first place, the futurity of Elijah's reappearance does not depend on an identification of him with one of the two witnesses. But if he will in fact be one of the two, he may well direct a judgmental ministry against the wicked and a gracious ministry toward those willing to be prepared for the Messiah's return.

John the Baptist did not exhaust the prophecy of Malachi. Gabriel explained that John was Elijah in the sense that he came "in the spirit and power of Elijah" (Luke 1:17). Jesus confirmed that "Elijah is coming and will restore all things" (Matt. 17:11). This He said *after* John's death. Elijah is yet to come.

The prophecy of Malachi, the reiteration of that prophecy by Jesus, the appearance of Elijah with Christ at the Transfiguration, and the likeness of Elijah's miracles in the OT to the miracles in Revelation 11:1-13 all unite to identify Elijah as one of the two witnesses. The early Church almost universally accepted the identification. John writes that the two witnesses will prophesy 1,260 days, apparently the *latter* half of Daniel's seventieth week, for "the nations" will surely not "tread under foot the holy city" until the Antichrist breaks his covenant with the Jews (Rev. 11:2, 3). The day of the Lord, then, cannot begin until the expiration of Elijah's ministry, which occupies the final half of the tribulation.

Conceivably, we might deny that Elijah will be one of the two

---

[10] *BibSac*, 100:89-97.

witnesses and place Elijah's reappearance within the Church age prior to the tribulation. But we have then a lack of imminence unacceptable in pretribulationism, for Elijah's ministry would still delay the day of the Lord. Or we might posit an interval between the rapture and the tribulation by interpolating Elijah's reappearance. But the very interval, by separating the rapture from the day of the Lord, would leave the difficulties about to be mentioned.

Certain celestial portents will both precede the day of the Lord (Joel 2:30, 31) and follow immediately upon the tribulation (Matt. 24:29). Clearly, the day of the Lord will not begin with the tribulation or any part of it, for otherwise the heavenly portents after the tribulation could not be said to precede that day. It cannot successfully be maintained to the contrary that the portents in Joel will find fulfillment toward the beginning of the tribulation under the sixth seal (Rev. 6:12-17) because, as we have seen, the sixth seal brings us to the end of the tribulation. And in 3:15 Joel mentions *in connection with Armageddon at the close of the tribulation* the same celestial portents which *precede* the day of the Lord according to 2:30, 31. Even if the sixth seal came shortly after the beginning of the tribulation and remained identical with Joel's portents, a considerable gap would still separate the rapture from the day of the Lord.

We might be tempted to think that an event in an early stage of the day of the Lord is said to happen before that day in the sense that it will precede a later stage.[11] But what is the sense in saying that something that happened Monday morning happened before Monday because it happened before Monday afternoon? Would we also want to say that the second coming will occur before the day of the Lord because it will occur before the millennial phase of the day, or that the millennium will precede the day of the Lord because it will precede the phase of final judgment?

We can hardly appeal to historical foreshadowings of the day of the Lord, such as the plague of locusts in Joel's day and the Babylonian invasion of Judah, to prove that a part of the day (the tribulation) precedes the posttribulational advent. The precursive and final fulfillments are self-contained units, separated by many centuries. The situation between them in no way

---

[11] Pentecost, 310.

parallels the successive events which will follow one right after another in the future and final fulfillment. "Before the day of the Lord" must mean before the whole period, before every event and episode within the day, else plain language loses its meaning.

Since the day of the Lord will begin after the tribulation, there would be a gap of seven years between a pretribulational rapture and the day of the Lord. Such an interval would destroy any relevance of the day of the Lord to members of the Church living on earth, for they would have been translated long before the day of the Lord set in. Yet Paul writes, "But you, brethren, are not in darkness, that the day [of the Lord—see v. 2] should overtake you like a thief; . . . so then let us not sleep as others do, but let us be alert and sober" (1 Thess. 5:4, 6). Paul's meaning is clear: upon the unsuspecting wicked the day of the Lord will come like a thief; upon the saints the day will not come like a thief, because they will be watching and therefore will not be surprised. But if the Church is to be removed years before the day begins, Paul's exhortation to be alert for the day becomes meaningless. And what point is there in saying that the day will not come like a thief upon Christians, who are watching, if it will not come upon them at all? Since the day of the Lord will begin after the tribulation and since Christians will not be taken by surprise at the arrival of that day, the Church will have come through the tribulation.

Paul, correcting false impressions concerning the day of the Lord, does not deny that Christians will meet that day, but rather gives them two signalling events by which they may recognize its approach—the apostasy and the revelation of the man of lawlessness (2 Thess. 2:1-5). If pretribulationism be true, Paul should have quieted the agitation of the Thessalonians by telling them that a pretribulational rapture will absent them long before the arrival of the day of the Lord. Instead, he informs them of harbingers within the tribulation by which they will see the approach of the day beforehand. So long as any gap (even three and one-half years) separates the rapture from the day of the Lord, the anomaly for pretribulationism remains. And if the day of Christ and similar expressions are equivalent to the day of the Lord, the connection between the Church and the day gains further strength.

A distinction is often made, however, between a pretribulational day of Christ and a following day of the Lord. The phrases "day of Christ" and "day" with a compound appellative appear in 1 Corinthians 1:8; 5:5 (perhaps); 2 Corinthians 1:14; Philippians 1:6, 10; 2:16. The arbitrariness of the proposed distinction becomes evident in the following observations:

In not one passage is the day of Christ construed with the rapture or a pretribulational coming of Christ. In the one reference where Paul connects the phrase with other eschatological terms (1 Cor. 1:8), those terms are at least ambiguous if not weighted on the posttribulational side (see below).

One of the six occurrences of the phrase rests on a highly questionable textual basis (1 Cor. 5:5). Since P[46] and B agree on the shorter reading with ample support from patristic literature, we should probably prefer "day of the Lord" over "day of the Lord Jesus." It might be argued that the added titles of Christ could easily have dropped out in transcription. But the variations among the manuscripts which carry our Lord's title and names in compound form suggest addition rather than subtraction, perhaps in conformity with Paul's frequent use of the compound title. At the very least, there is sufficient variation to prevent insistence upon the reading "day of the Lord Jesus" in this verse. And if "day of the Lord" be read here, as seems preferable, pretribulationism falls into difficulty, for Paul writes, "I have decided to deliver such a one to Satan for the destruction of his flesh, that his spirit may be saved in the day of the Lord." It would be highly anticlimactic for Paul to say that the spirit of a sinning Christian will be saved in the day of the Lord if that Christian will have been glorified seven years prior to that day.

Of the remaining five occurrences, there are four different combinations of the component names in the full title of Christ: "day of our Lord Jesus Christ" (1 Cor. 1:8); "day of our Lord Jesus" (2 Cor. 1:14); "day of Christ Jesus" or "Jesus Christ" (Phil. 1:6—again manuscripts vary); "day of Christ" (Phil. 1:10; 2:16). The variations suggest that we do not have a single technical phrase in contradistinction to the day of the Lord, but an expansion of the basic term "day of the Lord."[12] The more familiar names, "Jesus" and "Christ," are added, or substituted, to accentuate the

---

[12] Cf. Clarence E. Mason, Jr., *BibSac,* 125:352-359. Mason, a pretribulationist, recognizes the lack of hard and fast distinctions, but neglects to overturn the evidence that the day of the Lord (Jesus Christ) will not begin until after the tribulation.

relationship of Christians to the day of the Lord. In a context concerning the wicked, an undertone of dread and doom naturally pervades the passage. A reference to the saints' hope naturally vibrates with joy and anticipation. But the double relationship of the day to saved and unsaved no more proves a distinction between two days than the double relationship of Christ as ruler of Israel and as king over the nations proves two millenniums. And if mere differences in titles and names justified distinctions, we ought to distinguish between "the judgment-seat of God" (Rom. 14:10, correct text) and "the judgment-seat of Christ" (2 Cor. 5:10). Yet no one thinks of doing so. For that matter, we ought to distinguish among the *four* variations in the designations of Christ, because "day of Christ" differs just as much from "day of our Lord Jesus" as from "day of the Lord." Besides, the term "Lord" (κύριος) appears by itself many times with reference to Christ, and overwhelmingly so in Paul, who alone uses the phrases we are examining. What then is the essential difference between the various expressions if the proper names and titles all refer to the same person?

In the NT sixteen expressions appear in which the term "day" is used eschatologically.[13] Twenty times "day" appears without a qualifying phrase. In view of the wide variety of expressions and the numerous instances where "day" occurs without special qualification, it seems a very dubious procedure to select five out of the sixteen expressions, lump together four of the five as equivalent to one another, and distinguish the four from the one remaining. There is no solid basis, then, for distinguishing between the day of Christ and the day of the Lord. That day cannot begin until after the revelation of the Antichrist and the apostasy, after the ministry of Elijah, after the celestial phenomena between the tribulation and the posttribulational advent, in short, not until after the tribulation. Paul's admonition to be prepared for that day and his explanation that Christians will recognize

---

[13] See also "that day" (Matt. 7:22; 24:36; 26:29; Mark 13:32; 14:25; Luke 10:12; 17:31; 21:34; 1 Thess. 5:4; 2 Tim. 1:12, 18; 4:8); "day of judgment" (Matt. 10:15; 11:22, 24; 12:36; 2 Pet. 2:9; 3:7; 1 John 4:17); "the day" (Matt. 25:13; Luke 17:30; Rom. 2:16; 13:12; 1 Cor. 3:13; Heb. 10:25; 2 Pet. 1:19); "His day" (Luke 17:24); "last day" (John 6:39, 40, 44, 54; 12:48); "day of the Lord" (Acts 2:20; 1 Thess. 5:2; 2 Thess. 2:2; 2 Pet. 3:10); "a day" (Acts 17:31); "day of wrath" (Rom. 2:5; Rev. 6:17); "day of redemption" (Eph. 4:30); "day of visitation" (1 Pet. 2:12); "day of God" (2 Pet. 3:12); "the great day" (Jude 6; Rev. 16:14).

the approach of that day require a connection between the last generation of the Church and the arrival of the day of the Lord. Hence, the Church will continue on earth throughout the tribulation until the beginning of that day.

7

Comfort in 1 Thessalonians
4:13-5:11

Paul devotes 1 Thessalonians 4:13-5:11 to comfort of living saints concerning departed saints. The need for comfort arose out of a misconception on the part of the Thessalonian Christians with regard to the relationship of deceased believers to the second coming and kingdom of Christ.

CAUSE FOR SORROW

Paul implies that the misunderstanding derived from ignorance (v. 13). We might think that the sorrow of the Thessalonians derived from a mistaken belief in a remaining behind of deceased believers at a pretribulational rapture with a consequent later date of resurrection, perhaps after the tribulation. Thus, deceased believers, they thought, will miss the joy and blessing of the rapture.[1] Not objectionable in itself, this interpretation nevertheless rests on a pretribulational assumption and therefore does not provide support for pretribulationism unless another understanding equally or more harmonious with the text and background fails to surface.

But another, probably superior, explanation for the

---

[1] Walvoord, *RQ,* 80.

Thessalonians' sorrow does surface. The Thessalonians thought that only living believers will be raptured at the second coming and so the dead will not share in the meeting with Jesus and the honor of joining His retinue as He descends. The Thessalonians further thought that departed brethren, along with the wicked dead, will not rise until after the Messianic kingdom, and thus will miss the blessedness of Christ's earthly reign. This view gives a more substantial basis for the Thessalonians' sorrow than the notion that the dead in Christ will be left out of a pretribulational rapture. For what if deceased Christians will not rise till after the tribulation? Already they are in heaven with Christ and during the tribulation would continue there with pretribulationally translated saints. But if they are not to join Him in His public revelation and earthly dominion, real ground exists for sorrow concerning their disadvantage.

According to one line of reasoning, if the Thessalonians had thought that they were to go through the tribulation, they would have been concerned regarding their *own* welfare, not that of deceased believers. The way it is, Paul must have previously taught them pretribulationism.[2] But the Thessalonians, already suffering dire persecution, did not occupy themselves with cringing fears of future distresses. In this very epistle Paul commends them for their attitude toward suffering: they had "received the word in much tribulation with joy of the Holy Spirit" (1:6; cf. Acts 17:1-13; Phil. 1:29).

Even if Paul were comforting the living Thessalonians concerning their *own* fate, an intervening period of tribulation still would not clash with the comforting tone of the passage. In the Upper Room Discourse Jesus combined comfort with warning of persecution and distress. But it was not about *themselves* or about the possibility that *they* should go through the tribulation that the Thessalonians were thinking anyway. They were concerned about their departed brethren, who by decease could have no connection with a future tribulation on earth. To introduce the tribulation into the passage is to introduce an entirely foreign element. Indeed, the tribulation is not once mentioned or implied.

We might think that under posttribulationism Paul would have mentioned the antecedence of the tribulation to the rapture and that his failure to do so argues in favor of pretribulationism.

---

2 Wood, 47.

However, to have written that the tribulation will precede the rapture would have been quite extraneous to his purpose, for he was not discussing the time of the rapture but the chronological relationship of the resurrection of deceased saints to the translation of living saints. Hence, the nonmention of a preceding period of tribulation does not imply that there will be none. Paul's discussion in chapter four is "concerning those who have fallen asleep," not concerning those who, remaining alive, may go through the tribulation.

"BY THE WORD OF THE LORD"

Paul confirms what he has written with a revelation "by the word of the Lord" (v. 15). Just possibly he refers to a direct and special revelation from the Lord. Some have seized on the possibility to argue that the rapture has nothing to do with the already revealed posttribulational advent of Christ. But the new revelation would concern the synchronization of the resurrection of deceased saints with the translation of living saints, not the whole of the rapture and its relation to other events. Moreover, the phrase "by the word of the Lord" lends itself to several other interpretations:

"The word of the Lord" is Jesus' description of the second advent and gathering of the elect as recorded in the Olivet Discourse (Matt. 24:29-31; Mark 13:24-27). Perhaps Paul infers from the gathering of the elect at the posttribulational advent that resurrection and translation will follow in immediate succession. If he does indeed tie his description to the Olivet Discourse, the rapture will follow the tribulation ("immediately after the tribulation . . ."—Matt. 24:29).

Or, Paul may be referring to Jesus' statement that "he who believes in Me shall live even if he dies, and everyone who lives [or, 'is living'—the same word and form as in 1 Thess. 4:15, except there plural] and believes in Me shall never die" (John 11:25, 26). If so, Paul's point is that the juxtaposition of Jesus' two statements concerning the dead and those who will not die justifies the conclusion that the resurrection of deceased believers and the translation of living believers will occur in the same event. Of course, John wrote his gospel later than Paul wrote 1 Thessalonians. But Jesus' declaration, recorded in John, may well have come to Paul via the oral tradition of Jesus' teaching. The striking double parallelism between Jesus' and

Paul's statements regarding the dead who will rise and the living who will not die gives weight to the interpretation that "by the word of the Lord" harks back to the saying later recorded by John.

THE ADVENT

The revelation "by the word of the Lord" is that those living at the time of Jesus' coming will not precede those who have fallen asleep in Jesus. Paul expands this statement with a detailed description of the Parousia and rapture: "For the Lord Himself will descend. . . ." Do we here confront a contrast between the gathering of the elect through angelic agency at the posttribulational coming (Matt. 24:31) and the gathering of believers by Christ Himself in 1 Thessalonians 4:16?[3] A strong emphasis does lie on the word "Himself," but the Greek word αὐτός does not imply exclusiveness. And the very context forbids exclusiveness, for it speaks of the archangel who accompanies Christ. This same intensive pronoun appears with "our Lord Jesus Christ" in 2 Thessalonians 2:16, where He and the Father are the *compound* subject of the verbs "comfort" and "strengthen." But more noteworthily, Paul does not write that the Lord Himself will *gather* the saints. Rather, the Lord Himself will *descend*. Not a single word in the whole description identifies the gatherer as Christ. Rather, the reference to the "voice of the archangel" suggests angelic participation, in accordance with Matthew 24:31.

Other things being equal, the word "descend" (καταβαίνω) indicates a complete, uninterrupted descent, like that of the Spirit at Christ's baptism (Matt. 3:16; Mark 1:10; Luke 3:22; John 1:32, 33) and that of Christ in His first advent (John 3:13; 6:33, 38, 41, 42, 50, 51, 58). Where a reversal from downward to upward motion comes into view, a specific statement to that effect appears, as in Acts 10:11, 16 ("a certain object coming down, . . . and immediately the object was taken up into the sky"). In the absence of a statement indicating a halt or a sudden reversal of direction, we naturally infer a complete descent to the earth, such as will take place only at the posttribulational advent.

It is argued to the contrary that "the Lord does not come to earth in 1 Thess. 4:16, but meets the saints in the air. . . ."[4]

---

[3] Strombeck, 28.
[4] Ludwigson, 130; cf. Linton, 27, 28.

But surely it is strange that in this, the fullest description of the rapture, there should be no mention of a change in direction from earthward to heavenward, or of a halt. The absence of a specific phrase such as "to the earth" cannot be very significant, for there is not one NT account of the second coming which contains such a phrase. Yet all agree that at least the three accounts in the Olivet Discourse, 2 Thessalonians 1:7-10, and Revelation 19:11-16 portray the posttribulational descent of Christ to the earth. These passages and 1 Thessalonians 4:16, 17 share the implication that He will come all the way down. Thus, the saints will meet Christ in the air to join Him in His continued descent.

The "shout," "voice," and "trumpet" have led some posttribulationists to mock at a secret, pretribulational rapture by saying that this is the noisiest passage in the Bible. However, the matter of secrecy has very little to do with the validity or invalidity of the pretribulationalism. Posttribulationism gains nevertheless in the parallel between the "great [i.e., loud] trumpet," in which the emphasis lies on the publicity of the posttribulational advent (Matt. 24:27-31), and the "voice" and the "trumpet" in 1 Thessalonians 4:16. And there is good reason to connect the "voice of the archangel" (presumably Michael, the only archangel named in the Bible) with the resurrection of OT saints. Michael is specially associated with Israel in Daniel 10:21 and 12:1, 2, in the latter reference in close juxtaposition with the resurrection. If the resurrection and translation of the Church will occur simultaneously with the resurrection of OT saints, as indicated by the "voice of the archangel," the rapture will occur after the tribulation; for the resurrection of OT saints will not occur till then (Isa. 25:8; 26:19; Dan. 12:1-3, 13).

The raised and translated saints will be caught up "to meet [εἰς ἀπάντησις] the Lord in the air."

> When a dignitary paid an official visit or *parousia* to a city in Hellenistic times, the action of the leading citizens in going out to meet him and escorting him on the final stage of his journey was called the *apantēsis*. . . .[5]

This connotation points toward our rising to meet Christ in order to escort Him immediately back to earth. Although the connotation is not absolutely necessary, it does favor the posttribu-

---

[5] F. F. Bruce in *NBC*, 1159.

lational concept of the purpose and the manner of the rapture and presents an obstacle to the pretribulational concept of a return to heaven or a remaining "in the air" for seven years.

Paul breaks off his description with the statement, "And thus we shall always be with the Lord." Here again we miss any hint of a return to heaven or of a hovering over the earth. Quite simply, we shall be in Christ's presence forever, wherever He is. Paul reiterates his purpose by concluding, "Therefore comfort one another with these words" (v. 18). He has reassured his readers that the dead in Christ will rise immediately before the rapture in order to share equally with living saints in the blessedness of subsequent events.

THE RELATION OF CHAPTERS FOUR AND FIVE

The usual meaning of the Greek particle connecting chapters four and five (δέ) contains a mixture of a continuative sense and a slightly adversative sense. In other words, the particle implies a shift in thought, but not without close connection with the foregoing thought. Sometimes the adversative sense drops out altogether.[6] Therefore, it is wrong to claim that the "But" ("Now" in NASB) of 5:1 proves the beginning of a new thought in full contrast to and differentiation from the Parousia described in 4:15-18.[7] Nor does the shift from the pronoun "we" in 4:16ff. to the pronoun "they" in 5:1ff. imply a full contrast, for Paul uses the pronoun "you" in 5:1-5a in writing to the Christians more times than he uses "we" in 4:14-18. And in 5:5b-11 he again uses "we," more times than in 4:14-18. Hence, an entire shift in subject matter is not to be inferred from the usage of the pronouns. The appearance of "they" in chapter five is accounted for by the bringing into view of the wicked and their relationship to the Parousia. However, the saved also bear a relationship to that day. Therefore Paul retains the "you" and "we."

Walvoord succinctly and accurately states the relationship between chapters four and five: "the translation of the church . . . marks the beginning of the Day of the Lord."[8] The ease with which Paul moves from the rapture and Parousia into the day of

---

[6] *BAG*, 170.

[7] Strombeck, 90.

[8] Walvoord, *Thess*, 81.

the Lord without explanation or differentiation argues strongly for their identification. So also does Paul's exhortation to alertness and sobriety in order that the day of the Lord may not overtake Christians like a thief, for there would be no reason to watch for that day were not the rapture/Parousia a part of it.

Dissenting from Walvoord's view, Stanton seeks to destroy the identification by contrasting 4:13 ("But we do not want you to be uniformed") and 5:2 ("For you yourselves know full well"). He argues that since the Thessalonians did not know about the rapture but did know about the day of the Lord, the two must be different.[9] However, the Thessalonians were hardly ignorant of the rapture as a whole, for they wrongly thought that because of the rapture the living will precede the dead in resurrection. Rather, the Thessalonians mistook a detail within the larger event, viz., the time of the resurrection of deceased believers. On the other hand, their knowledge of the day of the Lord concerned the time of that day's arrival.[10] In context the two statements do not oppose each other.

Since the Parousia/rapture will mark the beginning of the day of the Lord for which we are to watch alertly and soberly, the rapture will follow the tribulation. For, as we have already seen, the day of the Lord will not include the tribulation.[11]

TIMES AND EPOCHS

The Thessalonians had no need for instruction regarding "the times and the epochs" (5:1). These refer to the final events which will presage the return of Christ, i.e., the beginning of the day of the Lord. But *why* had the Thessalonians no need for instruction? At least three possible answers present themselves.

First, the Thessalonians may not have needed instruction, says Walvoord, because the day of the Lord will be unheralded by signs and therefore will come unexpectedly upon all.[12] But that makes Paul's words vapid. If a professor of physics were to tell his class, "I do not need to explain the quantum theory to you," he would not be implying the impossibility of an explanation, but the needlessness of an explanation. Saying that instruction is unnecessary

---

[9] Stanton, 88.
[10] See below.
[11] See above, "The Day of the Lord."
[12] Culbertson and Centz, eds., *Understanding the Times,* 133, 134.

differs from saying that instruction is impossible. Moreover, the day of the Lord will come unexpectedly *only upon the wicked* ("upon them suddenly . . . they shall not escape"), who will not recognize the divinely appointed signs (vv. 2, 3). "But you, brethren," writes Paul with an emphatic ὑμεῖς to differentiate Christian believers from unbelievers—"but you, brethren, are not in darkness, that the day should overtake you like a thief" (v. 4). Besides, we can hardly hold that no signs will herald the arrival of the day of the Lord, for in his next letter to the Thessalonians Paul plainly states that that day "will not come unless the apostasy *comes first,* and the man of lawlessness is revealed" (2 Thess. 2:3).

Second, we might say that the Thessalonians had no need for instruction concerning "times and epochs" because instruction would have profited them nothing in view of the absence of the Church during the tribulational period of signs. But this explanation clashes with Paul's exhortation to alertness and sobriety in watching for the day of the Lord. If there exists instruction concerning the onset of the day's arrival, it is of great value for effecting the watchfulness to which Paul exhorts Christians.

We are led to the third possibility. Paul did not need to write concerning the times and the epochs because the Thessalonians already knew the appointed signs from his previous oral teaching. By recognizing the signs they did not need to be caught by surprise. The very fact that Paul had instructed and was yet to instruct them concerning the tribulational signs by which they might tell the approach of the day of the Lord implies the possibility that they might have lived to go through the tribulation and implies Paul's expectation that the last generation of the Church will go through it. This understanding is established by Paul's question—immediately after an emphatic declaration that the apostasy and the career of the man of lawlessness will precede the day of the Lord—"Do you not remember that while I was still with you, I was telling you these things?" (2 Thess. 2:5).

At first glance Jesus' statements in Acts 1:4-8 may seem to contradict the above view:

> And gathering them together, He commanded them not to leave Jerusalem, but to wait for what the Father had promised, 'Which,' He said, 'you heard of Me; for John baptized with water, but you shall be baptized with the Holy Spirit not many days from now.' And so when they had come together, they were asking Him, saying, 'Lord, is it at this time You are restoring the kingdom to

Israel?' He said to them, 'It is not for you to know times or epochs which the Father has fixed by His own authority; but you shall receive power when the Holy Spirit has come upon you; and you shall be My witnesses both in Jerusalem, and in all Judea and Samaria, and even to the remotest part of the earth.

If we did not have 1 Thessalonians 5:1, we still could not take the import of the passage in Acts to be that the disciples must be kept uninformed concerning what the *contents* of the times and epochs will be. This they already knew from the Olivet Discourse, where Jesus Himself had delineated tribulational events in some detail with prominence given to the abomination of desolation. Rather, in Acts 1:7 the disciples are not to know the *time* when that final series of events will begin its swift succession toward the Messianic kingdom. Jesus had just repeated the promise of the Spirit's baptism. "And so"—i.e., because in the OT the prophets connect the outpouring of the Spirit with the events which will usher in the millennial kingdom (Isa. 32; 44:1-5; Joel 2:28-3:1)—the disciples ask whether the Spirit's outpouring will set in motion the restoration of Israel. Jesus answers that they are to be kept uninformed of *that*.

We gather the import of Jesus' statement under three points: (1) the disciples had already received information concerning the series of events consummating the age; (2) the disciples could not know when these events were to begin or whether the outpouring of the Spirit was to launch the series; (3) in the meantime the disciples should concern themselves primarily with evangelization of the world (v. 8). Thus, according to Acts 1:7 the *time* of fulfillment is not for us to know. But according to 1 Thessalonians 5:1, especially with 2 Thessalonians 2:1-5, the content of the times and epochs is to be known beforehand and recognized during fulfillment.

READINESS FOR THE DAY OF THE LORD

In verses two and three Paul writes that the day of the Lord will overtake the wicked with sudden destruction, "like a thief in the night." For the figure of a thief in the night, we may recall Matthew 24:43, where the context is posttribulational (cf. also Luke 12:39); Revelation 3:3, where "like a thief" is qualified by the clause, "If therefore you will not wake up"; and Revelation 16:15, where the context again is posttribulational. But the day of the Lord will not overtake Christians like a thief (1 Thess. 5:4). Is it that Christians will be removed before the day of the Lord begins? But why then the contrast with the *unexpectedness* of the day's arrival for the wicked if the day will not arrive *at all* upon Christians? And why the exhortation to watchfulness (v. 6) if the Church will see (from the earthly standpoint, of course) neither the tribulational signs preceding the day nor the day of the Lord itself? And why the previous oral instruction and the written repetition of that instruction in 2 Thessalonians concerning the times and epochs?

Alternatively and preferably, the day of the Lord will not overtake Christians like a thief because they will be watching. They will have seen the tribulational signs and prepared themselves for the arrival of the day. This view comports with the wording of the statement, with the context here and in 2 Thessalonians 2:1-5 (and elsewhere) regarding precursive signs, and with the exhortation to watchfulness. And because of the posttribulational beginning of the day of the Lord,[13] the relevance of that day to the Church rules out a pretribulational rapture.

The figure of a thief in the night leads to an expansion of metaphor: "for you are all sons of light and sons of day. We are not of night nor of darkness" (v. 5). In the Greek text the absence of definite articles with the nouns "light," "day," "night," and "darkness" emphasizes the quality of the nouns, as opposed to the specifying of a particular day or night. The saints, by virtue of their being in the spiritual realm of light and day, have their eyes open to the signals and their hearts prepared for the day of the Lord. Thus its arrival will occasion no surprise. But the wicked, being in darkness, will fail to perceive the significance of tribulational events. Consequently, the day will catch them unprepared.[14]

W. K. Harrison objects that under this view the day of the Lord would come "as an enemy in the day to the saved," which "contradicts the specific declaration that 'the day of the Lord so cometh as a thief in the night.' "[15] Harrison simply overlooks that the day of the Lord comes as a thief only upon the wicked

---

[13] See above, "The Day of the Lord."

[14] For day and night as coexisting spiritual realms, see Luke 16:8; Rom. 13: 12, 13; Eph. 5:8; Col. 1:12, 13; 1 Pet. 2:9; 1 John 1:7; 2:9, 10.

[15] Harrison. *BibSac*, 114:321.

and that the day is no enemy to the saints, but a glorious deliverance. Harrison's own view is open to criticism: "Taking *night* and *day* as periods of time, they cannot exist at the same time. Since the Day of the Lord begins at night, the church being of the day necessarily will not be present. . . ."[16] But because the definite article is missing with "night" and "day," because "light" and "darkness" are not so readily taken as periods of time (Harrison omits these terms), and because all four terms are used figuratively throughout the NT for coexisting spiritual realms, we have no warrant to take "night" and "day" here as periods of time.

Some overcharge Paul's metaphor by arguing that the day of the Lord will not overtake sons of day because it will come during the night. But the parallel deals with the sudden unexpectedness of a thief's coming rather than with the night itself. And Paul does not state that the day of the Lord comes in the night, but that it comes like a *thief*. We may compare verse four, where the phrase "like a thief" appears without the phrase "in the night." "In the night" syntactically goes with "thief," not with "comes." And if the day of the Lord did include the tribulation and the tribulation were a period of night (as the pretribulational argument supposes), the coming of the day of the Lord would be tantamount to the coming of the night, so that that day could not be said to come *during* the night. Rather, it would come *with* the night because it would *be* the night. There results an impossible equation of day with night.[17]

Paul carries on the metaphors of night and day in an exhortation to be alert and sober, to live like sons of light (vv. 6, 7). That "God has not destined us for wrath, but for obtaining salvation through our Lord Jesus Christ" (v. 9) incites us to watch for the day of the Lord. For the day of the Lord will finalize our

---

[16] *BibSac,* 114:320.

[17] No pretribulation argument from the expression "like a thief" in verse four can rest on a completely solid basis, because rather weighty manuscript evidence supports the reading which would give the meaning "as day overtakes thieves." This reading has the support of A, B, and the bohairic version and has gained acceptance by many scholars, including Moffatt, Lightfoot, Frame, Wescott & Hort, and Milligan. In its favor, it is the more difficult reading and the one which best explains the origin of the other since it may be the more likely to have been changed to conform with verse two. Such a paronomasia and inversion of metaphor characterize Paul's style. If the day of the Lord will come both like a thief in the night (v. 2) and as day upon thieves (v. 4), we can hardly press the phrase "in the night."

salvation by our being "caught up" (4:16) as the Lord descends to deal out "retribution to those who do not know God and to those who do not obey the gospel of our Lord Jesus" (2 Thess. 1:8).

8

Correction in 2 Thessalonians

In 1 Thessalonians Paul offered comfort concerning deceased believers and issued exhortation to living believers. In 2 Thessalonians he corrects false teaching. According to the false teaching, the Thessalonians had already entered the day of the Lord, as was supposed from their severe persecution, and therefore the return of Christ lay in the immediate future. As a practical outcome, some had left their employment to wait for the advent of Christ. Meanwhile they were living off the means of others.

Posttribulational Release From Persecution

Paul begins by encouraging the Thessalonians in their endurance of persecution. Be patient, writes Paul in the first chapter, for two reasons: God will "repay with affliction those who afflict you" (v. 6), and God will give "relief" to you who now are persecuted. The double recompense will take place "when the Lord Jesus shall be revealed [literally, "in the revelation of the Lord Jesus"] from heaven with His mighty angels in flaming fire, dealing out retribution to those who do not know God . . ." (vv. 7, 8). This description fits only the posttribulational return of Christ in judgment. We might be tempted to stretch the meaning of the term "revelation" by inclusion of the tribulational period and a prior rapture.[1] But the context will not allow such a broadening of the term, because Paul unmistakably defines his meaning with a detailed description of the posttribulational advent and nothing else. Grammatically, that description is construed with "the revelation."

The word "when" goes back to the Greek ἐν (*in*). In its temporal sense ἐν denotes time within which or the point of time when something occurs. "When" provides a proper translation.[2] The resultant difficulty for pretribulationism is that Paul places the release of Christians from persecution at the posttribulational return of Christ to judge unbelievers, whereas according to pretribulationism this release will occur seven years earlier.

CONTEXT AND TRANSITION

Paul begins chapter two by beseeching the Thessalonians "with regard to (ὑπέρ) the coming of our Lord Jesus Christ, and our gathering together to Him." Although ὑπέρ occurred in early Greek (but not in the NT) in adjurations, practically all modern commentators agree that here it approximates περί, *concerning*. Paul, then, beseeches his readers in the interests of the Parousia and rapture, i.e., to rescue the doctrine from the Thessalonians' misconceptions regarding it.

But Paul neither makes nor implies any distinction between his description of the second coming in 2 Thessalonians 1:7-10 and that in 1 Thessalonians 4:16ff. He passes into the phrase "our gathering together to Him" (2:1) without an apparent shift of reference from the description in 1:7-10 of Christ's posttribulational advent "in flaming fire" to smite the wicked. In 2:8 Paul again refers to the posttribulational advent by writing of Christ's coming to slay the Antichrist. Hence, outstandingly posttribulational references surround the highly debated section 2:1-7. The very setting of the section should make us wary of unnecessarily interpolating the idea of a pretribulational rapture.

In 2:1 Paul mentions "our gathering" second in order to the Parousia. In the light of the immediately preceding description of the posttribulational advent, it seems natural to regard the Parousia as a reference to that event rather than a sudden

---

[1] English, 65.
[2] See BAG, who cite 2 Thess. 1:7.

switch to a pretribulational Parousia unmentioned in the first chapter and unsupported in 1 Thessalonians. Several verses later (2:8) the Parousia again refers to the posttribulational advent of Christ. If then the context of 2:1 leads us to regard the Parousia there as posttribulational, it is singularly strange that "our gathering together to Him" should be connected with it and mentioned second in order—unless the rapture, too, is posttribulational.

Paul now passes from the Parousia and rapture (v. 1) to the day of the Lord (v. 2), again without an apparent shift of thought. The identification of that day with the hope of Christians once more points to a posttribulational rapture since, as we have already seen, the day of the Lord will not begin until after the tribulation.

AN AGITATED STATE OF MIND

"Shaken from your composure," "disturbed"—these expressions describe the upset state of the Thessalonians. If the Christians mistakenly thought that they were experiencing the tribulation and believed posttribulationism because of Paul's previous teaching, they would have been rejoicing, we might suppose, rather than troubled at the prospect of quick deliverance.[3] But that line of reasoning sets up false alternatives, joy versus sorrow. Paul mentions neither. Instead, he directs his remarks to the problem of agitation among the Thessalonians, agitation at the prospect of an immediate return of Christ.

Paul does not leave us without clue concerning the outgrowth of the agitation among the Thessalonians, for he exhorts them to work for their daily living (3:6-15). Evidently some, having left their jobs, were shirking their responsibilities. Would Paul have dwelt upon an imminent, pretribulational rapture—even were the doctrine true—in order to quiet a disturbance which had its roots in the thought of a near return of Christ? Such an emphasis would only have aggravated the fanticism at Thessalonica. But emphasis on the precedence of obvious tribulational signs provides a real basis for Paul's restraining exhortation.

THE APOSTASY

The apostasy ($\dot{\alpha}\pi o\sigma\tau\alpha\sigma\acute{\iota}\alpha$) must take place before the day of the Lord will begin. English, followed by Wuest and others, has

---

[3] Wood, 68, 69.

suggested that the word here means *departure* and refers to the rapture itself, which would then come "first," i.e., before the tribulation.[4] Our examination of the word falls under two headings:

First, we need to consider the lexical evidence. English has noticed that LSJ give "departure" as a secondary definition and that the cognate verb, ἀφίστημι, literally means, *stand away from,* or *depart,* and is so used many times in the NT. Therefore, writes English, the correct and literal translation of ἀποστασία is "departure," with reference to "our gathering together to Him" (v. 1).

The meaning and connotation of a NT word are determined from four sources: (1) other appearances in the NT; (2) the LXX; (3) the *koinē* (of which NT Greek is a species); and (4) classical Greek. The last makes the least important of all sources and, significantly, it is from this least important source that English draws his argument. But even in classical Greek simple departure by no means predominates.

Evidence from the first three sources indicates that at the time the NT was written, ἀποστασία had acquired the limited meaning of departure in the spheres of religion and politics, i.e., political revolt and religious apostasy. The only other occurrence of the word in the NT (Acts 21:21) bears the sense of religious apostasy. Ἀποστασία and its cognate and earlier forms appear over forty times in the LXX (including several appearances in the versions of Aquila, Theodotion, and Symmachus)—every time with the meaning of religious or political defection. In matters of vocabulary and style the LXX strongly influenced the NT writers, whose Bible for the most part was the LXX. The high number of occurrences of ἀποστασία in the LXX and their broad distribution evince a well-established usage. And we ought to bear in mind that Paul was thoroughly familiar with and greatly influenced by the language of the LXX, for in quoting the OT he follows the LXX most of the time.

Our remaining primary source, the *koinē,* as given by MM, offers several examples of political rebellion and religious apostasy, but not one example of simple spatial departure. No wonder, then, that NT lexicons uniformly give ἀποστασία the special senses of religious apostasy and political rebellion—BAG, Kittel, Cremer, Abbott-Smith, Thayer, and others. No wonder also that scholarly commentators on 2 Thessalonians interpret ἀποστασία as bearing

---

[4] English, 67-71; Wuest, *BibSac,* 114:63-67.

this meaning—Alford, Ellicott, Moffatt, F. F. Bruce, Frame, Milligan, Morris, and others.

English appeals to translators who during the Reformation used the term "departure" for ἀποστασία: Tyndale (c. 1526), Coverdale (1535), Cranmer (1539), Geneva Bible (1557), and Beza (1565).[5] But the appeal to early English translations unwittingly reveals weakness, because in the era of those versions lexical studies in NT Greek were almost nonexistent and continued to be so for many years.[6] The papyri had not yet been discovered, and the study of the LXX had hardly begun. That subsequent versions uniformly departed from the earlier rendering points to a correction based on sound and scholarly reasons.

English and Wuest largely by-pass lexical evidence concerning the noun ἀποστασία in order to base their argument on the cognate verb ἀφίστημι. Of the fifteen occurrences of ἀφίστημι in the NT, only three refer to a religious departure. "And, since a noun takes its meaning from the verb, the noun, too, may have such a broad connotation."[7] The mistake comes in making the cognate verb determine the meaning of the noun in question. Many times nouns acquire special meanings. Ἀποστάσιον, another noun cognate to ἀφίστημι, means *divorce* or some other legal act of separation. Yet no one claims that this noun means *departure* in the wide, general sense of the cognate verb. By the same token, ἀποστασία does not need to have the wide, general sense of the same cognate verb.

It happens, then, that ἀποστασία had acquired the special sense of religious apostasy or political defection. Whereas ἀφίστημι very many times carries the simple meaning of spatial departure, ἀποστασία appears elsewhere in the NT and many times throughout the LXX *solely* with the special meaning. Such usage counts far more than etymology. We should take the meaning which a word had during the time and in the culture in which it was written instead of making recourse to a literal definition of the root. Thus, the terms "apostasy," "falling away," and "rebellion" do not overlay the Greek word with a questionable interpretation. They rather represent a valid and necessary recognition of the *usus loquendi*— i.e., they are true translations.

Second, we need to consider contextual evidence. English and Wuest argue several points from the context in 2 Thessalonians:

---

[5] English, 69.
[6] BAG, v.
[7] English, 69.

(1) the meaning of religious defection for ἀποστασία comes always from the context and qualifying phrases, not from the word itself; (2) the definite article with ἀποστασία in 2 Thessalonians 2:3 points to something well-known to the Thessalonians and explained in the previous context; (3) the context in 2 Thessalonians does not incorporate description of an apostasy, but does contain mention of the rapture (2:1 and 1 Thess. 4:16ff.).

There is a measure of truth in the statement that the idea of defection comes from the context. However, when the word appears exclusively or predominantly in such contexts—in the NT, the LXX, the *koinē*, and classical Greek—defection becomes inherent to the meaning. Where a question arises, therefore, we are bound to recognize the prevailing connotation of the word.

As for the use of the article with ἀποστασία, Wuest contends that individual identity must be explained in the foregoing context. But that is wrong. Although a writer may have already explained individual identity, he may just as well anticipate a following explanation. Or he may provide no explanation at all: the article then bears the sense, "the well-known . . ." or "the special. . . ."[8] Hence, we have at least three possible explanations:

First, the article points to a previous explanation (v. 1; 1 Thess. 4:16ff.). But it is unthinkable that Paul would use for the rapture a word the connotation of which overwhelmingly has to do with civil and religious defection.

Second, the article points to a well-known apostasy about which Paul had already informed the Thessalonians through his oral teaching. English calls this possibility "pure conjecture,"[9] *but the apostle himself writes,* "Do you not remember that while I was still with you, I was telling you these things?" (v. 5). The very fact that Paul inserts this rhetorical question suggests that we are not to look for an ἀποστασία which he delineated in 1 Thessalonians, but for an item in Paul's initial ministry by word of mouth.

Third, the definite article points to a special apostasy which gets further explanation in the ensuing discussion. One must read the passage blindfolded not to see that the immediately following context bristles with references to and explanations of "the apostasy." The man of lawlessness will lead a rebellion against God by opposing and exalting himself "above every so-called god or object of worship, so that he takes his seat in the

---

[8] BAG, 552.
[9] P. 70.

temple of God, displaying himself as being God" (v. 4). The sub-sequent verses abound with yet further descriptive expressions: "the mystery of lawlessness," "the lawless one," "the activity of Satan, with all power and signs and false wonders, and with all the deception of wickedness," "a deluding influence so that they might believe what is false." *The* apostasy will be a rebellion against God led by the Antichrist during the tribulation.

English objects that that cannot constitute apostasy because the Antichrist and his followers will never have known God. However, an apostate is not one who has known God truly, but one who has falsely *professed* to know God, in time has fallen away, and has thus revealed his true character. The piety of the Antichrist will be the key to his power of deceit. He will even agree to allow Jewish sacrifices in a rebuilt temple (Dan. 9:26, 27). But then viciousness and impiety will emerge in his breaking of that covenant, in his insolent assumption of deity, and in his ferocious persecution of all who resist his demand for worship. Thus, both lexical and con-textual considerations unite with unmistakable clarity to show that ἡ ἀποστασία does not represent the rapture, but the Antichrist's insurrection against the Almighty.

The Content of the False Teaching

What was the exact nature of the error which was troubling the Thessalonians? Taking the translation, "the day of the Lord *has come*" (2:2), we may follow either one of two lines of thought in looking at the passage from a pretribulational stand-point:

First, the Thessalonians, unaware of a pretribulational rap-ture, were led to believe that they had entered the tribulation, which they thought was part of the day of the Lord. To say this, however, is to invalidate the case for pretribulationism in both 1 and 2 Thessalonians. For if the Thessalonians themselves did not gather pretribulationism from 1 Thessalonians, it is at least doubtful that we who lack their advantage of having enjoyed Paul's oral ministry should find that doctrine taught there with any clarity. And in 2 Thessalonians Paul barely reminds them of what he had more fully taught while he was still with them (see 2:5). If his detailed teaching at that time had not made them cognizant of a pretribulational rapture, this skeletal review of that oral instruction could hardly have sufficed to inform and cor-rect them—or us.

Second, the Thessalonians thought that a pretribulational rapture had already occurred and that they had been left behind in the tribulation, which (as in the preceding view) they believed to be part of the day of the Lord. "Paul is answering this question in effect, 'No, you are not going to enter that period. The Lord will come for you first.' "[10] Paul omits making an outright statement of the most important point in such an interpretation of the passage—viz., a pretribulational advent and rapture. Yet according to pretribulationism, this was the very matter about which the Thessalonians were confused. Paul could not have taken for granted their understanding a pretribulational rapture from the former epistle, for then they would not have fallen into error in the first place. Correction of the error would have required a categorical statement to the effect that the rapture will take place before the tribulation. Such a statement nowhere appears.

The import of the passage, according to pretribulationism, may be summarized as follows: (1) the rapture will occur before the tribulation; (2) the tribulation will be recognized by the apostasy and the revelation of the man of lawlessness; and (3) since those events had not happened, the Thessalonians obviously had not entered the tribulation, the rapture had not occurred, and they had not been left behind.[11] The first statement, the basic premise, remains completely unexpressed in the text. Paul mentions the rapture in verse one and has described it in the first epistle. But neither here nor there does he write that it will take place before the tribulation. The statement that the tribulation will be recognized by the apostasy and the appearance of the man of lawlessness is true in itself, but it is neither the point nor the statement of Paul. He writes rather that these events will come to pass *before* the day of the Lord. If Paul were asserting a pretributional rapture, no relevance would attach to his writing, as he does, that the day of the Lord will not begin until after the tribulation. For the tribulation, with the two events Paul selects as signals of that period, would separate a pretribulational rapture from the beginning of that day with seven years or so. A pretribulational Paul should have written that events in the tribulation will follow the rapture. Instead, he writes that the day of the Lord will follow tribulational events.

---

[10] Walvoord, *RQ*, 164.
[11] See, e.g., Linton 78, 79.

For Paul to have pointed to the futurity of the apostasy and the revelation of the Antichrist as an assurance that the Thessalonians had not missed the rapture exceeds what he needed to write under pretribulationism. If in 1 Thessalonians he had taught that the rapture will precede the day of the Lord, here he would merely have needed to remind them of that fact. Rather, he explains that the apostasy and the man of lawlessness will precede that day. "Why did not Paul soothe their laments [sic, agitation] by referring to that rapture as a necessary precursor of the Day of the Lord instead of the Apostasy and Man of Sin as precursors?"[12] If, on the other hand, the Parousia and rapture will comprise the first event in the day of the Lord, then the rapture will take place after the tribulation, for the apostasy and career of the Antichrist will precede that day. The fact that Paul has already exhorted Christians to readiness for the day of the Lord (1 Thess. 5:4-11) establishes the relevance of those tribulational events for Christians: we shall see the apostasy and the man of lawlessness and thereby recognize the approach of the day of the Lord for which we look and prepare.

The statement that since those events had not happened, the Thessalonians obviously had not entered the tribulation, the rapture had not occurred, and they had not been left behind misses the intention of Paul altogether. He writes that the day of the Lord will not arrive before those events, not that those events will not happen before the rapture. Besides, it borders on absurdity to say that the Thessalonians thought that the momentous coming of Christ had already taken. place without their knowledge or participation. Did they think that all other Christians and the Apostle Paul himself had also been left behind? Surely the false teaching was more subtle than that. Conjecturing that the Thessalonian believers had been cut off from other Christians and that they thought the rapture had taken place since their last contact with Paul would be an adroit maneuver. But it would fail to carry conviction. These verses rather indicate that the Thessalonians were having contact with Paul and others, for the false teaching came by word or forged epistle from an outside source (v. 2). And Paul must have received communication from Thessalonica, else he could not have written to correct it. In fact, it is impossible that the Thessalonians supposed Paul (and

---

others) to have been taken in the rapture, because the erroneous doctrine purported to have come from the apostle himself (v. 2).

What then is the exact nature of the false teaching which had agitated the Thessalonians? First, they erroneously thought that the day of the Lord will include the tribulation. Paul both implies and answers this error with his statement that two conspicuous events representative of the tribulation must *precede* the day of the Lord. Second, the Thessalonians erroneously thought that they had entered the tribulation. Paul both implies and answers this error with the same statement concerning the two tribulational events which obviously had not taken place. Third, the Thessalonians erroneously concluded that Christ's coming lay in the immediate future, with resultant cessation of work, fanatical excitement, and disorder. Paul both implies and answers this error with his statement that the day of the Lord is neither immediate nor imminent because of the precedence of tribulational events. A similar corrective appears in Paul's exhortation to return to orderly living. Thus, it was not sorrow over a missed rapture which agitated the Thessalonians, but wild anticipations of an immediate return of Christ.

Several advantages attach to this posttribulational interpretation. It preserves the indications of other scriptures that the day of the Lord will begin only after the tribulation. It preserves the relevance of the day of the Lord to the Church, most clearly evident in Paul's exhortation to watchfulness and readiness for that day (1 Thess. 5:4-6), a relevance which we lose if any interval separates the rapture from the day. It assumes nothing not directly stated or implied in the text.

In the foregoing discussion we have worked with the translation "has come" for ἐνέστηκεν rather than the translation "is at hand" (AV). As the dominant meaning, the majority of modern scholars strongly favor the sense of arrival resulting in presence, rather than temporal proximity. In four of the six other appearances of the word in the Greek NT, the notion of presence is required (Rom. 8:38; 1 Cor. 3:22; Gal. 1:4; Heb. 9:9—in the first two references by contrast with futurity). In the remaining two occurrences (1 Cor. 7:26; 2 Tim. 3:1), either rendering will do. It has been objected to the translation "has come" in 2 Thessalonians 2:2 that in 1 Thessalonians Paul teaches that the day of the Lord will begin with the rapture; consequently, in 2 Thessalonians he would need only to refer to the former epistle.[13] However, although in 1 Thessalonians Paul implies that the rapture will fall within the day of the Lord, Paul does not expressly state that it will form part of the *first* event in that day. That is the natural conclusion apart from the false teaching, but it is the point which Paul later has to clarify because of the false teaching.

Should we nevertheless take the meaning "is at hand," a slight shift in interpretations would become necessary. Both pre- and posttribulationists would have to change the inference that the Thessalonians mistakenly believed in the presence of the day of the Lord into the inference that they mistakenly believed in its imminence. Pretribulationists would retain their basic but implausible contention that the Thessalonians regretted having missed the rapture. And the difficulty remains in explaining how the day of the Lord could have relevance to Christians, who are told to watch for that day, if the apostasy and the man of lawlessness will intervene between the rapture and that day. Posttribulationists would retain their primary contention that the Thessalonians mistakenly thought the return of Christ lay in the immediate future. Thus, the difference in the translation of ἐνέστηκεν does not touch the vital points of interpretation.

THE RESTRAINER

Enlarging on the career of the man of lawlessness, Paul reminds the Thessalonians that he had told them these things during his stay with them (v. 5). Therefore, he feels no need to write more specifically concerning the identity of the restraint which keeps the Antichrist from appearing ("... *you know* what restrains ..." [v. 6]). This vagueness has given rise to a great variety of interpretations regarding what or who is the restraint. But Paul's very vagueness ought to make all parties hesitant to use this part of the passage as proof for any view of the rapture.

The Thessalonians already understood what restrains (τὸ κατέχον, neuter) the appearance of Antichrist. Although the mystery of lawlessness is even now working, it cannot culminate in the revelation of the personal Antichrist until the restrainer (ὁ κατέχων, masculine) is removed (ἐκ μέσου γένηται, literally, "becomes out of the midst"). For a survey of the history of interpretation we may consult Alford, III, 55ff. and C. H. Giblin, *The*

---

[13] Douty, 81-83.

Threat to Faith, 13-22. Here we need to consider only some of the more prominent and contemporary views held among evangelicals.

There is a group of interpretations which differ widely in the identification of the restrainer, but which have close affinity in that they all regard ἐκ μέσου γένηται ("becomes out of the midst") as development or appearance onto the scene rather than removal from the scene:

	Ladd[14]	James Graham (A)	James Graham (B)[15]	Mrs. Needham[16]
The restraint	God's power	Anti-christ's self-restraint	Satan's power	Satan's power
The restrainer	God	Antichrist	Satan	Satan
That which is restrained	Anti-christ's appearance or mystery of law-lessness	Anti-christ's own appearance	Anti-christ's appearance	Anti-christ's appearance
That which becomes out of the midst	Antichrist	Antichrist	Antichrist	Mystery of wickedness

Apart from individual faults, these views share two serious flaws. First, if γένηται means to *appear on the scene,* the phrase "out of the midst" becomes an awkward insertion which adds no discernible meaning. By arbitrarily enlarging the expression with addition of the phrase "out of the earth," Graham merely draws attention to that awkwardness, since the phrase "out of the midst" stands without appendage in the text. Second, to "become out of the midst" signifies removal, not entrance. The translation which indicates entrance rather than exit rests on "failure to recognize this idiom."[17] The expression invariably denotes exit from a scene.[18]

[14] Ladd, 95; cf. Payne, 110.

[15] James Graham, *Watchman, What of the Night?* 82-85. Because Graham regards the Antichrist as Satan's *alter ego,* a variation arises within his own view.

[16] *The Antichrist,* 91; quoted by Thiessen, 40.

[17] F. F. Bruce, in *NBC,* 1164.

[18] Exod. 31:14; Deut. 4:34; Isa. 52:11; 57:2—all in the LXX; Matt. 13:49; Acts 17:33; 23:10; 1 Cor. 5:2; 2 Cor. 6:17; Col. 2:14; 1 Clement 29:3.

"Into the midst" (εἰς τὸ μέσον) is the proper phrase for entrance onto a scene.[19]

In the early church the view prevailed that Paul refers to the Roman Empire as the restraint, embodied in the emperor as the restrainer. As the conflict between the papacy and the imperial power grew, pre-Reformation evangelicals, and then Protestants, regarded the imperial or civil power as that which retards the destruction of the papacy (Antichrist) until the Parousia of Christ destroys the antichristian papal system. In favor of this view has been adduced Paul's vagueness, as though he were afraid the letter might fall into wrong hands and the removal of the imperial restraint be considered a teaching of sedition. However, the cryptic form of Paul's statement seems to stem rather from the fact that the Thessalonians already knew about the restrainer from oral teaching, as Paul himself indicates (vv. 5, 6a).

The Roman Empire has passed away. Yet the Antichrist has not appeared. Out of this historical fact has grown the interpretation that the restraint is divinely ordained human government, the rule of law, and that the restrainer is either the embodiment of human government in those who rule or the personification of the abstract principle.[20] This view has enjoyed wide popularity among scholars of all varieties, including a few pretribulationists.[21] It comes as close as possible to the prevalent view in the early Church and therefore might reflect the apostolic teaching. Also, restraint by the rule of law in human government admirably fits the context as a full contrast to "the man of lawlessness" and "the mystery of lawlessness." We cannot dismiss the view with the objection that the Antichrist will dictate with an *excess* of government, for, autocratic though he be, from the divine standpoint his rule will be a reign of lawlessness, a breakdown of justice, a corruption of morality—as the text itself unquestionably indicates by calling him "the man of lawlessness" and by referring to "the mystery of lawlessness." Of course, in times past human government has acted lawlessly toward God. But to the degree that it did so, it was not fully exercising the restraint of

---

[19] Jer. 21:4; 48:7—LXX; Mark 3:3; 14:60; Luke 4:35; 5:19; 6:8; John 20:19, 26. See BAG, 159, 508, 509, other lexicons, and the standard commentaries.

[20] "Comp. Rom. xiii. 4, where the personification is somewhat similarly introduced after, and elicited from, a foregoing abstract term [ἐξουσίαν]" (Ellicott, *Thessalonians,* 114).

[21] E.g., Hogg & Vine.

which Paul writes. The objection that restraint of the Antichrist calls for something more supernatural than human government overlooks Paul's conviction that God stands behind human govern-ment which praises good behavior and avenges evil (Rom. 13:1-7).

Many identify the restrainer with the Holy Spirit. Most pre-tribulationists believe in addition that the Holy Spirit restrains the appearance of the Antichrist *through the Church*. Hence, re-moval of the restrainer entails removal of the Church—out of the world, it is assumed. This removal will not be complete, however, because the Holy Spirit must still be present on earth during the tribulation for the work of evangelization and regeneration. "He will be here at that time in some such way as He was present in the world before the Day of Pentecost."[22] Stanton calls it a "re-versal of Pentecost" "as during the Old Testament economy."[23] Others believe that the Spirit restrains the Antichrist's appear-ance *directly* and *personally* rather than mediately through the Church.

Several considerations favor identification of the restrainer with the Holy Spirit. First, some in the early Church held this view. Theodoret, Theodore of Mopsuestia, and Chrysostom mention those who believe that the restraint is the Spirit's activity.[24] Far from being novel, the view just might reflect apostolic teaching. Second, it would seem that a person is required to restrain a person, that an omnipotent power is required to hold back a power so strong as Satan's. Third, this interpretation gives the most vivid force to the change from neuter gender ($\tau\grave{o}\ \kappa\alpha\tau\acute{e}\chi o\nu$) to masculine gender ($\acute{o}\ \kappa\alpha\tau\acute{e}\chi\omega\nu$). In his first reference to the Spirit as restrainer Paul conforms to the neuter gender of the Greek noun $\pi\nu\epsilon\hat{v}\mu\alpha$, *Spirit*. But in view of the personality of the Holy Spirit, Paul shifts to the masculine gender in his second reference.[25]

---

[22] Thiessen, 41.

[23] Pp. 105, 106.

[24] See citations in Alford, III, 57, 58.

[25] Some support this interpretation by saying that Jesus uses a similar grammatical construction in John 15:26; 16:13, 14, where the noun $\pi\nu\epsilon\hat{v}\mu\alpha$ and the article and the relative pronoun referring to $\pi\nu\epsilon\hat{v}\mu\alpha$ are neuter, but the demonstrative pronoun $\dot{\epsilon}\kappa\epsilon\hat{\imath}\nu o\varsigma$ is masculine. Jesus, they say, arranges His words so that the masculine noun $\pi\alpha\rho\acute{a}\kappa\lambda\eta\tau o\varsigma$ (*Paraclete, Comforter*) is the antecedent of $\dot{\epsilon}\kappa\epsilon\hat{\imath}\nu o\varsigma$ and thus emphasizes the personality of the Holy Spirit. However, because the masculine noun $\pi\alpha\rho\acute{a}\kappa\lambda\eta\tau o\varsigma$ is the prominent title of the Holy Spirit in the discourse and because there is no unusual arrangement of words in order to make $\dot{\epsilon}\kappa\epsilon\hat{\imath}\nu o\varsigma$ refer to $\pi\alpha\rho\acute{a}\kappa\lambda\eta\tau o\varsigma$ instead of $\pi\nu\epsilon\hat{v}\mu\alpha$, this corroborative argument has negligible value. The textual question of choosing between $\ddot{o}\varsigma$ and $\ddot{o}$ in Ephesians 1:4 undermines a supporting argu-ment from that source.

The charge of novelty against this view, as we have seen, does not survive investigation. We may ask why Paul should not have openly mentioned the Holy Spirit. But what reason would have prompted him to do so? For they knew what he was writing about (vv. 5, 6a). No other passage of Scripture teaches that the Spirit holds back the appearance of the Antichrist. But neither does any other Scripture teach that Satan, the Roman Empire, or human government holds back the Antichrist.

Grave difficulties, however, attend the pretribulational corollary to the identification of the restrainer with the Holy Spirit, viz., that the Church constitutes His special agency of restraint and that therefore His removal entails removal of the Church from earth even though He Himself stays in a retrogression of His ministry to a weaker, OT form. According to Acts 2:32, 33, the present fulness of the Spirit's ministry rests on the resurrection, ascension, and exaltation of Christ. Being historical facts not subject to negation, they assure eternal abundance of the gift of the Spirit. His partial withdrawal in a retrogression to the beggarly elements and immature status of the old covenant would amount to an annulment of Christ's exaltation. This is not to deny the possibility of a shift in the people to and through whom the Spirit ministers. It *is* to deny any diminishing of Pentecostal *fulness* and *power.* But the pretribulational argument requires the latter, because Pentecostal fulness and power in the saved Israelites and Gentiles of the tribulational period would restrain the Antichrist just as much as His alleged restraint by means of the Church presently.

Jesus clearly implies the indwelling of the Holy Spirit during the tribulation by saying to His witnesses during that period, "It is not you who speak, but it is the Holy Spirit" (Mark 13:11). During the tribulation the Holy Spirit will empower for evangelism and will regenerate on a scale even larger than now (Matt. 24:14; Rev. 7:9-14). In other words, the greater intensity of Satanic activity will find its match in a corresponding *increase,* not reduction, of the Spirit's activity. Within pretribulationism, there arises the practical impossibility that the 144,000 could evangelize the world in seven years—a task the Church has failed to accomplish in almost two millenniums—with less than NT fulness of the Spirit.

We have no warrant to infer from the residence of the Holy Spirit in the Church that He cannot work independently from the Church or that He limits Himself to the Church as His sole sphere and medium of activity. Neither in the present passage nor in any other do we catch so much as a hint that restraint of the Antichrist and of the mystery of lawlessness forms one of the purposes for the Spirit's residence in the Church. To think so assumes pretribulationism in the beginning. Of course, "the believers of this, as of every age, are 'the salt of the earth' and 'the light of the world' (Matt. 5:13-16): . . ."[26] But it is doubtful that Jesus had in mind anything like the restraint of the Antichrist's coming when He created those metaphors. Moreover, He made them long before the Day of Pentecost. Consequently, if restraint of the Antichrist were to come into view, it would be the ministry of the Spirit prior to the Church age which held back the man of lawlessness. We could not speak, then, of a reversion during the tribulation to the OT ministry of the Spirit, for that ministry likewise held back the Antichrist.

Some have also paralleled the restraining ministry of the Spirit now to His restraining ministry in Noah's day (Gen. 6:3). But the parallel subverts the pretribulational hypothesis. For when the Spirit ceased to restrain, the Lord did not transport Noah and his family to heaven, but preserved them on earth through judgment. Removal of restraint does not necessitate removal of saints.

"Become out of the midst" does not demand removal from the world. "Midst" more literally means "middle." The restrainer is standing in the middle, i.e., between the *person* of the Antichrist and the *revelation* of the Antichrist. It is as though the Antichrist stands in the wings, eager to break forth onto the stage of history. But the Holy Spirit blocks entrance until the appointed moment when He will step out of the way and allow the man of lawlessness to stride onstage before the admiring eyes of mankind. Perhaps a misunderstanding of the expression "become out of the midst" as passive has aided the pretribulational idea of withdrawal from the world. The expression is not passive. Lenski captures the meaning exactly with his idiomatic rendering "*get* out of the way."

To interpret the passage concerning the restrainer along pretribulational lines involves an unnecessary contradiction of the preceding context, which we have seen to be thoroughly posttribulational in import. On the other hand, the view that the Spirit restrains directly and personally, rather than mediately

---

[26] Thiessen, 38.

through the Church, harmonizes with the context and encounters no practical or theological difficulties. The special emphasis on the person of the Spirit in the change to masculine gender suggests a directness of personal restraint. And such restraint would seem to be required since not merely lawlessness in general is restrained, but the very person of the man of lawlessness.

The usual pretribulational interpretation of 2 Thessalonians fails at every point. It fails to explain why Paul places our release from persecution at the posttribulational advent (1:7ff.); fails to offer a reasonable basis for the Thessalonians' agitated state of mind; fails to maintain the relevance to the Church of the apostasy, of the revelation of the man of lawlessness, and of the day of the Lord; fails to establish ἡ ἀποστασία as the rapture; and fails to demonstrate that the Holy Spirit restrains through the Church and that the Church will be withdrawn from the earth in a retrogressive step to the OT economy.

At every point the posttribulational view of the passage commends itself. We shall be relieved from persecution at the posttribulational return of Christ. The Thessalonians mistakenly thought that Christ was about to return, that the day of the Lord was going to arrive in the immediate future. Paul reminds them that that will not happen until *after* the apostasy and the revelation of the man of lawlessness. Those events will take place during the tribulation yet *before* the day of the Lord, for which Christians are to be alert. The identity of the restrainer remains an open question, but even identification with the Holy Spirit poses no problem. Paul concludes the section with a restatement of Jesus' return after the tribulation to "slay" "the lawless one" and to "judge" those "who did not believe the truth" (vv. 8-12). From beginning to end posttribulationism characterizes the passage.

9

The Olivet Discourse

In discussing the Olivet Discourse as it relates to the rapture, we shall assume two postulates to which both pre- and posttribulationists generally agree: (1) the events centering around the destruction of Jerusalem in A.D. 70 did not exhaust Jesus' prophecy, with the result that a time of future tribulation immediately before the return of Christ is yet to be fulfilled; (2) the events centering around the destruction of Jerusalem did, however, constitute a fulfillment precursive to a larger and final fulfillment at the end of the age. The pretribulational interpretation of the Olivet Discourse rests on the additional assumption that later NT teaching fills the gap in the discourse regarding a pretribulational rapture. The posttribulational interpretation rests on what is believed to be confirmation of natural inferences from the discourse in subsequent NT teaching.

THE JEWISH REMNANT

To what group of redeemed do the Jewish saints addressed by Jesus and represented by the apostles belong, Israel or the Church? (It should be noted that the question is not whether the Church as a whole appears in the Olivet Discourse, but whether the Jewish remnant in the discourse comprises a segment of the Church.) Some hyperdispensationalists strike out the possibility that the Olivet Discourse has relevance to a

Jewish remnant belonging to the Church because the discourse appears in the synoptic gospels, which, they say, do not give truth for the Church. That line of reasoning, however, cannot adequately explain the instruction of Jesus concerning the Church in Matthew 16:18 and 18:15-18 except by positing a Jewish Church distinct from and prior to the present Church. The great objection to that position lies in its failure to recognize the organic unity between the teaching of Jesus as recorded in the synoptics and the teaching of Jesus through the apostles as recorded in the Acts, the epistles, and the Apocalypse. Jesus promises that the Comforter will "bring to your remembrance all that I said to you" (John 14:26). The "apostles' teaching" (Acts 2:42) is that which Jesus taught them (Matt. 28:20). Luke implies a continuance of Jesus' ministry through the Spirit-filled apostles (Acts 1:1b, 2a). Paul makes adherence to the "words ... of our Lord Jesus Christ" the test of orthodoxy (1 Tim. 6:3). And the Gospel for this age was "first spoken through the Lord" and "confirmed to us by those who heard" (Heb. 2:3).

Not *all* which Jesus taught directly applies to the present dispensation (e.g., the instruction concerning "presenting your offering at the altar," Matt. 5:23, 24). Necessarily, the fading days of the old economy still required some instruction. And Jesus withheld certain truths for later revelation through the apostles (John 16:12-15). But, although His teaching contains Mosaic elements incompatible with the present economy, the essential spirituality of the message of Jesus and His anticipation of Israel's rejection and the resultant present age make the bulk of His doctrine directly applicable to the Church. We dare not divorce the Olivet Discourse from the Church simply because of its appearance in the synoptics.

Others less strongly dispensational· regard Matthew alone among the synoptics as peculiarly Jewish and unchurchly. However, the Olivet Discourse appears in substantially the same form in Mark and in somewhat altered form in Luke. Consequently, it may still relate to the Church from the latter gospels. No one can miss the prominent Jewish element in Matthew. But we do wrong to leap from the Jewish cast of Matthew to the conclusion that this gospel falls outside the immediate concerns of the Church. The correct explanation for the Jewish element in Matthew is simple. As a Jew himself, Matthew writes an account of the incarnation, life, death, and resurrection of Jesus the Messiah from a Jewish standpoint for the purpose of winning Jews to Christianity and/or confirming Jewish believers in their Christian faith. That the only two references to the Church in any of the gospels both occur in Matthew (16:18; 18:15-18) disagrees with an exclusion of the Church from the applicability of Matthew.

Pretribulationists further argue that the context of the Olivet Discourse stamps it unmistakably with a Jewish impress. But we must take care not to miss the import of the context by drawing a false deduction in dislodging the discourse from churchly teaching. Rather, the context indicates that the Jewish nation has passed into a state of divine disfavor because of their rejection of Jesus the Messiah.[1] Since Jesus speaks from that standpoint, we might think it better logic to conclude that the discourse relates to the present dispensation characterized by Israel's setting aside.

On Palm Sunday Jesus rode into Jerusalem amid the Hosannas of the Galilean pilgrims, only to be met by the rebuff of the Pharisees. As He drew near the city, He wept over it. The following day He reentered Jerusalem and judgmentally cleansed the temple. The chief priests and scribes again rebuffed Him. On Tuesday the chief priests, scribes, and elders challenged His authority. Jesus retorted with three parables of judgment which signify that because the Jewish nation had rejected Him, the King's son, God the King had rejected the Jewish nation. The second parable climaxes with these terrible words: "the kingdom of God will be taken away from you, and be given to a nation producing the fruit of it" (Matt. 21:43). The disciples of the Pharisees together with the Herodians, the Sadducees, and the Pharisees quickly rebounded with attempts to trap Jesus in His words. There follows His scathing denunciation of the scribes and Pharisees. Then comes His sorrowful farewell to the Jewish nation (Matt. 23:37-39).

John comments that "though He had performed so many signs before them, yet they were not believing in Him," and cites the divine, judicial rejection of Israel in Isaiah 53:1 and 6:10 as fulfilled on this occasion (John 12:37-40). Jesus then withdrew from the temple—His final exit—and from the city, crossed Kidron, and sat upon Olivet, where he spoke His discourse. We can hardly ask for more evidence that Jesus takes the standpoint

---

[1] As premillennialists, posttribulationists agree to the temporariness of God's rejection of Israel. J. F. Rand mistakenly imputes the usual amillennial position to premillennial posttribulationists (*BibSac*, 113:202).

of His rejection by the Jewish nation and His Father's rejection of the Jewish nation. It is the chronology of the resultant present age which Jesus now outlines. The context supports the relationship of the Olivet Discourse to the Church.

But in the discourse, do not Jewish elements indicate a Jewish rather than a churchly application? The truly significant question regarding the Jewish elements is whether they indicate that the Jews addressed in the discourse are Jews religiously, or only nationally. The demands of the Jewish cast of the discourse are fully met by our considering the Jewish remnant as Jews nationally but not religiously because they belong to the Church (cf. Rom. 11:5). It is fitting that Jesus should give special instructions to Jewish Christians who reside in Jerusalem and environs concerning the future crises of that city, especially since He is answering the apostles' question regarding the fate of the temple and the city. We do not, and should not, relegate the books of Hebrews and James to another dispensation because of their Jewish coloring. Their authors simply address Jewish Christians who belong to the Church. So it is with the Olivet Discourse.

Several Jewish aspects of the discourse deserve specific attention. Jesus warns of persecution from Jewish leaders in synagogues (Mark 13:9; Luke 21:12). But He likewise warns of persecution by ostracism from synagogues in the Upper Room Discourse (John 16:2), to which only extreme dispensationalists deny churchly application.

According to some interpreters, "the gospel of the kingdom" (Matt. 24:14) preached during the tribulation will differ from the Gospel preached in the Church age even though both gospels agree in their soteriology. Doubtless the tribulational witness will contain emphasis on the near return of Christ to establish His Messianic kingdom on earth. But that falls short of proof that the heralds of the coming King will be Jewish witnesses who will not belong to the Church. We have no reason to deny that the Church will, and does, preach the Gospel of the kingdom. Indeed, Paul, the apostle to the Gentiles and outstanding custodian of ecclesiological truth, preached to Gentiles as well as Jews concerning the kingdom (Acts 20:25; 28:23, 30, 31) and taught a present spiritual aspect of the kingdom in the Church (Col. 1:13). If "the gospel of the circumcision" (Gal. 2:7, 8) fits the Church, we go beyond the evidence to find any incompatibility between the Gospel of the kingdom and the Church. That we cannot regard the Gospel of the kingdom as exclusively

Jewish arises also from the lack of Jewish exclusiveness in the millennial kingdom itself. The Church will rule with Christ (1 Cor. 6:2; Rev. 20:6), and the apostles, the foundation of the Church (Eph. 2:20), will judge the twelve tribes of Israel in that kingdom (Matt. 19:28).

Regarding the abomination of desolation and the flight from Judea, Jesus says, "And pray that your flight may not be . . . on a Sabbath" (Matt. 24:20). Stanton asks whether members of the Church are bound by Sabbath regulations, and gives the obvious answer, no.[2] However, restrictions on Sabbath travel were not divine injunctions, but rabbinic traditions (cf. "a sabbath day's journey" [Acts 1:12], less than a mile, i.e., far less than would be required for a safe flight from Jerusalem). Such traditions Jesus Himself repeatedly violated with His disciples (see, e.g., Matt. 12:1-14). Indeed, the violations formed one of the sorest spots in the animosity between Jesus and the Pharisees. Certainly Jesus does not contradict His own actions and teaching by implying that during the tribulation God will hold Jewish believers responsible to keep rabbinical restrictions concerning travel on Sabbaths. He merely recognizes that reduction of services to travellers and extra-scriptural restrictions imposed and enforced in Jewish society might hamper the flight of Judean Christians.

A destruction of Jerusalem took place in A.D. 70. The occurrence of that precursive fulfillment within the Church age negates the contention that Jewish elements in the discourse require the absence of the Church. Cf. the flight of Christians from Jerusalem to Pella in A.D. 68, though Pella is not in the "mountains," to which Jesus tells His disciples to flee. We may reason further. The falling of the precursive fulfillment within the Church age establishes a precedent which makes it probable that the final, tribulational fulfillment will likewise take place while the Church is still present on the earth.

Pretribulationists regard the apostles to whom Jesus spoke the Olivet Discourse as representative of a Jewish remnant belonging to redeemed Israel. Posttribulationists regard the apostles as representative of a Jewish remnant belonging to the churches of Jerusalem and Judea and in turn to the Church at large. If we may determine from other Scriptures whether the apostles usually represent Israel or the Church, we shall have data for a deci-

---

[2] Stanton, 59.

sion concerning the group to which the Jewish remnant belongs and therefore to which Jesus addresses the Olivet Discourse.

To propose the enquiry is almost to answer it. The apostles had previously received instruction concerning ecclesiastical discipline (Matt. 18:15-18). Only two days later they were to receive the Upper Room Discourse (including the promise of the rapture, John 14:1-3) and participate in the institution of the Lord's Supper, an ordinance of the Church. A few weeks following they were to be baptized in the Holy Spirit and form the nucleus of the first church in Jerusalem. The apostles were the foundation of the Church (Eph. 2:20). Their doctrine was that of the Church (Acts 2:42). They were God's gift to the Church (Eph. 4:11) and the highest officers in the Church (1 Cor. 12:28). They were the recipients of distinctively ecclesiological truth (Eph. 3:5, 6). And their names will be inscribed on the foundations of the New Jerusalem *in contradistinction to* the names of the tribes of Israel (Rev. 21:12-14). Clearly, the apostles stand as representatives of the Church, not of Israel. Hence, their representative role in the Olivet Discourse leads to the conclusion that the tribulational saints addressed through them belong to the Church.

THE PLACE OF THE RAPTURE IN THE OLIVET DISCOURSE

Where in the Olivet Discourse are we to place the rapture? There is no mention of a rapture prior to the tribulation. It might be said that mention of a pretribulational rapture would have violated the dispensationally Jewish nature of the discourse. But we have just rejected that view of the discourse. It might also be said that mentioning a pretribulational rapture of the Church would have meant nothing to the apostles since they were still thinking as Jews concerned with Israel. However, the Church had been revealed to some extent in the predominantly Jewish setting of Christ's identity as the Messiah of Israel (Matt. 16:13-18) and even to the length of instructions for ecclesiastical discipline (Matt. 18:15-18). Furthermore, only two days following the Olivet Discourse, Jesus talked about the rapture in the Upper Room (John 14:1-3). We know of no intervening instruction which would have made a pretribulational rapture any more understandable to the apostles in the Upper Room than on the Mount of Olives. The disciples were still thinking as Jews when they asked about the restoration of the kingdom to Israel in Acts 1:6, and some continued to think as Jews even later in the Church age when the Judaizing question arose (Acts 15:1ff.; Gal. 2:1ff.). Yet the rapture had long since become the subject of divine revelation. We have yet to discover convincing reasons for Jesus' omission of a pretribulational rapture—if such there will be—in an otherwise fairly comprehensive sketch of final events.

Posttribulationists equate the rapture with the gathering of the elect by angels at the sound of a trumpet (Matt. 24:31). The Lukan parallel supports the equation, for there Jesus says, "But when these things begin to take place, straighten up and lift up your heads, because your redemption is drawing near" (Luke 21:28). The posttribulational view gains further support from parallel terminology in Paul's Thessalonian discussion of the Church's rapture, where we read of a trumpet, clouds, and a gathering of believers just as in the Olivet Discourse (1 Thess. 4:16, 17; 2 Thess. 2:1).

Most pretribulationists refer the gathering of the elect after the tribulation to the gathering of the remaining dispersed Jews into the promised land. In support of this view are cited Isaiah 27:12, 13 and Deuteronomy 30:4, passages in which phraseology very similar to that in the Olivet Discourse portrays the gathering of Israel. Walvoord would broaden the gathering of the elect to include the confluence of *all* saints at the second coming.[3] Posttribulationists might incorporate the thought of Israel's regathering in consonance with the allusion to Isaiah and Deuteronomy. But by the same token, Paul's allusive quotations of the Olivet Discourse in his descriptions of the rapture broaden the reference to include the rapture of the Church.

The general term "elect" may refer to Israel, to the Church, or to both. But whereas pretribulationists cannot allow the expression in its posttribulational context to signify the rapture and cannot find another expression to fit the rapture in an equally definite pretribulational context (either in the Olivet Discourse or in any other passage), posttribulationists can point to the posttribulational gathering of the elect as an expression which easily lends itself to the rapture. The burden of proof falls then on those who would put the rapture before the tribulation.

Equation of the rapture with the gathering of the elect after the tribulation immediately runs into the objection that angels

---

[3] *RQ*, 63.

gather them in the Olivet Discourse, but Jesus Himself does so in Paul's description of the rapture (1 Thess. 4:16). However, it is a genius of Semitic thought that the medium or agency through which an action is accomplished often drops out of sight. The ultimate cause then appears as the direct cause.[4] But even that explanation is unnecessary in 1 Thessalonians, for there we do not read, "The Lord Himself will *gather* . . . ," but, "The Lord Himself will *descend*. . . ." The question "Who will catch up the saints?" remains completely open in the Pauline passage. Even had Paul identified Jesus as the gatherer, we still could not press a disagreement with the Olivet Discourse. For if, in line with the pretribulational understanding, angels will gather the Israelites into Palestine, we face the same "disagreement" elsewhere in that according to Isaiah 43:5 and Deuteronomy 30:4, 5 God Himself will bring His people back into the land.

Equation of the rapture with the gathering of the elect also runs into the objection that Jesus mentions no resurrection in connection with the gathering of the elect. But neither did He mention a resurrection in John 14:1-3. Nor did Paul mention a resurrection in 2 Thessalonians 2:1. Yet all parties agree that in both passages the rapture comes into view. Not every detail of the Parousia gains mention in every description of the event. We know, positively, from Revelation 20:4-6 that a resurrection of the saints will occur on the same posttribulational occasion which will feature the gathering of the elect. That is enough.

Armerding adds two minor objections to our taking the gathering of the elect as the rapture: "(1) The powers of the heavens, a reference to Satan and his hosts, will be dealt with upon this occasion, which will not be true of the rapture." But why may not the rapture and the dealing with the powers of the heavens take place at the same time? "(2) The tribes of the earth shall mourn. while the rapture will be an occasion of rejoicing."[5] However, since the reference to mourning appears in an allusive quotation of Zechariah 12:10-14, where the tribes of Israel will mourn in repentance throughout the land ($\gamma\hat{\eta}$—LXX) when they look upon their Messiah, it is better to take Jesus' meaning as the same. And

---

[4] Cf. Matt. 8:5-13, where the centurion appears to beseech Christ personally to heal his servant. But the Lukan account shows that the centurion was doing it through a delegation of Jewish elders and a further delegation of "friends" (Luke 7:1-10).

[5] Armerding, *Moody Monthly*, 51:788, 809; cited by Rand, *BibSac*, 113:201.

under any view of the rapture, the return of Christ after the tribulation will occasion rejoicing on the part of tribulational saints. The event will have two sides and elicit different reactions from saints and from sinners.

ONE WILL BE TAKEN

Then there shall be two men in the field; one will be taken, and one will be left. Two women will be grinding at the mill; one will be taken, and one will be left (Matt. 24:40, 41, paralleled in Luke 17:34, 35 with omission of the two in the field and addition of two in one bed).

How are we to understand this event, as judgment or as rapture? If as judgment, posttribulationists face the following challenge: if at the close of the tribulation the wicked will all be taken in judgment and the saints all raptured, who will remain in natural bodies to populate the millennial earth? Two weaknesses appear in that line of argument:

First, if the taking is judgmental and the argument is to be sustained against posttribulationism, we must suppose the destruction of the entire unsaved population of the earth. By no means does the text authorize the supposition. On the other hand, a partial destruction would leave the remaining unsaved to populate the millennial earth.[6] Thus, posttribulationists can regard the clause as a reference to judgment without damage to their view.

Second, if we regard the judgment as complete, rather than partial, the pretribulational view of the judgment of the nations (Matt. 25:31-46) runs into trouble. For if all the wicked will be taken away in judgment at Christ's advent, who will remain to be the goats in the judgment of the nations? The difficulty presents a formidable argument against understanding the statement "one will be taken" as a reference to judgment. We cannot resolve the difficulty by equating "one will be taken" with the judgment of the nations, for the two scenes obviously differ. Here people are scattered throughout the earth. There all nations assemble before Christ's throne. Nor can we resolve the difficulty by saying that the taking is *for* judgment instead of *in* judgment, for then we lose the parallel with Noah's Flood in the previous verses. God did not take away the wicked with the Flood for the

---

[6] See below, "The Judgment."

purpose of *subsequent* judgment. The Flood *was* the judgment. Furthermore, saints as well as sinners are brought to the judgment of the nations.

The argument is put forward that the context requires us to regard "one will be taken" as judgmental. The preceding verses do, indeed, draw upon the Deluge: "the flood came and took them all away" (v. 39). Notably, however, two different words appear for the action of taking, αἴρω (v. 39) and παραλαμβάνω (vv. 40, 41). The same word could easily have been employed had an exact parallel between the two takings been intended. Instead, we have the employment of another word which only two days later describes the rapture (John 14:3). The example of the Deluge illustrates not so much the judgmental character of the Parousia as its unexpectedness so far as the wicked are concerned. But granting that the context indicates judgment, we are not forced to conclude that "one will be taken" in judgment and "one will be left" in safety. The reverse may just as easily be understood: "one will be taken" in rapture and "one will be left" for judgment.

As mentioned, two days later the same word for taking appears in description of the rapture: "I will come again, and receive (παραλήμψομαι) you to Myself" (John 14:3). The apostles would naturally have associated the two expressions. Jesus probably so intended, else He would have drawn a distinction. The thought underlying παραλαμβάνω militates against our treating the word as descriptive of judgment. The prefix παρα- (*alongside*) denotes accompaniment and association (though not always of a friendly or joyous sort—cf. John 19:17) following the action of taking: "take (to oneself), take with or along" (BAG).[7] Subsequent association and accompaniment with the one who takes or receives admirably suits the rapture but clashes with the sudden stroke of judgment at Armageddon, where a terrible, eternal separation follows. In this light, the change from αἴρω to παραλαμβάνω indicates a change in topic and connotation: the former term refers to judgment similar in unexpectedness to the Flood, the latter to reception of the saints at the rapture to be forever with their Lord (cf. 1 Thess. 4:17; John 14:3).

Finally, we should note the characteristics of the event de-

---

[7] BAG. The prefix παρα- does not carry an ablative sense, *from the side of,* for in the usage of παραλαμβάνω elsewhere the thought is always one of accompaniment *by the side of* the one taking rather than separation from the side of one left.

scribed in the words "one will be taken, one will be left." It will happen instantaneously. It will affect people simultaneously. It will separate those who are in close physical proximity, even two in one bed. We know also that the event commands our watchfulness and readiness ("Therefore be on the alert," v. 42a). Where in prophetical literature of the Bible do we find a judgment which fits Jesus' description? Yet the rapture fits easily— and by context is tied closely to the foregoing description of the Parousia and the gathering of the elect "immediately after" the tribulation. The very preceding verse mentions this "coming of the Son of Man," the same phrase which appears with undeniably posttribulational import in verse twenty-seven.

Jesus speaks the Olivet Discourse from the standpoint of God's rejection of Israel. The discourse, therefore, relates to the dispensation of the Church. Confirmation of such a relationship comes from the role of the apostles as representatives of the Church and from the falling of the precursive fulfillment within the present age. Jewish elements in the discourse refer to conditions in Jewish society, not to divinely required keeping of Mosaic legislation on the part of Christians. The gathering of the elect at Jesus' return after the tribulation lends itself as a description of the rapture, in contrast to the inexplicable absence of an allusion to or mention of a rapture prior to the tribulation. "One will be taken" is best understood as the rapture in connection with the posttribulational Parousia just described.

10

The End of the Age

NT writers use two words for the end of the age, τέλος (*end*) and συντέλεια (*consummation*). The latter word may denote a more or less extended period of time. But we confront a different situation in the term τέλος. It can hardly include the period of tribulation. For in speaking of the tribulation, Jesus promises that "the one who endures to the end, it is he who shall be saved" (Matt. 24:13). The end must come at the close of the tribulation if one is to endure the tribulation to (εἰς) the end. Otherwise, Jesus' words make nonsense. Furthermore, "this gospel of the kingdom shall be preached in the whole world for a witness to all the nations, and then the end shall come" (Matt. 24:14). By preceding the end, the tribulational witness prevents the end from including the tribulation.

Paul writes that the "Lord Jesus Christ ... shall also confirm you to the end" (1 Cor. 1:7, 8). The reference in the preceding clause to "the revelation of our Lord Jesus Christ" fixes the eschatological connotation of the term "end." Although it may be questioned whether the term bears an eschatological significa-tion, the "end" is associated with the perseverance of Christians in Hebrews 3:6, 14; 6:11. Because "the end of all things is at hand" (1 Pet. 4:7, 8), Peter exhorts Christians to be "of sound judgment and sober spirit for the purpose of prayer ... [and] fervent in your love for one another." Jesus admonishes the saints in the Thyatiran church to "hold fast until I come.

And he who overcomes, and he who keeps My deeds until the end, to him I will give authority over the nations" (Rev. 2:25, 26). Here the "end" links with the coming of Christ (only the posttribulational has received mention—1:7) and the inauguration of the millennial kingdom (see also 2:27). In other words, Christians must go through the tribulation if they are to be confirmed to the end, to persevere till the end, to prepare themselves for the end, and to hold fast until the end.

It may be countered that "end" is a loosely used term, the meaning of which we ought to determine from immediate context rather than from indications in the Olivet Discourse alone. However, several considerations favor our taking the usage in the Olivet Discourse as definitive for other passages. In the entire NT there is but one place where we can determine with exactness the eschatological meaning of the "end." That place is the Olivet Discourse, where the term indubitably refers to the close of the tribulation. None of the subsequent references to the "end" distinguishes a different end from that of which Jesus spoke. And although in other connections "end" is a common, general term, because of Jesus' instruction in the Olivet Discourse it carries a technical sense in subsequent eschatological teaching. We see confirmation of the technical eschatological meaning of the "end" in the lack of qualifying phrases and clauses when the term appears in the epistles and Revelation. That lack implies something well-known and already defined.[1] The association of the "end" with the inauguration of the millennial kingdom, when the Christian who "overcomes" will receive "authority over the nations" and will "rule them with a rod of iron" (Rev. 2:25-27), further favors, though does not demand, a posttribulational location of the end.

If another end will close the Church age prior to the tribulation, we should need to regard the tribulation as a distinct age with its own end. But the NT knows only one more age, "the age to come" (Matt. 12:32; Mark 10:30; Luke 18:30; 20:34, 35;

---

[1] An exception to the technical eschatological meaning seems to crop up in 1 Corinthians 15:24, where the "end" is postmillennial. But, in accordance with the context and with premillennialism, the "end" may here refer to the end of the resurrection, i.e., the final resurrection—that of the unjust—following the millennium. In any case, Paul makes it clear in context that this "end" *follows* the Parousia and first resurrection. The passages above deal with the "end" *at* the Parousia and first resurrection, in the framework of which it remains legitimate to speak of a technical usage.

Eph. 1:21; Heb. 6:5).[2] "The age to come," a technical term in Jewish eschatology, properly denotes the final state *after* the Messianic reign.[3] Therefore, the day of the Lord, which encompasses the Messianic reign from the second advent to the last judgment, forms a pivotal "day" which at once connects and divides "this age" and "the age to come." How then can we think of two separate termini for the one present age? To the contrary, the "end" uniformly denotes the close of the present age at the conclusion of the tribulation and beginning of the day of the Lord. And the scripturally stated relevance of the "end" to Christians requires that the last generation of the Church pass through the tribulation in order to arrive at that "end."

Excursus on the Consummation (συντέλεια) of the Age

Different views concerning the consummation of the age alternate between regarding it as the closing point of the tribulation (cf. the "end") and as the whole or part of the tribulation. Some posttribulationists have regarded the consummation of the age, when the tares and wheat and the good and bad fish will be separated (Matt. 13:39, 40, 49), as the single crisis at Jesus' posttribulational advent. The gatherings of the wheat (v. 30) and of the good fish (v. 48) then represent the rapture, which is thereby posttribulational. It is objected against this interpretation that in the parable the wicked are gathered before the saints whereas at the Parousia the saints will be gathered prior to the judgment of the wicked. But the objection is not entirely convincing. Although the tares are bound or prepared for burn-

---

[2] Sometimes the plural "ages" appears for the final state. But that only emphasizes the interminable extent of the eternal age.

[3] Strack-Billerbeck, *Kommentar zum NT*, IV/2, pp. 799ff. Sometimes a certain confusion existed between the Messianic reign and the age to come (see J. Klausner, *The Messianic Idea in Israel*, 408ff.).

ing before the gathering of the wheat, the actual burning, or judgment, is not stated to occur before the gathering of the wheat and may, instead, occur afterward in the field.

A number of other interpretations have been suggested. (1) The parables refer to the millennial age and its close. But how then could the Devil, who will be bound in the abyss (Rev. 20:2), sow the tares? (2) The separation is that of the sheep and goats at the judgment of the nations between the Parousia and the millennium (Matt. 25:31ff.).[4] However, in Matthew 13 the separation takes place in the field, which represents the world-wide extent of the kingdom of heaven (v. 38); but in Matthew 25 the separation takes place before the throne in the immediate presence of the King. (3) The "consummation of the age" is the tribulational period, during which the wicked will be harvested in judgment and at the close of which the Gentile and Jewish saints will be gathered for the inauguration of the millennial kingdom. Adopting this view, Walvoord and Wood needlessly contend that the parables do not teach an order of separation.[5] But there is an explicit emphasis on the gathering of the tares first (vv. 28-30, 40-43). Stanton equates the reaping in Matthew 13 with Revelation 14:15, but fails to explain the order of reaping.[6] (4) The consummation is Jesus' coming to earth at the close of the tribulation when false disciples will be judged immediately before the true saints are gathered for the inauguration of the millennial kingdom. Both pre- and posttribulationists might hold this view, only they would differ on the nature of the gathering—general confluence *versus* rapture.

Two primary difficulties beset the interpreter of the twin parables of the tares and wheat and the good and bad fish. (1) The tares are gathered first. We may resolve this difficulty by regarding the gathering of the wheat as intervening between the binding of the tares and their burning, by regarding the consummation as a period of time, or by limiting the judgment to that by which false disciples are judged. (2) The gathering and burning of the wicked must not include the entire unsaved population of the earth, else none would be left to be the goats in the judgment of the nations (in the pretribulational scheme) or to

---

[4] English, 54.
[5] Walvoord, *RQ*, 160; Wood, 82-84.
[6] Stanton, 199.

enter the millennium (in the posttribulational scheme). We may solve this problem by limiting the sphere of judgment to false disciples in the kingdom. The fact that the parables concern the kingdom of heaven, not the world at large (though the kingdom is, of course, *in* the world), seems to require some such limitation. That the Devil specially sows the tares in the midst of the wheat accords with a limitation to the sphere of Christian profession. The judgment of false Christendom might well correspond to the divine overthrow of Babylon (Rev. 17). We must interpret Jesus' statement that "the field is the world" (v. 38) as a reference to geographical extent, not to content. In other words, the outward manifestation of the kingdom will be worldwide—the tares and wheat are scattered throughout the field—but will not include the world's entire population.

The question remains whether the consummation denotes an extended period of time or a single crisis at the posttribulational advent. Wood argues that all forms of the Greek word "end" refer to a goal accomplished, not a period of time closed. The effectuation of the completeness may occupy at least a short period, just as a harvest occupies a short period in the total time between planting and storage.[7] Frost, a posttribulationist, likewise proposes that the consummation will be a period of time, and adds the observation that the prefix $\sigma\upsilon\nu$ - (*with*) may imply a number of events which will combine to consummate the age.[8] In contrast to Wood, Frost holds that the "end" ($\tau\acute{\epsilon}\lambda o\varsigma$) denotes only the point of time at the posttribulational advent. "Consummation" does seem to mean an extended period in Hebrews 9:26b ("but now once at the consummation He has been manifested to put away sin by the sacrifice of Himself"). On the other side, the disciples evidently understood the consummation as the single crisis at Jesus' advent (Matt. 24:3, where a single definite article governs both $\pi\alpha\rho o\upsilon\sigma\acute{\iota}\alpha\varsigma$ and $\sigma\upsilon\nu\tau\epsilon\lambda\epsilon\acute{\iota}\alpha\varsigma$). Yet Jesus' use of the term "end" instead of "consummation" possibly intimates correction of a misconception on their part.

"The consummation of the age" appears in the great commission (Matt. 28:18-20), but there is little in those verses to define its meaning. Whether the consummation is a point or a

[7] Wood, 74-77.
[8] Frost, 21-23.

period of time, both pre- and posttribulationists share common problems of interpretation and, in large measure, common solutions.

11

The Resurrection

The resurrection of the dead in Christ will immediately precede the rapture (1 Thess. 4:16-18). Therefore, if Scripture places the resurrection of saints in general after the tribulation and does not specifically put the resurrection of deceased members of the Church before the tribulation, it is natural to understand that the deceased of the Church will be raised after the tribulation. Such a resurrection would of course draw the translation of living members of the Church and the rapture of the whole Church into a posttribulational orbit.

A perusal of Isaiah 23-26 reveals that the resurrection spoken of in 25:8 and 26:19 will occur after the tribulational anguish of Israel and the nations (24:1-13, 16b-22; 26:16-18, 20, 21) and at the establishment of the Messianic kingdom and conversion of Israel (24:14-16a, 22-25:12). Paul quotes Isaiah 25:8 as fulfilled at the resurrection and translation of the Church (1 Cor. 15:54). If the defeat of death for the Church will fulfill the posttribulational defeat of death prophesied by Isaiah, the translation and rapture will likewise be posttribulational.

In 12:1-3, 13 of his book, Daniel puts the resurrection after the time of unprecedented tribulation, at the downfall of the Antichrist (11:45), at Israel's deliverance, and at the "end" (elsewhere in Daniel indicated to be the time of the Antichrist's downfall, the establishment of God's kingdom on earth, and the close of the seventieth week—cf. 7:26, 27; 9:26, 27 and Jesus' use of the term "end" in the Olivet Discourse).

In Luke 14:14, 15 Jesus links "the resurrection of the righteous" with the millennial kingdom. Again, Jesus links "the resurrection from (ἐκ, indicating the first resurrection, that of the just from among the unjust) the dead" with the attainment of "that age" (Luke 20:34-36). The juxtaposition by καί of entrance into the eternal state ("that age") and attainment of the resurrection of the righteous indicates a point of time after the tribulation and within the pivotal day of the Lord, which at once divides and connects "this age" and "that age."

The raising of "all that the Father has given Me," which certainly includes the Church, will take place "on the last day" (John 6:39, 40, 44, 54; 11:24). "The last day" refers to the close of the present age. Pretribulationists might include within the last day the whole period from the beginning until the end of the tribulation in order to accommodate a pretribulational resurrection. But by its use as a chronological signpost, the last day appears to be a point of time at the end of the tribulation rather than the extended period of tribulation. Cf. Jesus' contrast between the "days" (plural) of the tribulation and the "day" (singular) of His coming (Matt. 24:19, 22, 29, 36-38, 50; 25:13; Mark 13:17-32; Luke 17:22-31; 21:6, 22, 23, 34).[1]

In Revelation 11:15-19 it is implied that the resurrection of the saints will occur under the seventh trumpet inasmuch as the time of the saints' rewards will then arrive. And the seventh trumpet brings us to the posttribulational advent.[2] From Revelation 20:4-6 we learn that "the first resurrection" of the "blessed and holy" will take place at the inauguration of the thousand years' reign of Christ.

Contemporary pretribulationists explain that the posttribulational resurrection will concern only saints who lived and died outside the age of the Church, but that the deceased of the Church will enjoy a pretribulational phase of the first resurrection.[3] In 1 Corinthians 15:23, 24 Paul distinguishes at least

---

[1] Some hold that "life from the dead" at Israel's posttribulational conversion denotes the bodily resurrection of the saints (Rom. 11:15). The interpretation is questionable.

[2] See above on Revelation.

[3] Walvoord, *BibSac,* 124:3-15, and *MK,* 278-284. If the resurrection of OT saints be posttribulational, their judgment must also take place some time after the tribulation. Hence, pretribulationists can ill afford to criticize posttribulationists for placing the judgment of the Church after the tribulation. They must do the same with OT saints. Nor can they then argue from the supposed necessity of an interval so far as the judgment is concerned (see below, "The Judgment").

two phases of the first resurrection: "Christ the first fruits, after that those who are Christ's at His coming." If two phases, why not three or more? Cf. the raising of the two witnesses in Revelation 11:11, 12 (but this may coincide with and be included in the posttribulational resurrection) and the casting of the beast and the false prophet into the lake of fire as a preliminary phase of the second death (but in Revelation 19:20 the phrase "second death" fails to appear in this connection and we are left uncertain).

The first resurrection does, in fact, take place in phases. But only *two* phases of the first resurrection can be determined from clear and specific chronological notations: that of Christ, the first fruits, and that of the saints who are raised at the close of the tribulation. In principle we should not consider a pretribulational phase of the first resurrection impossible, but we need scriptural evidence. Paul might have stated that the resurrection of the deceased of the Church will take place before the tribulation just as easily as John, in Revelation 20, puts the first resurrection after the tribulation. But Paul does not. It seems that a pretribulational phase, the only stage relevant to the Church, should have been stated to be pretribulational just as clearly as the posttribulational phase is indicated to be posttribulational. As it is, we naturally conclude that the resurrection of the deceased of the Church will occur in connection with the only future event specifically revealed to be the occasion of the first resurrection, viz., the posttribulational return of Christ.

Paul places the translation of living Christians "at the last trumpet" (1 Cor. 15:51, 52). Because the sounding of trumpets gains considerable prominence in John's apocalyptic description of tribulational events, the "*last* trumpet" doubtfully sounds before the subsequent tribulational trumpets. It is far more natural to regard the "last" as one sounded at the end of the age, after the sounding of the seven apocalyptic trumpets, or to identify the last trumpet of the translation with the last trumpet in the series of seven at the close of the tribulation. For at that time Christ will come in great power to make the kingdom of the world His own and to reward the prophets, saints, and all who fear His name (Rev. 11:15-18). We may well equate the "great trumpet" at the posttribulational advent in Matthew 24:31, the last trumpet in 1 Corinthians 15:52, the trumpet of God in 1 Thessalonians 4:16, and perhaps the seventh trumpet in Revelation 11:15-18 as well.

Some have resisted the equation by drawing contrasts between the last trumpet and the seventh trumpet. Thus, the trumpet at the rapture will be a trumpet "of God," whereas an angel will sound the seventh trumpet. But the alleged contrast is superficial. Since angels do God's bidding, an angel might sound the trumpet of God.[4] Besides, the last trumpet may *follow* the seventh trumpet or be included among events within the seventh trumpet. Pretribulationists need not only to prove a distinction, but also to explain the incongruity of the adjective "last" for a pretribulational trumpet. Again, it is claimed that the seven trumpets will be long blasts in contrast to the trumpet at the rapture, which will be blown "in a moment, in the twinkling of an eye."[5] But where do we find evidence that the trumpets of Revelation will be long blasts? Purported evidence in the expression, "the days . . . when he shall begin to sound" (Rev. 10:7), rests on the very questionable translation of the AV. We are not to think that the seventh angel "*begins* to sound," but that he is "*about* to sound" (NASB; $\mu\epsilon\lambda\lambda\eta$). Furthermore, Paul does not write that the last trumpet will be *blown* in a moment, but that "we shall all be *changed* in a moment" (1 Cor. 15:51, 52). This will take place "at" the last trumpet. The Greek word translated "at" ($\epsilon\nu$) indicates the time when or during which the last trumpet will sound without specifying how long or short the blast may be. And once more, an inclusion of the last trumpet within the seventh trumpet or a *following* of the seventh trumpet by the last trumpet would allow a distinction yet dissipate the argument against the posttribulationalism of the last trumpet.

Almost all who wish to drive a wedge between the last trumpet at the rapture and the final trumpet at the close of the tribulation stress that the joyous content of the last trumpet points to translation whereas the dreadful content of the seventh trumpet points to judgment. But in the very nature of the event the dreadful judgment of the wicked will occasion the joyous deliverance of the saints. Revelation 11:18 clearly states that blessing as well as judgment will characterize the contents of the seventh trumpet ("the time to give their reward to Thy bond-servants . . ."). Yet a third time, distinction between the seventh trumpet and a subsequent last trumpet would dissipate the argument.

But in writing of the last trumpet, how could Paul have had an eye on the seven trumpets when John had not yet written Rev-

[4] So also the pretribulationists English, 107, 108, and Stanton, 195, 196.
[5] Stanton, 195, 196; Pentecost, 190.

elation? On the purely naturalistic level, the seven trumpets in Revelation might hark back to Paul's "last trumpet," and Paul might have looked back to the trumpet at the end of the age in the oral tradition of Jesus' discourse on the Mount of Olives. Apart from the possibility of knowledge of and conformity to previous tradition, the superintendence of the Holy Spirit would have brought about a harmony of meaning.

Pretribulational writers have proposed several arrangements of trumpets as alternatives to the harmonistic approach of posttribulationists. Stanton maintains that the seventh trumpet will not be the last because the trumpet of Matthew 24:31 will follow it.[6] But on what grounds should we accept the dictum that the seventh trumpet will fall within the tribulation instead of at its close in connection with the second coming? We have already seen good reasons to regard the seventh trumpet along with the seventh seal and the seventh bowl as dealing with the Parousia and attendant events. But even though we accept a distinction between the seventh trumpet and a final trumpet blown at the following Parousia, the "*last* trumpet" hardly deserves its designation apart from posttribulationism. Stanton also separates the trumpet of God (1 Thess. 4:16) from the last trumpet in order to make a series of two. At the rapture the trumpet of God will awaken the dead in Christ, and then the last trumpet will summon the resurrected and living saints.[7] But, as another pretribulationist writes, "That 'the last trump' and 'the trump of God' are identical seems quite clear. The context in both cases has to do with the resurrection. . . ."[8]

Others connect the last trumpet with the sounding of the trumpet at Mt. Sinai (Ex. 19:9-11, 13, 16-20) in order to form a series of two.[9] The reason given is that these are the only two trumpets *of God* mentioned in Scripture. The passage in Exodus, however, does not say that the trumpet was of God or that it was sounded by God. From the angelic participation in the giving of the law we might justifiably surmise that an angel sounded the trumpet of God on that occasion (cf. Deut. 33:2; Acts 7:53; Gal. 3:19; Heb. 2:2). Strombeck also supposes that the trumpets mentioned in Isaiah 18:3 and Zephaniah 1:14-

---

[6] Stanton, 194.
[7] Stanton, 194, 195.
[8] Armerding, *The Olivet Discourse,* 88.
[9] Strombeck, 110, 111; Hoyt, in *Understanding the Times,* ed. Culbertson and Centz, 282.

17 will be blown at the beginning of the tribulation. He then equates them with the "last trumpet" at the rapture. But in both references the trumpet merely symbolizes battle. In neither reference do we confront evidence that the trumpet will sound at the beginning of the tribulation. And the problem of the designation "last" for a pretribulational trumpet remains.

We may regard as more restrained the explanation that a pretribulational trumpet will be last in its sphere, i.e., in the Church age, rather than last in a series. But so long as there are only the present age and the coming age connected by the day of the Lord noninclusive of the tribulation, the "last" in the present age carries us to the end of the tribulation. And it is quite improbable that the adjective "last" should describe a trumpet never explicitly stated to be blown before the tribulational period during which the blowing of trumpets figures strongly.

On the one hand, saints of one sort or another will rise from the dead at the posttribulational advent. This resurrection will coincide with the gathering of the elect, with the occasion when "one will be taken, and one will be left," and with the blowing of a trumpet at the end of the age. On the other hand, the resurrection, translation, and rapture of the Church will take place at "the last trumpet." Scripture nowhere indicates that a trumpet will sound before the tribulation. At the same time we know that various trumpets will sound during and at the close of the tribulation. Hence, chronological data in passages concerning the resurrection uniformly point in a posttribulational direction.

12

The Promise in John 14:1-3

Let not your heart be troubled; believe in God, believe also in Me.
In My Father's house are many dwelling places; if it were not so,
I would have told you; for I go to prepare a place for you. And
if I go and prepare a place for you, I will come again, and receive
you to Myself; that where I am, there you may be also.

In this passage Jesus promises to return and receive His disciples to Himself.[1] Jesus tells them, it is usually understood, that
He will go back to heaven for the preparation of heavenly "mansions" (AV) to which He will take the disciples at His return.
From this the argument develops that Jesus must come to take
believers to heaven before the tribulation, because at His
posttribulational return He will reign upon the earth rather than
return to heaven. But notable weaknesses appear in the argument:

---

[1] Payne adopts the view that Jesus here promises to come and receive to
heaven believers *at their deaths* because Jesus has just spoken of His own
death and of the disciples' following Him in death (13:36, 37) and because
the statement "I will come" in 14:18 carries a spiritual sense (p. 74). But
in the exchange between Jesus and Peter concerning Peter's boisterous
faith (13:36, 37) Jesus implies that Peter will *not* follow Him in death, at
least not on this occasion. Nothing is said concerning the death of believers
generally. In 14:18, "I will come" refers to Jesus' coming in the person of the
Comforter, the Holy Spirit, for the believers' earthly lifetime, not to a
spiritual coming of Christ at a Christian's death. The additional clauses in
14:1-3, "and receive you to Myself; that where I am, there you may be
also," rule out a reference to the Spirit's descent as in verse eighteen.

Jesus does not promise that upon His return He will take believers to mansions in the Father's House. Instead, He promises, *"Where I am,* there you may be also." The pretribulational interpretation would require us to believe that the Church will occupy heavenly mansions for a short period of seven years, only to vacate them for a thousand years in order to reign with Christ "upon the earth" (Rev. 5:10; 20:4-6). A thousand years' delay before habitation of the mansions poses no greater problem for posttribulationists than a thousand years' vacating them does for pretribulationists. In order to maintain pretribulationism we might avoid the difficulty by regarding the New Jerusalem (where the mansions are assumed to be) as a millennial as well as an eternal city. Then the Church would not have to leave her mansions during the millennium because they, too, will descend from heaven after the tribulation. But if this view be adopted, no difficulty arises for posttribulationism either! For if the mansions in the New Jerusalem will descend at the beginning of the millennium, the Church will not need to return to heaven before the tribulation in order to dwell in them.[2]

Although in John 14:1-3 we may solve any difficulty for posttribulationism by taking the widely accepted millennial application of the New Jerusalem, another view of the passage better accords with the larger context:

> Christ is promising to take His disciples to the Father's house when He comes again. . . . The passage . . . clearly teaches that the disciples will go from earth to heaven. . . .[3]

That, however, is exactly what the passage does not state. Indeed, the absence of such a statement makes one of the most remarkable features of the passage and holds the clue to a deeper and truer understanding.

---

[2] Those who believe that the Church will hover in mid-air for seven years at the point where they meet Christ prior to the tribulation cannot use John 14:1-3 argumentatively, for like posttribulationists they do not believe that Jesus and the Church will return to heaven upon His advent. Doubtless, the theory of a lengthy stay in the sky offers some advantage. It slightly alleviates the problem of two second comings instead of one and provides a reason why no passage concerning the rapture incorporates a return to heaven. However, neither do we read any place of a seven years' waiting in the sky. And those who hold such a view have to let go supposed indications in Revelation that the Church has moved entirely to heaven by the time the tribulation begins.

[3] Walvoord, *BibSac,* 112:2; and *RQ,* 76, 77; see also Linton, 33, 34.

In order to console the disciples concerning His going away, Jesus tells them that His leaving will work to their advantage. He is going to prepare for them *spiritual abodes within His own person.* Dwelling in these abiding places they will belong to God's household. This He will accomplish by going to the cross and then ascending to the Father. But He will return to receive the disciples into His immediate presence forever. Thus, the rapture will not have the purpose of taking them to heaven. It rather follows from their being in Christ, in whom each believer already has an abode.

The crucial point is that Jesus does not speak about a work of construction in the New Jerusalem. He rather speaks along a line which runs through the entire Upper Room Discourse, that of the position "in Christ" of believers. The word "place" (τόπος) easily lends itself to the thought. The verb "prepare" (ἐτοιμάζω) often refers to a spiritual work.[4] And the figure of a house (οἰκία), in its various nominal and verbal forms, appears frequently in the NT as a metaphor for the place of believers in the Father's domestic domain.[5]

The use of μονή and its associated verb confirms the above understanding. Unfortunately, the familiar term "mansion" does not project the correct connotation in contemporary English. The Greek word carries no thought of a stately house of imposing size and luxurious style. It means simply an *abode* or an *abiding place* (the meaning of "mansion" in early English). And the rest of the Upper Room Discourse indicates that μονή and its verbal cognate μένω have to do with a spiritual abode in Christ rather than a material structure in heaven. Μονή appears only once elsewhere in the NT, and that, significantly, only a few verses after John 14:2. Referring to the Father and Himself, Jesus says, "We will come to him, and make Our abode [μονή] with him" (John 14:23). The two appearances of μονή denote a reciprocal relationship: as believers will have abiding places in Christ, so the Father and the Son will have an abiding place in believers. The plurality of the term "abodes" in verse three emphasizes the individuality of each believer's place in Christ.

In confirmation, "abiding" in a spiritual sense forms a leading

---

[4] Matt. 3:3; 25:34; Mark 1:3; Luke 1:17, 76; 2:31; 3:4; 12:47; 1 Cor. 2:9; 2 Tim. 2:21.

[5] Acts 9:31; Rom. 8:9, 11; 14:19; 15:2; 1 Cor. 3:9, 16; 8:1; 10:23; 14:3, 4, 5, 12, 17, 26; 2 Cor. 10:8; 12:19; 13:10; Gal. 6:10; Eph. 2:19, 21; 4:12, 16, 29; 1 Thess. 5:11; Heb. 3:2-6; 10:21; 1 Pet. 2:5, 7.

motif throughout the Upper Room Discourse: "the Father abiding in Me" (14:10); "He [the Comforter] abides with you, and will be in you" (14:17); "abide in Me, and I in you ... abides in the vine, ... abide in Me" (15:4); "if anyone does not abide in Me, ... (15:6); "if you abide in Me, and My words abide in you, ..." (15:7); "abide in My love" (15:9); "you will abide in My love; even as I ... abide in His love" (15:10). Jesus could hardly have made it clearer that the abode of a disciple in the Father's house will not be a mansion in the sky, but a spiritual position in Christ. The larger context of Johannine literature bears out the same thought. See John 6:56; 1 John 2:6, 10, 14, 24, 27, 28; 3:6, 9, 17, 24; 4:12, 13, 15, 16.

We can now easily understand why Jesus said, "I ... will receive you to Myself; that where I am, there you may be also," instead of, "I ... will receive you to myself; that I may take you to the heavenly mansions." Believers already dwell in Christ, their abiding place. Hence, all that is needed at their meeting with Him is to be kept in His immediate presence for evermore. We are not to deny a literal heaven, of course, but only to regard the context of John 14:1-3 as indicative of a spiritual relationship to the Father through union with Christ.

The interpretation gains further substantiation from the depth of meaning it gives to verse six. In Christ their abode, believers have the "way" into the Father's presence. In Christ, they have the "truth," revealing the Father's innermost character. And in Christ, they have the "life," infusing into them the Father's very nature. These are the present consequences of a position in Christ, just as reception into His immediate presence will be the future consequence.[6]

---

[6] We read that "the hope of the return of Christ to take the saints to heaven is presented in John 14 as an imminent hope. There is no teaching of any intervening event" (Walvoord, *RQ,* 78). However, the Upper Room Discourse does disclose that at least one outstanding event, the coming of the Holy Spirit, must precede the return of Christ to receive His disciples. Furthermore, Jesus also predicts an intervening period of persecution and tribulation (John 15:18-21; 16:1-4, 33). (And elsewhere Jesus gives the great commission to be carried out in an intervening period.) Thus, Jesus does *not* put forward His promise to return as an imminent hope.

13

Silence, Harmonization, and Differentiation

SILENCE

With due appreciation of the weakness inherent to the argument from silence, both pre- and posttribulationists have appealed to such reasoning. Sometimes a tit-for-tat becomes apparent. "If posttribulationists had one positive Scripture on the time of the translation, it would save them much complicated argument."[1] But if *pre*tribulationists had one positive Scripture on the time of the translation, it would save *them* much complicated argument. "The whole point of posttribulationism would be conclusively won by just one reference placing the Church in the tribulation."[2] But the argument would be conclusively won for *pre*tribulationism by just one reference placing the whole Church in heaven during the tribulation, or placing the return of Christ or the resurrection or the rapture of the Church before the tribulation. "In the Old Testament the tribulation passages refer to both Israel and the Gentiles and to the saved among either group [Although saved Gentiles appear in *millennial* passages, do they appear in OT *tribulational* passages?] but never to a corporate body of Jew and Gentile combined as they are in

---

[1] Walvoord, *RQ*, 155.
[2] Walvoord, *RQ*, 145; cf. Linton, 22.

the church."[3] That is true, for the reason that the uniting of Jew and Gentile into a corporate body awaited revelation in the NT. But the lateness of the revelation of the corporate body in no way tells us whether or not that body will be present in the tribulation.

Posttribulationists are charged with failing to distinguish two phases of the second coming just as OT prophets failed to distinguish the two advents of Christ (1 Pet. 1:10-12). The lack of chronological exactness and the merging of separate events in OT prophecy then become crutches to explain the lack of pretribulational explicitness in the NT.[4] But appeal to such "prophetic perspective" fails. At least a couple of OT passages imply the present hiatus between the first and second comings of Christ (Ps. 110:1; Dan. 9:26). Moreover, OT saints were not expected to understand clearly a distinction between different comings of the Messiah. If the NT situation were similar, we would not be expected to understand a distinction between two phases of the second coming. But the NT is far clearer than the OT in the details of prophetic chronology. Hence, a lack of distinction in the OT does not justify the lack of distinction in the NT. The details of the two comings of the Messiah as given in the OT could not be harmonized into one event because of the antithesis between His suffering and glory. In the alleged two phases of the second coming, however, the descriptive details are markedly parallel and quite harmonious.[5] At most, an appeal to OT vagueness might turn up the *possibility* that the Parousia will take place in separate phases. But the line of reasoning would lead only to an agnosticism. Perhaps the Parousia will take place in three or four or many more phases. How could we know?

In sharp contrast to the absence of scriptural statements explicitly setting forth the resurrection, translation, and rapture of the Church and the Lord's return as pretribulational stand the acknowledged statements that after the tribulation Jesus will come, the elect will be gathered, and the first resurrection will occur. Pretribulationists place the rapture at an advent nowhere stated to be pretribulational. Posttribulationists place it at an advent, gathering, and resurrection indisputably located after the tribulation. Surely the advantage lies with the posttribulational view.

---

[3] Walvoord, *RQ*, 61.
[4] See, e.g., Wood, 107.
[5] See below.

Viewed as a whole, the NT addresses Christians in the present age. Why in the entire NT do we meet not one unambiguous statement that Jesus will come before the tribulation? Is it not strange that what is supposed to be the blessed hope of the Church is not once chronologically pinpointed in the book of the Church, while that "phase" of the second coming which is supposed *not* to be the hope of the Church *is* categorically stated to occur after the tribulation—and that it is so stated several times?

HARMONIZATION AND DIFFERENTIATION

"Distinguish the things that differ." But the question is not whether we should distinguish the things that differ. Rather, what things really differ? Here the argument revolves around various eschatological terms and passages descriptive of the second coming.

Three main terms appear in the NT for the second coming: "revelation" (ἀποκάλυψις), "appearing" (ἐπιφάνεια), and "coming" or "presence" (παρουσία, *parousia*). Almost all contemporary pretribulationists acknowledge that the three terms are used indiscriminately for what they regard as the two phases of Jesus' return. Ἀποκάλυψις appears in 1 Corinthians 1:7 and 1 Peter 1:7, 13; 4:13 concerning the hope of believers in the present age. And παρουσία appears in Matthew 24:3, 27, 37, 39 and 2 Thessalonians 2:8 concerning the posttribulational advent. Thus, the distinction which used to be made between the pretribulational Parousia and the posttribulational revelation breaks down.[6]

Parousia literally means "presence," "a being alongside." It is therefore argued by some that the word favors the presence of Christ with the Church during the tribulation more than the arrival of Christ after the tribulation. But Christ will be present with the Church after the tribulation just as pretribulationists say He will be during the tribulation. And although in 2 Corinthians 10:10 and Philippians 2:12 *parousia* contrasts with absence, scholarly authorities concur that "arrival" came to be an integral and many times the predominant idea in the word (see any of the standard dictionaries and lexicons). Deissmann has

---

[6] Payne's argument that the definite article with "coming," "appearing," and "revelation" demonstrates the singleness of the event (pp. 47, 48) fails to recognize that the exact force of the Greek definite article is a delicate question. Cf. Payne's similarly tenuous emphasis on the definite article in the phrase "the last trumpet" (pp. 58, 59).

shown that *parousia* was commonly used in NT times for the visits of kings and emperors to their provinces. Events were even dated from such *parousiai*.[7] This connotation beautifully fits the return of Jesus as King of kings and Lord of lords at the close of the tribulation (cf. Rev. 19:11-16).[8]

Pretribulationists see great and numerous contrasts between pre- and posttribulational advents. We read long lists of alleged contrasts in detail.[9] But the contrasts possess negligible argumentative value. Many of the contrasted details do not contradict one another, but lend themselves to harmonization in a single event. For example, the fact that the saints will meet the Lord in the air in no way implies that He will not continue His descent to the Mount of Olives. In other contrasts we are dealing with mere assertions or the taking of disputed points for granted. As an example of assertion which entirely begs the question, we may take the statement "At the time of the translation, the earth is not judged and sin continues." Yes, if we assume pretribulationalism. No, if we assume posttribulationism. An example of taking a disputed point for granted emerges in the statement, "The translation is before the day of wrath from which the church is promised deliverance." That is so only if God will use a pretribulational rapture as His method of deliverance. But this is the very matter in question.

There is no reason why Jesus cannot come *for* His saints and continue to descend *with* them. The meeting in the air does not preclude a descent to the earth. Even in the first stage of His descent, Jesus will come with the disembodied spirits of deceased saints. A judgment of the Church concerning rewards need not conflict with a judgment of Israel and of the Gentiles concerning entrance into the kingdom. The blessing of being taken at a posttribulational rapture will not take away the privilege of entrance into the millennium. Those who rise in the first resurrection will reign with Christ. The marriage supper of the Lamb will not clash with the judgmental supper. The one involves the Church and the other involves the wicked. Jesus' coming as

---

[7] Deissmann, *LAE*, 368-373.

[8] Although the OT knows no terminological distinction between the first and second comings of Christ, terms comparable to ἀποκάλυψις, ἐπιφάνεια, and παρουσία, with special reference to our Lord's advents, do not appear in the OT. Therefore the two testaments are not comparable in the matter of terminology.

[9] See, e.g., Walvoord, *RQ*, 101-103.

Bridegroom and Head of the Church will not exclude His Messiahship and Kingship. The banner of love in the rapture (a doubtful figure) in no way needs to clash with Christ's rule with a rod of iron over the nations. To say that judgment falls upon the earth after the rapture, whereas the liberation of nature follows the revelation, completely takes for granted a pretribulational occurrence of the rapture. The resurrection of the deceased of the Church does not rule out the resurrection of OT saints at the same time.[10]

We read further of contrasts between Matthew 24 and 1 Thessalonians 4:[11]

In Matthew 24, signs precede the coming, but not in 1 Thessalonians 4. But, to quote one writer against himself, "there is no need that all the accompaniments of the rapture be restated at every mention of the event."[12] Paul does imply that signs will precede the second coming and that the Thessalonians already knew them (5:1ff.). And in 2 Thessalonians 2:1-5 he reiterates two of the outstanding signs.

In Matthew 24 the Son of Man comes, in 1 Thessalonians the Lord Himself. Are we then to infer a different event every time a different title for Jesus is used? Is the glorious appearing "of our great God and Savior, Christ Jesus" (Tit. 2:13) to be distinguished from the coming of "the Lord Himself" (1 Thess. 4:16)?

In 1 Thessalonians we read of the trumpet of God, but in Matthew 24 of the trumpet of the angels. However, Jesus does not identify the one who will blow the "great trumpet." Even did an angel blow it, it might still be the trumpet of God. "The sword of the Lord" was also called "the sword of Gideon." "The rod of God" was Moses' rod. Jesus baptized, yet not Jesus, but His disciples (John 4:1, 2). Similarly, there is no problem in the gathering of the elect by angels.

In Matthew 24 we read of judgment, but not in 1 Thessalonians. However, we *do* read of judgment in 1 Thessalonians: "destruction will come upon them suddenly" (5:3).

In Matthew 24 the tribes of the earth mourn. But the figure of "birth pangs upon a woman with child" in 1 Thessalonians

---

[10] See Stanton, 265, for the alleged contrasts implied and countered in this paragraph.

[11] English, 45; Stanton, 62, 63.

[12] Stanton, 199.

5:3 also expresses anguish. Besides, in Matthew 24 Jesus probably refers to the repentance of Israel.[13]

In 1 Thessalonians the Church is gathered to Christ, in Matthew 24 the Jewish elect. But that is the very question: might not the elect be, or include, the Church?

In 1 Thessalonians there is resurrection, but not in Matthew 24. To be sure, there is no *mention* of resurrection in Matthew 24. But the very writers who draw out this contrast place the resurrection of OT saints at the posttribulational advent, where the apostle John indubitably places the first resurrection (Rev. 20:4-6).

On the other hand, we may observe that in both accounts there is a personal return of Christ. In both, a gathering of saints. In both, angelic participation. In both, the sounding of a trumpet. In both, clouds. We know that in the gospels, certain narratives—say, of the feeding of the five thousand—concern the same incident because a number of the main details are identical and because we can harmonize the varying details. So it is with the accounts of our Lord's return. Certain details may vary, but they do not contradict one another. The main features stand out in bold relief as identical.

There is force in the hermeneutical principle that "in disputed questions of interpretation, the simpler view is to be preferred; the burden of proof rests upon the more elaborate explanation."[14] Pretribulationism is the more elaborate view in that without explicit scriptural statements it divides the second coming and the resurrection of the saints into two phases. "Pretribulationists do not believe that there are two second comings, . . . but that there is one coming incorporating two separate movements. . . ."[15] We may detect a struggle to maintain unity and separateness at the same time. But two separate movements from heaven to earth cannot by any stretch of fancy be considered one coming. Jesus' first advent involved a somewhat lengthy period of sojourn upon the earth, but there was only one movement from heaven to earth.[16] The two movements posited in pre-

---

[13] See above, "The Olivet Discourse."

[14] Ladd, 165.

[15] Stanton, 19.

[16] Walvoord erroneously writes, "Posttribulationists themselves consider the doctrine of the second advent a series of events rather than one great climactic act of God," and cites only Rose (Walvoord, *RQ*, 136). Rose's peculiar view can hardly be taken as representative of the posttribulational school. The second advent will climax a series of events, but in itself will be single.

tribulationism do indeed violate the law of parsimony in interpretation.

Two of the clearest methods by which Jesus and the writers of
the NT might have distinguished separate phases of His return—
differentiation in terminology and contradictoriness in descriptive
details—were not employed. Yet we might have expected Jesus and
those writers (especially Paul, the most prominent expositor of
ecclesiological truths) to have distinguished carefully in one or
the other manner if not in both. On the contrary, the identity of
terminology and the harmoniousness of the descriptive details
create a presumption in favor of the view which regards the second advent as a single, uninterrupted event.

14

The Judgment

It has been argued that if the rapture were to take place after the tribulation, all believers would be caught up and glorified, with the result that no "sheep" would remain to be present at the judgment of the nations or to populate the millennial earth (cf. Matt. 25:31-46). On the other hand, pretribulationism provides between the rapture and the judgment of the nations an interval of seven years during which a new generation of believers will arise. These will be the "sheep," who in their natural bodies will populate the millennial earth.

Several questions arise. Are the "brothers" of Jesus in Matthew 25 Jews? Will the kingdom into which the sheep enter be the millennial phase or the eternal phase of God's rule? Will the judgmental scene in Matthew 25 occur at the *beginning* of the millennium? May it not be the description of a general judgment of "all the nations" of men from all ages at the close of the millennium (and thus be parallel to Revelation 20:11ff.)? Many have believed the latter: "Some pre-millennialists make it to be the kingdom of Christ here on earth during the Millennium. . . , while Alford, Lange and all other premillennialists who place this judgment scene at the end of the Millennium, refer the kingdom to the time of the new heavens and the new earth after the Millennium."[1] Hence, the understanding of one general judgment at the end of the millennium does not merit the designation "amil-

---

[1] Biederwolf, 359.

lennial," for the early champions of premillennialism in modern times held to this view. Rather, the understanding of Matthew 25:31-46 as a separate judgment prior to the millennium is an innovation which arose with pretribulationism itself.[2]

If the judgment in Matthew 25 will take place after the millennium, the unregenerate who survive the tribulation and second coming will go into the millennium in their natural bodies. Were such a general judgment after the millennium rejected, however, posttribulationists might still place the judgment of believers immediately after the second coming (cf. Daniel's seventy-five extra days beyond the seventieth week—Dan. 12:12). Pretribulationists can hardly object, for that is exactly the place where they provide room for the judgment of the nations.

In the pretribulational scheme separate judgments are usually listed as follows:

1) the judgment of the Church in heaven during the tribulation concerning reward for works (2 Cor. 5:10),

2) the judgment of the nations living on earth immediately before the millennium concerning entrance into the millennium (Matt. 25:31-46),

3) the judgment of the living nation of Israel immediately before the millennium concerning entrance into the Davidic kingdom of the millennium (Ezek. 20:33-38), and

4) the judgment of the wicked dead after the millennium concerning degrees of punishment (Rev. 20:11-15).

A scheme of prophetic chronology ought to explain the data of Scripture adequately with a minimal number of "loose ends" and extra-scriptural assumptions. In the above list of judgments a disconcerting number of "loose ends" and extra-scriptural assumptions do appear in the form of four groups of people unaccounted for, who require the assuming of four additional judgments never mentioned in Scripture:

1) the judgment of OT saints, raised after the tribulation,

2) the judgment of tribulational martyrs, who will remain under the altar in heaven until the close of the tribulation (Rev. 6:9-11) and who cannot be included by pretribulationists in the judgment of the living nations because the martyrs will have left their natural bodies through death,

3) the judgment of those who will be saved during the millennium (Isa. 2:2, 3; 11:10; 55:1-7), and

---

[2] *Ibid.*, 355-357.

4) the judgment of the wicked living at the close of the millennium (other than the armies which will come against the holy city and be destroyed—Rev. 20:7-9).

The extra-scriptural multiplication of judgments required by the exigencies of the pretribulational scheme does not commend the theory which generates it.

We may also observe that those who maintain the necessity of an interval between two phases of the Parousia in order to provide time for the judgment of Christians and the marriage supper of the Lamb themselves have crowded together four judgments—that of martyred tribulational saints, that of OT saints, that of the living nation of Israel, and that of the living nations—between the posttribulational advent and the millennium. What has become of the necessity for an interval in the pretribulational outline of events?

Within pretribulationism we may attempt to harmonize the judgments of the disregarded groups with the four judgments already appearing in the list. But the moment we begin the attempt, we adopt the very principle of harmonization which leads to our understanding a single general judgment. (The principle also leads to a blending of descriptions of the Parousia which in pretribulationism must be kept apart.)

Not only does the pretribulational scheme require the assuming of additional judgments. It also takes much for granted concerning each individual judgment. "According to 2 Corinthians 5:10, all believers of this age must appear before the judgment-seat of Christ in heaven. . . ."[3] But neither this verse nor any other indicates that Christians will be judged in heaven or in the air or during the tribulation. And although Paul writes in the first person plural, he does not specifically limit the judgment to the believers of this age, or, for that matter, to believers.

The pretribulational view of the judgment of the nations is likewise beset by difficulties and based on unproved premises. All parties acknowledge that the treatment of the "brothers" of Christ will constitute outward evidence of inward salvation. But who will be those "brothers"? According to the pretribulational understanding, they will be the Jews as a nation. But that assumption becomes dubious when we recall that in this same book

---

[3] Walvoord, *BibSac,* 113:197; cf. Walvoord, *RQ,* 89.

(Matt. 12:49, 50) Jesus defines His brothers as "whoever shall do the will of My Father."

We do better to take the meaning that the sheep showed their love for Christ in their love to one another as Christ's brothers (cf. 1 John 3:14), or even more specifically, in their loving acceptance of persecuted Christian witnesses and their message (cf. Matt. 10:11-42). It may be objected that the change from "you" to "these brothers of Mine" makes a distinction between the sheep and the brothers. But in this very discourse we can count no less than six shifts between the second and third persons. Yet all the while the same people stay in view (Matt. 24:3-28). Cf. the Beatitudes: "Blessed are they. . . . Blessed are you" (Matt. 5:10, 11). Even Walvoord comments on "the frequent interchange of the second and third persons."[4] In the passage before us, Jesus does not say "to yourselves," for that might have implied individual self-love. And He does not say "to one another," because He wished to give a different emphasis. The clue that the shift in persons does not imply another group of people appears in the shift from the plural "you" to the singular "one." The resultant emphasis is that a loving deed to *just a single one of Christ's most insignificant disciples* is done to Christ Himself and demonstrates true salvation. With this understanding of the "brothers," the sheep represent the saved of all time and the goats the lost of all ages. Christ's commendation will surprise the sheep, not because they will be unaware of having ministered to one another as fellow-believers, but because Christ's first statement will sound as though they have ministered to Him directly and personally.

We need to question the assumption that the immediate issue of the judgment of the nations will have to do with entrance into the millennial kingdom. The statement that the sheep will go into "eternal life" (Matt. 25:46) better lends itself to the view that Jesus refers to the eternal phase of the kingdom (cf. Luke 1:33). The immediate and prime issue of the judgment will then concern entrance into eternal bliss versus eternal punishment.

It can be demonstrated that some of the wicked will survive the tribulation and Parousia and that those who do will enter the millennium. We are therefore forced to put the judgment of the nations after the millennium. For if it were to take place be-

---

[4] *RQ*, 112.

forehand, none of the wicked (goats) could enter the millennium. In Zechariah 14:16ff. we read that

> any who are [better, "everyone (כֹּל) who is"] left of all the nations that went against Jerusalem will go up from year to year to worship. . . . And it will be that whichever of the families of the earth does not go up to Jerusalem to worship the King, the Lord of hosts, there will be no rain on them.

That those who enter the millennium will include wicked survivors of the tribulation derives from the phraseology—*"everyone who is left of all the nations."* It also derives from the inclusion of those who attacked Jerusalem—i.e., the armies of the wicked who will converge on Palestine at the close of the tribulation—and from the implication that some of those who will enter the millennium may refuse to go to Jerusalem for the worship of the Lord, a refusal hardly characteristic of the righteous. This passage, therefore, goes against any interpretation which would prohibit the wicked from entering the millennium.

The judgment of the sheep and the goats becomes the pattern for the great general judgment at the end of time. Epistolary writers refer to that aspect which has to do with Christians simply because they address only Christians in their letters (Rom. 14:12; 1 Cor. 3:12-15; 2 Cor. 5:10). In Revelation 20:11-15 John mentions only the wicked dead because he has already mentioned, repeatedly and prominently, the saints of the first resurrection (vv. 4-6, 9). Even in a pretribulational scheme, we would have to place here the final judgment of both the righteous and the wicked who will live on earth as subjects of Christ's millennial rule. The conditional clause "And if anyone's name was not found written in the book of life" (v. 15) naturally implies the presence of believers whose names *will* be found written in the book of life.

Contrasting Matthew 25 and Revelation 20, Scofield writes, "Here there is no resurrection; the persons judged are living nations; no books are opened; three classes are present, sheep, goats, brethren; the time is at the return of Christ (v. 31); and the scene is on the earth."[5] However, although Jesus does not *mention* the resurrection in Matthew 25, contemporary pre- as well as posttribulationists place the resurrection of OT saints after the tribulation. In Matthew 25 Jesus designates the people

---

[5] *SRB,* note on Matt. 25:32.

judged as "*all* the nations" (v. 32), not "living" nations. The books may be an added detail given in Revelation. A previous paragraph has shown the probability of only two groups in Mat-thew by virtue of an identification of the sheep and Christ's brothers. A gap may intervene between the second coming and this judgment: "But when the Son of Man comes in His glory, and all the angels with Him, [millennium] then He will sit on His glorious throne." Or, "He will sit on His glorious throne. [Millennium] And all the nations will be gathered before Him." The prophets frequently fail to mention intervals of time such as the millennium. But better yet, the statement, "He will sit on His glorious throne," itself summarizes the millennial reign of Christ. Finally, Jesus does not identify the place of the judgment in Matthew 25. Consequently, Scofield's last alleged contrast lacks textual basis.

Walvoord, drawing from Peters, argues that the term "nations" is never used of the dead.[6] But the nations gathered in general judgment after the millennium will have come to life through resurrection (Rev. 20:5, 12, 13). It is further argued that the term "nations" ($\xi\theta\nu\eta$) refers exclusively to the Gentiles whereas a general judgment would involve the Jews as well. However, there are numerous exceptions in which the Jews are included along with the Gentiles. For example, "all the nations" in the great com-mission (Matt. 28:19) hardly excludes the Jews (cf. Acts 1:8, "both in Jerusalem . . ."). Especially when $\pi\acute{a}\nu\tau a$ modifies $\xi\theta\nu\eta$, the term may incorporate the Jews.[7] The references listed from Peters[8] have to do with the confluence of nations at Armageddon, and therefore in no way connect with a judgment of sheep and goats following Armageddon.

The next judgment in the pretribulational scheme is that of the living nation of Israel in accordance with Ezekiel 20:33-38. But that passage may not portray a formal judgment at all. Rather, under the figure of a shepherd and his flock the Lord likens the restoration of Israel to Palestine to another Exodus, a recurrent comparison in the prophets.[9] The Lord will purge out the rebels as He brings His people toward the land through heathen countries. Those countries are like the wilderness where

---

[6] Walvoord, *MK*, 287, and *BibSac*, 114:300.

[7] Cf. Rom. 4:17, 18; 16:26; Rev. 5:9; 10:11; 14:6, 8; 18:3; 21:24; 22:2; see Alford's note on Gal. 3:8.

[8] Isa. 66:15-21; Joel 3:9-21; Zeph. 3:8-20; Rev. 16:13-16; 19:17-20.

[9] Isa. 41:17-20; 43:16-21; Jer. 23:7, 8; Hos. 2:14-20; Mic. 7:15-17.

God judged the generation of Israel which came out of Egypt. The repentance and salvation of "all Israel" right at the second advent (Zech. 12:9-13:1; Rom. 11:26, 27) preclude that Ezekiel refers to a subsequent judgment in which some will still be found "rebels."

Several Scripture passages associate the reward of believers with the second coming. From the association it is sometimes argued that the judgment of believers will not occur after the millennium, but just after a pretribulational coming of Christ and prior to His engagement in millennial rule of the earth. Certainly at the Parousia believers will enjoy the rewards of glorification and vindication. But their formal judgment is another matter. The reception of crowns merely indicates victorious finishing of the earthly race (2 Tim. 4:8; 1 Pet. 5:4; Rev. 3:11). And there is reward right now for believers who through death have gone to be with the Lord (Phil. 1:21, 23). Yet the formal judgment of their works has not taken place. Deceased believers' presence with the Lord also destroys the argument that divine holiness demands a formal judgment of believers immediately upon the Parousia.[10] Neither does the present suffering of punishment by unbelievers in the fire of hades imply that their formal judgment has already taken place. Hence, a further delay of the formal judgment for the thousand years following the Parousia should occasion no surprise.

The gap of two millennia which now exists between the first and second comings of Christ goes unnoticed in a number of passages (Isa. 9:6; 61:2; Zech. 9:9, 10; cf. Luke 4:16-21). And, as all premillennialists quickly agree, the millennium itself goes unnoticed in many passages. For example, the first and second resurrections stand side by side as though occurring at the same time (Dan. 12:2; John 5:28, 29). Yet one thousand years intervene (Rev. 20:4ff.). Therefore, objection to a millennial gap between the Parousia and the formal judgment of believers' works ignores the common and much more crucial contention of pre- and posttribulationists *as premillennialists* that the same gap exists between the two resurrections. Even more pointedly, Jude 14, 15, places the judgment of "all," *including the "ungodly,"* in conjunction with Christ's coming. Similarly, Revelation 11:18 puts the "time . . . for the dead to be judged" in conjunction with the second advent. Matthew 16:27 and Reve-

---

[10] Strombeck, 126.

lation 22:12 likewise connect the judgment of "every man" with Christ's advent. Since the judgment of the wicked, admittedly postmillennial (Rev. 20:11-15), is joined with the second coming, nothing keeps the judgment of the righteous from being postmillennial, too. (The day of the Lord covers the whole period from the Parousia to the final judgment; hence, separated events appear in conjunction because they will occur within the same unit of time, the day of the Lord.)

When we come to specific verses concerning the judgment of believers, explanations become still easier. The statement, "You will be paid at the resurrection of the righteous" (Luke 14:14), need not imply a formal judgment. The immediately following reference to those "who shall eat bread in the kingdom of God". and the consequent parable of the great banquet point rather to the wedding supper of the Lamb (Rev. 19:9). In 1 Corinthians 4:5 Paul merely states that Christ will come and bring the hidden things to light. If the phrase "praise . . . from God" indicates a formal judgment—though it need not—the phrase "and then" (also Matt. 16:27) may simply denote a progression of time beyond the second advent.[11] The expression "shrink away from Him in shame" in 1 John 2:28 need not imply a formal judgment. But even so, the "Parousia" with which it is associated might include the presence of Christ from His arrival through the end of the millennium when a general judgment takes place. A correct reading and translation of 2 Timothy 4:1 will resolve any problem there: "I solemnly charge you . . . *by* His appearing and His kingdom" (NASB), not "judge . . . at his appearing" (AV). "The great white throne" and "the judgment-seat of Christ" are easily synonymous. If distinctions were to be inferred from such slight differences in terminology, we ought to distinguish "the judgment-seat of Christ" (2 Cor. 5:10) from "the judgment-seat of God" (Rom. 14:10, correct text). Yet they are clearly the same in that the final examination of Christians forms the topic of both verses. From none of these passages, then, is it necessary to deduce that Christ will judge the works of believers immediately upon the rapture of the Church.

At the very least we can say that not enough scriptural data about the judgments is available for the establishing of a decisive argument in favor of pretribulationism. On the other hand,

---

[11] Cf. Stanton, 233, 234.

several serious difficulties adhere to the scheme of judgments proposed in pretribulationism. And weighty considerations favor a general judgment, which leaves pretribulationism without arguments favoring itself and disfavoring posttribulationism.

15

Historical Confirmation

"Finding it difficult to sustain their contention solely on the basis of Scripture, these authors [posttribulationists] endeavor to discredit the teaching that the Church will be caught up before that awful period begins by asserting that this is a recent teaching."[1] Whatever posttribulationists have done in the past, hopefully the foregoing pages here have dispelled the notion that posttribulationism leans on tradition rather than Scripture. Nevertheless, an understanding of the history of the doctrine will help to establish a proper perspective and will confirm the scriptural arguments adduced for posttribulationism.

The novelty of an eschatological view requires that evidence put forward in its favor be weightier than usual since it is unlikely that saintly and learned scholars or the mass of pious Christians should for centuries have misconstrued the teaching of Scripture on so important a point as the blessed hope. On the other hand, the antiquity of a view weighs in its favor, especially when that antiquity reaches back to the apostolic age. For those who received their doctrine first-hand from the apostles and from those who heard them stood in a better position to judge what was apostolic doctrine than we who are many centuries removed.

---

[1] Thiessen, *BibSac*, 92:188.

Ante-Nicene Eschatology

Until Augustine in the fourth century, the early Church ·generally held to the premillenarian understanding of Biblical eschatology. This chiliasm entailed a futuristic interpretation of Daniel's seventieth week, the abomination of desolation, and the personal Antichrist. And it was posttribulational. Neither mentioned nor considered, the possibility of a pretribulational rapture seems never to have occurred to anyone in the early Church.

Clement of Rome exhorts the Corinthian Christians to watchfulness and purity on the basis of Jesus' coming as prophesied in Habakkuk 2:3 (with Hebrews 10:37) and Malachi 3:1:

> Of a truth, soon and suddenly shall His will be accomplished, as the Scripture also bears witness, saying, "Speedily will He come, and will not tarry;" and, "The Lord shall suddenly come to His temple, even the Holy One, for whom ye look" (*I Clement* xxiii).[2]

The quotation stands alongside the illustration of a tree budding and putting forth leaves and fruit which finally ripens—an illustration which hardly conveys imminence. The OT passage undeniably speaks of Christ's sudden advent to the earth after the tribulation, for the context discusses the tribulation, the reappearance of Elijah, and the millennium. Clement holds forth *this* coming to the Christians as their hope and object of watchfulness. In similar vein Clement speaks of watching and waiting for the arrival of the kingdom. This passage can hardly be claimed for the doctrine of imminence (as has been done) when it clearly pertains to the posttribulational advent. Similarly Cyprian can write about the suddenness of the world's end without implying imminence, for he also writes of a future, prior coming of the Antichrist (*Treatise* xii, 3, 89).

In the *Epistle of Barnabas* Christians are exhorted to stand fast in the present evil time and in the coming period of tribulation:

> The final stumbling-block (or source of danger) approaches, . . . [here the author launches into a discussion of the Antichrist]. We take earnest heed in these last days; for the whole [past] time of your faith will profit you nothing, unless now in this wicked time we also withstand coming sources of danger, as becometh sons

---

[2] Quotations come from the readily available edition of *The Ante-Nicene Fathers* by Robertson and Donaldson.

of God. That the Black One may find no means of entrance, let us flee from every vanity, let us utterly hate the works of the way of wickedness (*Epistle of Barnabas* iv).

Plainly, Barnabas could not exhort his readers in this manner unless he believed the Church to go through the tribulation and encounter the Antichrist.

Justin Martyr places the resurrection and gathering of Christians at the beginning of the millennium and equates their hope with Christ's return to earth as prophesied in the OT (*Trypho* lxxx, lii). Still more directly, he writes:

> The man of apostasy [Antichrist] . . . shall venture to do unlawful deeds on the earth against us the Christians . . . (*Trypho* cx).

In *The Pastor* (*Shepherd*) *of Hermas* the writer describes a vision:

> I was going . . . along the Campanian road. . . . I advanced a little, brethren, and, lo! I see dust rising even to the heavens. . . . I see a mighty beast like a whale, and out of its mouth fiery locusts proceeded. . . . I came near it, and the monstrous beast stretched itself out on the ground, and showed nothing but its tongue, and did not stir at all until I had passed by it. . . . Now after I had passed by the wild beast, and had moved forward about thirty feet, lo! a virgin meets me, adorned as if she were proceeding from the bridal chamber. . . . I knew from my former visions that this was the Church, and I became more joyful. . . . And she . . . said to me, 'Has nothing crossed your path?' I say, 'I was met by a beast . . . , but through the power of the Lord and His great mercy I escaped from it.' 'Well did you escape from it' says she, . . . 'You have escaped from great tribulation on account of your faith, and because you did not doubt in the presence of such a beast. Go, therefore, and tell the elect of the Lord His mighty deeds, and say to them that this beast is a type of the great tribulation that is coming. If then ye prepare yourselves, and repent with all your heart, and turn to the Lord, it will be possible for you to escape it. . . . Cast your cares upon the Lord, and He will direct them. Trust the Lord, ye who doubt, for He is all-powerful, and can turn His anger away from you, and send scourges on the doubters. . . . Those, therefore, who continue steadfast, and are put through the fire, will be purified by means of it. . . . Wherefore cease not speaking these things into the ears of the saints. This then is the type of the great tribulation that is yet to come. If ye wish it, it will be nothing (*Pastor of Hermas*, Vision Fourth).

Occasionally we read quotations of just enough of the passage to give the impression that the "pastor" teaches pretribulationism."[3] In reality, the gist of the vision is that the Church will encounter the great tribulation, but that she need not fear it if she casts her fears upon the Lord. A perfectly clear statement in the Second Vision confirms this understanding:

> Happy ye who endure the great tribulation that is coming on. . . .

Twice in *The Teaching of the Twelve Apostles* Matthew 24:31, which concerns the gathering of the elect at the posttribulational advent, is quoted with the substitution of "Church" for "elect"' (chapters ix, x). Christians are then exhorted to stand fast through the reign of the Antichrist until the posttribulational advent and resurrection:

> Watch for your life's sake. Let not your lamps be quenched, nor your loins unloosed; but be ye ready, for ye know not the hour in which our Lord cometh. [Here Walvoord, Stanton, and Pentecost break off the quotation in an endeavor to make the passage establish a belief in imminence by the early Church[4]] . . . for the whole time of your faith will not profit you, if ye be not made perfect in the last time. . . . then shall appear the world-deceiver as Son of God, and shall do signs and wonders. . . . Then shall the creation of men come into the fire of trial, and many shall be made to stumble and perish; but they that endure in their faith shall be saved from under the curse itself (chapter xvi).

Irenaeus, who claims to hold that which was handed down from the apostles, was as forthright a posttribulationist as could be found in the present day:

> And they [the ten kings] shall . . . give their kingdom to the beast, and put the Church to flight (*Against Heresies* V, 26, 1).

> But he [John] indicates the number of the name [Antichrist, 666] now, that when this man comes we may avoid him, being aware who he is (*Against Heresies* V, 30, 4).

Irenaeus also places the resurrection of the Church after the rule of the Antichrist and in conjunction with the resurrection of OT saints (*Against Heresies* V, 34, 3; V, 35, 1).

---

[3] Thiessen, *Theology,* 476; Stanton, 221, 222.
[4] Walvoord, *BibSac,* 111:200; Stanton, 221; Pentecost, 169.

Hippolytus writes:

> Now concerning the tribulation of the persecution which is to fall
> upon the Church from the adversary [he has been speaking of
> the Antichrist and the Antichrist's persecution of the saints and
> continues in the same vein]. . . . That refers to the one thousand
> two hundred and threescore days (the half of the week) during
> which the tyrant is to reign and persecute the Church (*Treatise
> on Christ and Antichrist* 60, 61).

Then in chapters 62-67 Hippolytus quotes extensively from passages concerning the tribulation and the posttribulational advent (Dan. 11, 12; Matt. 24; Luke 21; 2 Thess. 2; Rev.
20), connects these passages with the future experiences of the
Church, and equates them with 1 Thessalonians 4.

Melito of Sardis teaches exemption for Christians from the
conflagration of the earth by fire (generally considered among
the early fathers to be premillennial). But it is exemption by
preservation *through* the conflagration as Noah was preserved
through the Flood. In the letter of the churches of Vienna and
Lugdunum to the churches of Asia and Phrygia the persecution
of the Gallic churches is made precursive to the unrestrained persecution of the Church by Satan during the great tribulation:

> For with all his strength did the adversary assail us, even then
> giving a foretaste of his activity among us which is to be without
> restraint. . . .

And Methodius makes the resurrection of Christians coincident
with the millennial renewal of nature after the tribulation (*Discourse on the Resurrection* i, 8).

Tertullian identifies the rapture à la 1 Thessalonians 4 with
Christ's coming to earth to destroy the Antichrist and to establish His kingdom. Likewise, he connects the resurrection of the
"Church" with that advent (*Against Marcion* iii, 25; *On the Resurrection of the Flesh* xxiv).

> Now the privilege of this favor [viz., to go without dying at the
> translation] awaits those who shall at the coming of the Lord be
> found in the flesh, and who shall, owing to the oppressions of the
> time of Antichrist, deserve by an instantaneous death [Tertullian's
> way of expressing "translation"], which is accomplished by a sudden
> change, to become qualified to join the rising saints; as he writes to
> the Thessalonians (*On the Resurrection of the Flesh* xli).

. . . That the beast Antichrist with his false prophet may wage war on the Church of God. . . . Since, then, the Scriptures both indicate the stages of the last times, and concentrate the harvest of the Christian hope in the very end of the world . . . (*On the Resurrection of the Flesh* xxv; cf. *Scorpiace* xii).

Cyprian comments on the purpose of the tribulational passage in the Olivet Discourse:

With the exhortation of His foreseeing word, instructing, and teaching, and preparing, and strengthening the people of His Church for all endurance of things to come . . . (Treatise VII).

He further discusses the persecution of the Christians by the Antichrist (Treatise XI, 12).

Commodianus places the resurrection of Christians after the reign of the Antichrist, between the tribulation and the millennium (*Instructions* xliv, lxxx).

In *The Constitutions of the Holy Apostles* appears an exhortation to watchfulness for the Lord's coming—but not for an imminent, pretribulational coming because the immediately following section, joined to the exhortation by the causal conjunctive adverb "for," contains an admonition to steadfastness throughout the tribulation. The utilizing of terminology from 1 Thessalonians 4 for a description of the posttribulational advent deserves note:

Be watchful for your life. "Let your loins be girded about, and your lights burning, and ye like unto men who wait for their Lord, when He will come, at even, or in the morning, or at cockcrowing, or at midnight. For at what hour they think not, the Lord will come; and if they open to him, blessed are those servants, because they were watching." [Again Walvoord breaks off the quotation in an endeavor to make the passage teach imminence.[5]] . . . for through the abounding of iniquity the love of many shall wax cold. For men shall hate, and persecute, and betray one another. And then shall appear the deceiver of the world, the enemy of the truth, the prince of lies, whom the Lord Jesus "shall destroy with the spirit of His mouth, who takes away the wicked with His lips; and many shall be offended at Him. But they that endure to the end, the same shall be saved. And then shall appear the sign of the Son of man in heaven;" and afterwards shall be the voice of a trumpet by the archangel; and in that interval shall be the revival of those that were asleep. And then shall the Lord come, and all His saints with Him . . . (*Constitutions* VII, ii, xxxi, xxxii).

---

[5] *BibSac*, 111:200; 129:31.

The presence of the Church in the tribulation forms the substratum of Victorinus' entire *Commentary on the Apocalypse.* For example:

> He speaks of Elias the prophet, who is the precursor of the times of Antichrist, for the restoration and establishment of churches from the great and intolerable persecution [followed by a lengthy discussion of the persecution of the Church by the Antichrist] (VII, 351ff.).

Finally, Lactantius describes the plagues of the tribulation, the Antichrist, the persecution of the righteous, the coming of Christ and the resurrection, the millennium, and the final judgment. "The righteous" quite obviously include the Church in the terminology of Lactantius because his prevailing purpose is one of encouragement for Christians to remain steadfast throughout the last times. Yet in his outline of coming events Lactantius gives but one advent and one resurrection of the righteous, both after the tribulation (*Institutes* VII, xv-xxvii; cf. *Institutes* IV; and *Epitome* lxxi, lxxii).

We can conclude from the above survey of Ante-Nicene writings that the early Church was as explicitly posttribulational as it was premillennial. Wherever chiliasm appears in early patristic literature, the coming of the Messianic kingdom, not a rapture preceding by several years, appears as the hope of the Church. We discover not even a passing reference to, much less a refutation of, any who believed otherwise. This cannot be said even of premillennialism. Every Ante-Nicene writer who touches in any detail upon the tribulation, resurrection, rapture, or second coming displays a posttribulational persuasion. The number of those is about equal to those whom we can quote directly in favor of premillennialism.[6] Almost every time, premillennialism and posttribulationism coincide in the early fathers.

Therefore, to the degree that the historical argument for

---

[6] Some early fathers who cannot be cited by means of direct quotation are claimed by premillenarians through inferential and indirect evidence. For example, it is inferred that Polycarp was premillenarian because Irenaeus, his pupil, was so, and that Pothinus was premillenarian from the chiliasm of the churches of Vienne and Lyons, over which he presided, and from his association with Irenaeus. We might use such lines of reasoning to swell the ranks of early posttribulationists, also. To use the same examples, the posttribulationism of Irenaeus would imply that Polycarp, his teacher, was posttribulational and that Pothinus, whom Irenaeus succeeded, was likewise posttribulational.

posttribulationism is discredited, the historical argument for premillennialism loses ground. Premillennialists cannot legitimately appeal to Ante-Nicene chiliasm without accepting the posttribulationism which formed an integral part of the premillennial outline of coming events. If the premillennialism of the early Church favors apostolicity of the belief, the posttribulationism of the early Church likewise favors the apostolicity of that belief. Furthermore, the coupling of premillennialism and posttribulationism in the early Church invalidates the claim that pretribulationism is necessary to a scriptural kind of dispensationalism. An approach dispensational enough to be premillennial and futuristic concerning Daniel's seventieth week has been known for almost twenty centuries. But pretribulationism appeared only in the last century. A necessary correlation between the two becomes very difficult to prove.

It has been objected that the number of Ante-Nicene writers whom we can cite for posttribulationism is too small to establish a general belief in the early Church.[7] The fact of the matter is that the writings which are regularly quoted in favor of premillennialism may also be quoted in favor of posttribulationism. And who among the outstanding early fathers is missing from the list of posttribulationists? Only Clement of Alexandria and Origen, whose names have become trademarks for the mystical, allegorical method of interpretation and who strongly opposed premillennialism, especially as manifest among the Montanists. The evidence that the early Church was posttribulational needs no apology for lack of numbers.

Pretribulationists urge that the early Church held an incipient pretribulationism in the doctrine of imminence.[8] But the early Church did *not* hold to the doctrine of imminence. The very passages cited for imminence reveal a belief that the Church will pass through the tribulation. For example, probably the strongest exhortations to watch, often cited by pretribulationists, are the above-quoted passages from *The Teaching of the Twelve Apostles* and *The Constitutions of the Holy Apostles*. But in each passage the exhortation to watch for the Lord's return is immediately followed by a section which shows an expectation of going through the intervening period of the tribulation. The early Christians were not so devoid of common sense as to believe

---

[7] Walvoord, *BibSac,* 113:291, 292.

[8] Walvoord, *BibSac,* 113:291, 292; Thiessen, *BibSac,* 92: 193.

that Christ might come at any moment and at the same time believe that they must first experience the tribulation. The opposition of the two thoughts is not a subtle point of theology. It makes an obvious contradiction. To say that early Christians simultaneously held such plainly conflicting beliefs is to say they were stupid. Rather, "the expectation of the coming of Christ included the events which would attend and precede His coming."[9] Although watching for the Lord's coming implies imminence to some people, it does not to the minds of others and did not do so to the early Church.

Statements about the suddenness of Jesus' return and the end of the world by context refer only to the crisis after the tribulation. The most ardent devotees of imminence cannot thoughtfully claim, for example, that the statement of Malachi quoted by Clement, "The Lord shall suddenly come to His Temple," refers to a pretribulational advent. An event may take place with suddenness and be speedily approaching, yet not be imminent.

Although Payne is not a pretribulationist,[10] he does strongly advocate imminence as the belief of the early Church.[11] In so doing he shows an almost total disregard for context by failing to put statements from which he infers imminence in the framework of perfectly clear statements concerning the future persecution of the Church by the Antichrist. Thus, he quotes *Barnabas* iv, "The Lord has cut short the times and the days that His Beloved may hasten" (and a similar statement in xxi), without regard for Barnabas' warning in the very same paragraph to stand fast against the coming Antichrist. Similarly, the statement of Hermas concerning Jesus' coming "suddenly" (iii, 9, 7) is quoted without regard for the perfectly clear beatitude, "Happy ye who endure the great tribulation that is coming on" (ii, 11). Again, Justin Martyr's statement that the Antichrist "shall venture to do unlawful deeds on the earth against us the Christians" (*Trypho* cx) and his placing of the resurrection and rapture of Christians at the beginning of the millennium (*Trypho* lxxx, lii) do not deter Payne from inferring that the phrase "look for His future appearance" (*Trypho* lii) shows a belief in imminence on the part of Justin.

Payne also attempts to show that the early fathers thought

---

[9] Ladd, 20.
[10] See "Addendum on Imminent Posttribulationism."
[11] Pp. 12-17.

the tribulation possibly to have been fulfilled in the persecutions they had already endured. In *Barnabas* iv, "We enquire much concerning events at hand," Payne prefers to read "things present" in support of his view. But we cannot read potential fulfillment into the statement, because Barnabas speaks of the *approach* of the final stumbling-block. The admonition, "Hate the error of the present time," is also cited. But that error has nothing to do with the Antichrist or the tribulation. It is the Judaizing error against which Barnabas has been warning. In the citation "Now in this wicked time we also withstand coming sources of danger," the word "coming" rules out any thought that the tribulation might have already been fulfilled.

Payne presses the present tense in certain patristic passages to support his contention that the early fathers thought that the tribulation might have reached fulfillment in their persecutions with the result that they viewed Jesus' return as an imminent possibility. Thus, *Hermas* i, 4, 3 is quoted: "The golden part *is* you . . . so you who *live* among them *are being tried*." "Them" is taken as the fire and blood of the tribulation. But it can just as easily be taken as the people of the world. In fact, the usual reading is singular, "in it," with reference to the world. More importantly, the whole passage in *Hermas* and the very paragraph from which the quotation is taken speak of the tribulation as yet to come. Future tenses surround and almost smother the present tense of the main verb, which is utilized only in the interpretation of the symbols and therefore is roughly equivalent to an equal sign without temporal value. Some subsidiary verbal forms conform to the main verb merely as a matter of style. We must recall Hermas' clear statement, "Happy ye who endure the great tribulation that is coming on."

Cyprian writes that "the day of affliction has begun to hang over our heads, and the end of the world and the time of the Antichrist to draw near, so that we must all stand prepared for the battle. . . . A severer and a fiercer fight is now threatening." It is obvious that although Cyprian believed the tribulation was impending, he did not believe it possible that the tribulation had already taken place (*Epistle* 55, 1). Cyprian's comment, "Nor let anyone wonder that we are . . . tried with increasing afflictions, when the Lord before predicted that these things would happen in the last times," mentions present persecution, but not tribulational persecution at the hands of the Antichrist (*Epistle* 55, 2). The "last times" include the whole of this age (2 Tim.

3:1-9; Heb. 1:2; cf. Ignatius, *Epistle to the Ephesians* 11), and Cyprian's indication that the persecutions are increasing may even imply they have not yet reached their climax under the Antichrist. It is true that Cyprian writes, "The enemy [the Antichrist according to Payne] *goeth* about and *rageth,* but immediately the Lord follows to avenge our sufferings" (*Epistle* 55, 7). But this follows hard upon a statement, unquoted by Payne, that the Antichrist is yet to come before Jesus returns: "Antichrist is coming, but above him comes Christ also." Moreover, "the enemy that goeth about and rageth" may not be the Antichrist at all, but Satan, who presently inspires persecution. The phraseology alludes to 1 Peter 5:8: "Your adversary, the devil, prowls about like a roaring lion. . . ." Yet again, in this same passage from Cyprian we read, "Nor let any of you, beloved brethren, be terrified by the fear of future persecution, by the coming of the threatening Antichrist." Payne quotes this statement, but omits the words "by the fear of future persecution."

Finally, Payne appeals to Ignatius: "Weigh carefully the times. Look for Him who is above all time" (*Epistle to Polycarp* 3). But the phrase "above all time" bears no relationship to imminence. It refers to the eternality of the Son of God: "above all time, eternal and invisible," or as the alternate version reads, "before time, yet appeared in time." The admonition to "weigh carefully the times" may indicate a looking for tribulational events as precursive of the second coming.

We may fairly conclude that both pretribulationists and others who find imminence in the Ante-Nicene fathers are grasping at straws. The early fathers uniformly expected a yet future persecution by the Antichrist prior to the Lord's return.

Appealing to the progress of doctrine, we might think that pretribulationism represents a refinement of an early belief in imminence. However, developments of primitive beliefs have usually come in response to novel and erroneous teachings. Hence, the undoubted progress of doctrine *may* be, not a justification for, but an indictment against pretribulationism as a novel and erroneous teaching which now requires in rebuttal an expansion and refinement of the primitive posttribulationism. Since the early Church did not hold to imminence, but to the intervention of the tribulation, pretribulationism appears to be just such an innovation rather than an extension.

But, we may ask, was not the eschatology of the early Church so immature and general that we cannot reasonably expect to find a detail such as a pretribulational rapture? No, it simply is not true that the Ante-Nicene eschatology lacked maturity and detail. For example, in long eschatological passages in the writings of Irenaeus, Hippolytus, and Lactantius we confront full and challenging discussions concerning Daniel's seventieth week, the 1,260 days, the abomination of desolation, the ten toes, the mixture of iron and clay, the ten horns, the little horn, the Antichrist, the false prophet, the apostasy, the reappearance of Elijah, the restoration of worship in the Jewish temple, the significance of 666, comparison of Daniel and Revelation, Babylon, Armageddon, the first resurrection, the rapture, the second advent, millennial conditions, the final resurrection, and the last judgment. The only significant eschatological matter of which the early fathers were incognizant appears to be a pretribulational rapture!

It is said that pretribulationism might have been lost just as the doctrine of justification by faith.[12] However, early patristic evidence is extant that the early Church *did* hold to justification by faith. The doctrine shines brightly in *The Epistle to Diognetus* viii-xi. That other writers who mention the doctrine also extolled the value of Christian virtue does not negate their belief in justification by faith, for the same situation prevails in the NT between Paul and James, and indeed within Paul's writings alone. Are we to suppose that the early Christians were not trusting in Christ's righteousness and so were not actually saved? Admittedly, the James-like point of view became prevalent and ultimately perverted, but it cannot be said that the Pauline point of view faded out of existence. On the other hand, pretribulationism is entirely absent in patristic literature. The doctrines of justification and the rapture are not only dissimilar in their history, but neither are they parallel in Scripture, since the NT categorically affirms justification by faith, but not a pretribulational rapture. Thus the comparison between them breaks down.

Of course, obvious unscripturalness and fancifulness characterize many teachings of the early fathers. But that hardly renders patristic evidence useless. Despite the appearance of individual idiosyncrasies, general unanimity of opinion among the fathers—as in the matters of the rapture and the millennium—should keep us from dismissing patristic testimony lightly. If we were to dismiss that testimony in favor of posttribulationism,

---

[12] Pentecost, 166.

we ought to do the same with the testimony favoring premillennialism. Patristic evidence only confirms scriptural evidence. But it does do that much. Where a teaching obviously contradicts Scripture, patristic testimony will not carry weight. Where the scriptural evidence lies in question, patristic testimony gains in value.

MEDIEVAL ESCHATOLOGY

After Constantine wedded Christianity to the Roman Empire, the eschatology of the Church began to change. Augustine fostered amillennialism. The millennial reign was spiritualized into the present age, which was to terminate about A.D. 1000. When Jesus failed to return at that time, the chronology was necessarily modified, but the amillennialism remained basically the same. The sway of Roman Catholic Christianity gave rise to postmillennialism. Also, during the Middle Ages the historical interpretation of the Apocalypse came into vogue. The beast and the false prophet were often identified with Islam and Mohammed, though even some Roman Catholics expected an Antichrist to usurp the papacy.

POST-REFORMATION ESCHATOLOGY

The reformers, concerned in the main with soteriology, carried over amillennial and historical approaches to eschatology and identified the Antichrist with the papacy. But premillennialism soon found advocates among Protestants in Spener, Cocceius, Bengel, and Van Oosterzee. These men retained the historical interpretation of Revelation, as did also some later premillennialists—Mede, Isaac Newton, Whiston, Cuninghame, Brooks, Bickersteth, Birks, Elliott, and, in some measure, Alford. In this general period Whitby, Vitringa, and David Brown advanced postmillennialism with its optimistic hope of the world's conversion. Meanwhile, against the prevalent Protestant identification of the Antichrist with the papacy, the Jesuit Ribera revived the futuristic approach to Revelation.

Historicism having discredited itself through the fixing of dates and fantastic interpretations of current events, Maitland, Todd, Burgh, and Isaac Williams restored premillennial futurism to Protestant circles. Tregelles, B. W. Newton, Nathaniel West, and many others followed. Both premillennialism and futurism revived before the first glimmer of pretribulationism. We can marshal as fine an array of scholars and Bible teachers for posttribulationalism as for any moot question of theology.[13] This is mentioned only lest too much stock be placed in the present popularity of pretribulationism within a large segment of American evangelicalism.

THE RISE OF PRETRIBULATIONISM

Pretribulationism arose in the mid-nineteenth century. The likelihood is that Edward Irving was the first to suggest the pretribulational rapture, or at least the seminal thought behind it. Premillennialism had aroused great interest in prophetic study. To Henry Drummond's conferences at Albury Park (1826-30) came Irving, then a minister of the Church of Scotland. According to an unpublished manuscript of reminiscences by B. W. Newton, who was one of the original leaders of the Plymouth Brethren and a close personal friend of Dr. William Marsh of the Albury circle, Newton says concerning the Albury group: "Soon Irving joined, and ruined it all by suggesting the Secret Coming."[14] S. P. Tregelles, an outstanding scholar whose objectivity in the early Brethren controversies is highly regarded on all sides, makes a similar statement concerning the Irvingite origin of pretribulationism.[15] Both Newton and Tregelles were contemporary to the rise of the teaching within their own group.

An independent testimony comes from Mr. Robert Baxter, an Irvingite, who in his *Narrative of Facts Characterizing the Supernatural Manifestations in Members of Mr. Irving's Congrega-*

---

[13] Gleaned primarily from Alexander Reese, *The Approaching Advent of Christ*, 18, James Graham, *Watchman, What of the Night?* 92, 93, and Ladd, 35-60, is the following list of premillennial posttribulationists: Mede, Bengel, Spener, Cocceius, Van Oosterzee, Auberlen, Bleek, Christlieb, Delitzsch, De Wette, Dusterdieck, Ebrard, Ewald, Godet, Hofmann, Lange, Luthardt, Orelli, Rothe, Stier, Volck, Zahn, Isaac Newton, Whiston, Cuninghame, Trench, Alford, Andrews, Birks, the Bonar brothers, Ellicott, Maitland, Brooks, Bickersteth, Elliott, Ryle, Saphir, Stifler, Tregelles, B. W. Newton, West, David Baron, Guiness, A. J. Gordon, Erdman, Kellogg, Moorehead, Cameron, Frost, R. V. Bingham, Bishop Frank Houghton, Oswald J. Smith, Ockenga, J. Sidlow Baxter. Some of these men were not full-fledged futurists, with the result that their value in the list is somewhat diminished.

[14] This manuscript is reported to be in the Isle of Wight. I owe my information concerning it to Mr. F. R. Coad of Sutton, Surrey, England, and to Professor F. F. Bruce of Manchester.

[15] *The Hope of Christ's Second Coming*, 35.

tion, and Other Individuals in England and Scotland, and formerly in the Writer Himself[16] describes a revelation given to him on January 14, 1832, that in 1,260 days from that date Jesus would return, the saints would be raptured to heaven, the Antichrist would reign, and then Jesus would return *with* the saints. In the preceding year Baxter had come to the ideas of a future advent of Christ in two phases and of the removal of the saints before the final period of judgment. Baxter attributes these ideas to earlier statements by Irving but gives no references to specific writings of Irving. Nevertheless the present writer would suggest Irving's *Babylon and Infidelity Foredoomed of God*[17] and a lecture delivered in 1829 in Dublin and contained in Irving's *Thirty Sermons, to which are added Five Lectures,*[18] in which Irving implies and expounds the view that the Church must be taken to heaven before she returns with Christ in judgment.

In the above-mentioned manuscript of reminiscences, Newton also says concerning the Brethren chapel at Plymouth, opened in 1831: "On the very second Sunday that the chapel was used, a divergence arose. In the morning the Secret Rapture was preached by Capt. Hall, and in the evening it was denounced by Wigram." Wigram later changed and became Darby's closest lieutenant. Lady Powerscourt, who was favorably disposed toward Irving, established prophetic conferences similar to those at Albury, and to these came followers of Irving and J. N. Darby himself.[19] With the intermingling of Irving, Irvingites, and early Brethren at such conferences, it is easy to see how Irving's suggestion could have passed to the Brethren.

Darby's own account, according to W. Kelly,[20] is that he came to a pretribulational view around 1830—or after Irving first propounded the theory, we may note—from a consideration of 2 Thessalonians 2:1. This does not mean that Darby had not received influence from a different quarter. Brilliant but eccentric, Darby is usually considered a poor witness in his own behalf, for

[16] 2nd ed., London, 1833, pp. 17ff.

[17] 2nd ed., Glasgow, 1828, pp. 337-339.

[18] London, 1835, pp. 60, 61.

[19] See *Letters and Papers by the Late Theodosia A. Viscountess Powerscourt,* edited by Robert Daly (London, 1838), 68, 69; J. N. Darby, *Letters* (London, n.d.), I, 5ff.; W. B. Neatby, *A History of the Plymouth Brethren* (London, 1901), 38ff.

[20] *The Rapture of the Saints: Who Suggested It, or rather, On What Scripture?*

he did not like to acknowledge the priority of another in putting forward his teachings. An ex-clergyman of the Church of Ireland by the name of Tweedy seems to have played a minor role in helping Darby and the Dublin group of Brethren to skirt the post-tribulational import of the Olivet Discourse by relegating it to a dispensationally Jewish application.[21]

In fairness, we should make additional observations. First, the origin of an interpretation of Scripture is not the measure of its correctness. *At this point we are engaged in an enquiry of purely historical interest.* Second, although the Brethren may have borrowed from Irvingism, they also rejected its applications of biblical apocalyptic to current events and built a much more sane and coherent system of prophetic interpretation. Apparently the two movements interacted, for later Irvingite teaching shows influence from the Brethren.[22] Third, pretribulationism should not be stigmatized through association with the heresies of Irving and the outbreak of "tongues" and prophetic ecstasies in his movement. His first suggestion which led to pretribulationism came in the late 1820's. His first condemnation for heresy came in late 1830 and his final excommunication from the Church of Scotland in 1833. Tongues and prophetic utterances did not begin to appear in his church until late 1831, i.e., after the appearance of pretribulationism.

Broadcast by Darby's six visits to America and by the extensive literature campaign of the Brethren and other writers under their influence, pretribulationism spread rapidly. Today some argue that the popularity of pretribulationism has derived from the upsurge of Bible study during the last hundred years.[23] However, the majority believe what they are taught. And the wide-

---

[21] R. Cameron, *Scriptural Truth About the Lord's Return,* 70-72.

[22] See R. Norton, *Memoirs of James & George Macdonald* (London, 1840), 10ff., 145, 156, 171-176—the outpouring on Margaret Macdonald did not include revelation of a pretribulational rapture, as has falsely been alleged (see 101ff.); *idem, The Restoration of Apostles and Prophets in the Catholic Apostolic Church* (London, 1854), 9; W. W. Andrews, *The Catholic Apostolic Church* (London, 1867), 46, 47; George C. Boase, *The Restoration of Apostles* (London, 1867), 29, 30; *The Nearness of the Second Coming of Christ* by the Minister of the Parishioners of Holbeck (London, 1852), 6, 9-11; and the anonymous tracts *A Letter on Certain Statements Contained in Some Late Articles in "The Old Church Porch" Entitled "Irvingism"* (London, n.d.), 61ff; *Apostles: Given, Lost, and Restored* (London, 1853); and *The Chronology of Scriptures* (London, 1854), 43-48. See also Edward Miller, *The History and Doctrines of Irvingism* (London, 1878), I, 1-47, 53ff., 79, 156; II, 1-8.

[23] Walvoord, *BibSac,* 113:293.

spread interest in prophecy at the time pretribulationism arose facilitated the spread of the new theory. But from the rapidity of its diffusion we can determine neither its origin nor its scripturalness.

We may summarize the historical arguments:

First, the eschatological chronology of the early Church displays enough detail to have included an imminent, pretribulational rapture in its premillennial scheme had pretribulationism been held as the apostolic doctrine.

Second, all the early fathers who touch upon final events speak with an explicitly posttribulational accent and assume this to be universal language in orthodox Christianity.

Third, the early Church did not hold to the imminence of Jesus' return. Most of the passages cited in favor of imminence exhibit in the immediate context an expectation of passage through the tribulation. The few and isolated remaining passages use no stronger language than the Scripture itself employs in admittedly posttribulational passages.

Fourth, the early Church received its doctrine directly from the apostles. If the earliness of posttribulationism does not indicate apostolicity, neither can we say that the earliness of premillennialism indicates apostolocity. And if the late origin of a- and postmillennialism indicates human invention, the still later origin of pretribulationism indicates the same.

Fifth, the premillennialism and futurism revived after the Reformation was posttribulational.

Sixth, pretribulationism did not become known and widely held until the mid-nineteenth century.

In view of the foregoing, we ought to regard pretribulationism as a late innovation, not an extension or refinement of the doctrine of the early Church. By adding to the burden of proof which pretribulationism is unable to bear in scriptural exegesis, the historical argument confirms posttribulationism.

Addendum on the Futurity of
the Seventieth Week

To those who regard the seventieth week of Daniel as already fulfilled, the debate whether the Church will be raptured before, during, or after the seventieth week seems pointless. They explain Daniel 9:24-27 as follows: the finishing of the transgression, ending of sin, making atonement for iniquity, bringing in of everlasting righteousness, sealing up of vision and prophecy, and anointing of the most holy place (v. 24) all refer to Christ and to His redemptive work in the first advent. The sixty-ninth week expired when Jesus was anointed with the Spirit at His baptism (v. 25). The cutting off of the anointed one "after" the sixty-two weeks (added to the first seven, making sixty-nine *in toto,* v. 26a) refers to Christ's crucifixion and occurred in the middle of the seventieth week. Verse 26b describes the destruction of Jerusalem under Titus in A.D. 70. The end of the seventieth week, being undefined, either expired three and one-half years after the crucifixion or extended by divine grace until A.D. 70. The making of a firm covenant (or confirming or causing to prevail of a covenant, v. 27a) refers to Christ's securing the benefits of the Abrahamic covenant of grace during His earthly ministry. (The subject of the verse according to this view is not "the prince who is to come," but another prince, "the Messiah.") The causing of the sacrifice and oblation to cease (v. 27) has to do with the abrogation of animal sacrifices by Christ's self-sacrifice. In verse 27b there appears another reference to the destruction of Jerusalem.

The opposite view regards the seventieth week as a future prelude to the restoration of the kingdom to Israel at Jesus' return. The seventieth week will begin when the Antichrist confirms a covenant with the Jews, a covenant he will later break by stopping sacrifices in the temple and by setting up the abomination of desolation.

The weaknesses in the historical view and the advantages of the futurist view are these:

The seventy weeks have to do with the Jews. We cannot spiritualize the phrase "your people" (v. 24) into a spiritual Israel inclusive of the Gentiles without doing violence to the plain sense of the passage. For example, the destruction of Jerusalem, spoken of prominently in the prophecy, deals with Israel *the nation.* And yet, since in the seventy weeks the goals listed in verse twenty-four were to be accomplished, the seventy weeks cannot have entirely elapsed, for the finishing of Israel's transgression, the purging of her iniquity, and the bringing in of her everlasting righteousness have not reached completion. Paul writes of these as still in the future for Israel (Rom. 11:25-27).

It is doubtful that "the most holy" which is anointed refers to Christ, for nowhere in the OT does this expression refer to a person—hence the translation, "the most holy *place*" (NASB).

The extension of the sixty-ninth week to the Messiah does not necessarily fix the termination of the sixty-ninth week at the baptismal anointing of the Messiah.

If the cutting off of the Messiah occurred in the middle of the seventieth week, it is very strange that the cutting off is said to be "after" the sixty-nine weeks (figuring the sum of the seven and the sixty-two weeks). Much more naturally the text would have read "during" or "in the midst of" the seventieth week, as it does in verse twenty-seven concerning the stoppage of the sacrifices. The only adequate explanation for this unusual turn of expression is that the seventieth week did not follow on the heels of the sixty-ninth, but that an interval separates the two. The crucifixion then comes shortly "after" the sixty-ninth but not within the seventieth because of an intervening gap. The possibility of a gap between the sixty-ninth and the seventieth weeks is established by the well-accepted OT phenomenon of prophetic perspective, in which gaps such as that between the first and second advents were not perceived.

For the seventieth week to expire at an indefinite time some years after the culmination has been reached is highly anti-climactic especially in view of the impressive goals laid out. The remaining years after the crucifixion become superfluous, with little intent, purpose, or meaning.

If the alternative of extending the seventieth week to A.D. 70 be taken, it seems far more strained to stretch the week five or six times beyond the usual length of seven years than to retain the normal length with a hiatus between the sixty-ninth and the seventieth weeks.

Christ did not make or confirm a covenant for one week. He established the new covenant forever.

Payne argues that a covenant by the Antichrist with the Jews would be a new—i.e., previously nonexistent—covenant. But the expression "cause to prevail" implies that the covenant already exists and therefore refers to the covenant of grace. "Thus Christ could announce at the last supper, 'This is my blood of the testament, . . .' For Matthew 26:28 does not say, according to the oldest manuscripts, 'the *new* testament,' . . ."[1] *Pace* Payne, the

---

[1] Payne, 150, 151.

accounts in Luke 22:20 and 1 Corinthians 11:25 *do* use the term "*new* covenant" and the writer to the Hebrews twice quotes Jeremiah 31 (cf. 33) concerning the "*new* covenant" effected by Christ's sacrificial death. Therefore we cannot accept the argument that the expression "cause to prevail" rules out a covenant made by the Antichrist, because historicists themselves apply the phrase to a previously nonexistent covenant, the one inaugurated by Jesus' death. Besides, it is more natural to understand that a covenant is "put in force." when it is first made.

The redemptive work of Christ rendered the animal sacrifices obsolete, but did not "put a stop" to them. They did not cease being offered until A.D. 70 at the destruction of Jerusalem and the temple under Roman violence (cf. Heb. 8:4).

Jesus speaks of Daniel's abomination of desolation as signalling the great tribulation, "immediately after" which will come heavenly portents and the second advent. The events in A.D. 70 may be percursive, but they cannot constitute the full and final fulfillment, for Christ did not immediately return. Moreover, to place the complete fulfillment of the seventieth week at A.D. 70 or before severs the obvious connection between Daniel 9, Matthew 24, and Revelation. (Compare "in the middle of the week" [Dan. 9:27], forty-two months and 1,260 days [Rev. 11:2; 12:6; 13:5], and time, times, and half a time [Dan. 12:7; 7:25; Rev. 12:14].) Under the historical view, if the relationship between Daniel and Revelation were retained, Revelation, which was written probably a quarter century after the destruction of Jerusalem, would be history instead of the prophecy it purports to be. (On account of this Payne feels forced to adopt a date for the Apocalypse prior to A.D. 70.[2])

Syntactically, it is at least as good to make the subject of verse twenty-seven the coming prince, who is the nearer possibility, as it is to make the Messiah, previously mentioned, the subject. The entire passage is *not* Messianic, as historicists often assert,[3] for verse 26b speaks of another prince, Roman, whose people, the Romans, are to destroy the city and the sanctuary. Immediately after mention of this non-Messianic prince and his destroying people and without indication of a shift in reference, we read that "he" will "make a firm covenant with the many for one week." Although the covenant is to be in force for one week, not

---

[2] P. 173.
[3] E.g., Payne, 151.

till the middle of the week does he put a stop to the sacrifice and grain offering. *If the reference were to the covenant by the blood of Christ which outmoded the Mossaic sacrifices, the covenant would have come into force three and one-half years before Jesus shed His blood to put that covenant into effect.*

Although the lack of certainty regarding the exact dates of our Lord's ministry demands some reserve, the futuristic view rests on a more exact chronology, best and fully set forth in Sir Robert Anderson's *The Coming Prince*. Very briefly, it is common ground that the seventy sevens are weeks of years. Anderson reckons a year at 360 days from the equation of 1,260 days with forty-two months (Rev. 12:6, 7, 13, 14; 13:4-7), from the equation of five months with 150 days (Gen. 7:11; 8:4; 7:24; 8:3), and from other evidence of unequal value. By calculating from the only known decree to rebuild the *city* of Jerusalem (Neh. 1:1-11; 2:1-8) sixty-nine weeks of seven 360-day years, we are brought to Palm Sunday, the only time Jesus was publicly acclaimed King, Prince, and Messiah and shortly after which He was cut off.

It is objected that the short years of 360 days with which Anderson works make no provision for leap days and leap years. To make such provision, however, would involve the chronology in abstruse mathematical and astronomical calculations and, more seriously, would push back the beginning of the seventy weeks to a decree regarding the rebuilding of the Temple, not of the city itself. This is a serious difficulty for the historical view. It must take as its point of departure a decree many years prior to the decree for the rebuilding of the city. It is true that the remnant built houses in which to live before Nehemiah's time. But the *decree* for rebuilding the city with its walls and streets was not issued and the actual reconstruction carried out until the time of Nehemiah, as his midnight ride through rubble and debris gives evidence. It is further objected that the day of the decree in Nehemiah is not given, only the month Nisan. But according to Jewish custom, where the day was not specified, time was reckoned from the first of the month.

The accuracy is so remarkable that the objections seem paltry by comparison. The best answer to the objections is the failure of the historical view to provide an exact and accurate chronology and the resultant substitution of chronologies dealing in wide approximations, with the result that the seventy weeks of years become half-literal and half-symbolic. The futuristic view can be established apart from Anderson's calculations, but they endow the futuristic view with a chronology far superior to chronologies under the historical view.

Finally, the view that the seventieth week will be fulfilled immediately before Jesus' return was held by the early Church, which received its doctrine from the apostles themselves. See the eschatological sections in Irenaeus, Hippolytus, Lactantius, and others which are noted in the chapter "Historical Confirmation." Payne calls patristic futurists "exceptions."[4] The fact is that in the early Church these very writers had by far the most to say about eschatology.

Addendum on Imminent Posttribulationism

In his book *The Imminent Appearing of Christ,* J. Barton Payne has revived a form of historicism. He calls it "classical posttribulationism."[1] According to his view, Daniel's seventieth week is history (for refutation see the preceding addendum) and all necessary antecedents to Jesus' return might now be fulfilled. Thus Christ might appear at any moment.

Such an imminent posttribulationism or potential historicism is not "classical" at all. Reformation and 'post-Reformation historicism was merely held over from Roman Catholic eschatology. The appeal to patristic writings is equally futile. For, although it is true that some patristic passages display a feeling that the Church had entered into the *beginning* of the tribulation, imminent posttribulationism requires the possibility that we have progressed to the very *end* of the tribulation. But the early fathers uniformly place the career of the Antichrist and his persecution of the Church *yet in the future, even in those passages concerning expectancy which Payne cites as proof of their belief in imminence.* Paul does the same when he places the Antichrist

---

[4] Pp. 149, 150.
[1] Pp. 40-42.

in the future, yet exhorts Christians to watch for the day of the Lord, which will *follow* the Antichrist (1 Thess. 5; 2 Thess. 2). Jesus does the same when He speaks the most elaborate warnings to watch in the entire NT in immediate connection with a description of His return after the tribulation and relates our watching to tribulational events. Both the NT and early patristic writings lack the doctrine of imminence. The terms for expectancy bear the nonimminent connotation they commonly have in other connections throughout Greek literature, both biblical and extra-biblical. See the chapters "Expectation and Imminence" and "Historical Confirmation."

According to Payne, should Jesus return today, we could look *back* to see that events in recent years had fulfilled the predictions of events necessarily preceding Jesus' return; and any generation of the Church, except the apostolic, could have done the same.[2] But the NT uniformly tells us to look *forward through* the signalling events *toward* the second advent and not to look for the second advent as an imminent possibility until we see the signalling events come to pass (Matt. 24:32, 33; Mark 13:28, 29; Luke 21:28-31; 2 Thess. 2:1-3). Payne himself correctly interprets 2 Thessalonians in terms of Paul's quelling the excitement at Thessalonica by insistence that Christians should not look for Jesus to come until after the Antichrist, who obviously has not appeared.[3] Yet this exhortation by Paul and the relating of expectancy to signalling events by Jesus require that the events preceding Jesus' return be recognizable by Christians beyond reasonable doubt at the time of their occurrence. The time of unprecedented trouble, the world-wide plagues, the meteoric career of the man of lawlessness, the abomination of desolation in connection with this evil personage—after every allowance has been made for symbolism, we still cannot suppose that all these and others have possibly passed unnoticed. They are *revelatory* signs and must therefore be recognizable upon occurrence. It is on the stumbling-block of the obviousness of tribulational events that Payne's potential but uncertain fulfillment falls to the ground.

As noted above, Payne excepts the apostolic generation from the generations of the Church able to see potential fulfillment of all antecedents to the second coming, because the apostolic Church had to wait for the destruction of Jerusalem predicted

---

[2] Pp. 106, 107, 120, 121.
[3] Pp. 59-61, 76, 77.

by Jesus and because some years had to elapse in order that the disciples might obey the great commission.[4] Since Jerusalem was destroyed in A.D. 70 and sufficient time has long since elapsed, Payne sees no difficulty for imminence now. But the point remains that if the return of Christ was not imminent for the very generation which was originally exhorted to watch and did watch (1 Thess. 1:9, 10), watching does not necessitate imminence; and potential fulfillment is not needed to meet the demands of expectancy.

In order to evaluate imminent posttribulationism more in detail, we need to examine Payne's denials of double (precursive and final) fulfillment and of a revival of the Roman Empire and then examine potential fulfillment in relation to Daniel, Revelation, and the Olivet Discourse. To ease the task of finding in contemporary and recent history potential fulfillment of events antecedent to the second coming, Payne relegates as much as possible to ancient history and denies that any future and more exact fulfillment remains.[5] But the denial of precursive and final fulfillments, i.e., double fulfillment, is not justified. Jesus Himself established the principle when He predicted, "Elijah is coming and will restore all things" (Matt. 17:11)—after the death of John the Baptist and in connection with His statement, "Elijah already came" (Matt. 17:12). Gabriel had said that John the Baptist would minister "in the spirit and power of Elijah" (Luke 1:17). Elijah had come and was yet to come. That is double fulfillment of Malachi 4:5.

Similarly, many OT passages about the day of the Lord had near future fulfillments in plagues and invasions by Assyrians and Babylonians and in the post-exilic restoration. But NT writers quote these passages and refer them to a far future fulfillment in and around the second coming of Christ, when their cosmic and Messianic language will receive larger due. For example, in describing His return, Jesus utilizes Isaiah's description of the impending Babylonian invasion and the following restoration (Isa. 13:10; 27:13; 34:4—Matt. 24:29-31; Mark 13:24-27). Also, Peter says that the speaking with tongues at Pentecost fulfilled Joel 2. But Joel 2, 3 also provides a source for the NT picture of the Battle of Armageddon yet in the future. Payne admits far future fulfillment, but claims that each separate part

---

[4] Pp. 89-91.
[5] Pp. 115, 116.

of the passage has but one fulfillment. For example, Joel 2:28, 29 refers to Pentecost (Acts 2:16-21), the following verses to the second coming and the day of the Lord.[6] Even a cursory reading of the passage, however, shows that the pouring out of the Spirit primarily refers to the time of Israel's millennial restoration after the Battle of Armageddon. The preceding verses describe that final restoration when Israel "will never be put to shame" (v. 27—certainly not fulfilled in the post-exilic period). The promise of the Spirit is introduced by the words, "And it will come about *after* this that I will pour out My Spirit. . . ." In conjunction with the promise are the celestial signs which signal Christ's return and the preservation of a remnant in Jerusalem (vv. 30-32). The fulfillment at Pentecost must therefore be the first or precursive part of a double fulfillment. Payne himself unconsciously subverts his denial of double fulfillment by seeing a first fulfillment of the abomination of desolation in the desecration of the temple by Antiochus Epiphanes and a second in the erection of Roman standards over the site of the temple in A.D. 70.[7]

It would be difficult for a premillennialist who recognizes a fulfillment of OT prophecy in this age to deny double fulfillment and retain premillennialism. For many of the OT passages applied in the NT to the Church age have clearly millennial settings. See, for example, Isaiah 11 (Rom. 15:12); Jeremiah 31:27-37 (Heb. 8:8-12; 10:15-17); Joel 2:21-3:21 (Acts 2:16-21); Amos 9:11-15 (Acts 15:15-18). To affirm exhaustive past or present fulfillment of these prophecies is to retreat into an amillennial denial of their future millennial setting or to wrest them from context. On the other hand, when we recognize the validity of double fulfillment and see that there remains for Israel a period of unprecedented distress unfulfilled by the northern invasions described in the OT, intolerable stress afflicts the theory of potential fulfillment at the present moment.

More specifically, Scripture indicates that the Antichrist will arise out of a revived Roman Empire just prior to Christ's kingdom on earth. In his discussion of Daniel 2 and 7 and Revelation 17, Payne holds that Krushchev may be the Antichrist and that the demise of the ancient Roman Empire fulfilled the prediction of Rome's overthrow by the ten horns. The overthrow of three of

---

[6] P. 139.

[7] Pp. 118, 119, 146, 153.

the ten kingdoms which replaced the Roman Empire may have its fulfillment in events such as Krushchev's overthrow of Hungary.[8] Against the possible (but now anachronistic) identification of Krushchev with the Antichrist, Daniel 7:7, 8 indicates that the Antichrist will arise out of the Roman territory. And since the people of the coming prince (the Antichrist) were the Romans who destroyed Jerusalem in A.D. 70 (Dan. 9:26), the Antichrist himself will have to be a Roman. And although some Christians now endure persecution, evangelical Christian activity enjoys more than enough freedom to prevent our saying Krushchev or any other Antichrist is presently "prevailing" against the saints (Dan. 7:21, 22; Rev. 13:7). Furthermore, the Antichrist will lead the final apostasy by setting himself forth as God in the temple (2 Thess. 2:3, 4). This cannot refer to general apostasy within the temple of the Church,[9] for what individual of the stature of the Antichrist at the present time is attempting *within the Church* to replace God as the object of worship? Certainly Krushchev did not. The pope himself does not claim divinity, and he does not possess enough political power to qualify as the Antichrist. Even were we to take Payne's figurative interpretation of the word "temple" in 2 Thessalonians 2:4, no present leader of apostasy answers the biblical description of the Antichrist. Therefore fulfillment must be future and antecedent to the second coming.

The fall of Rome 1,500 years ago did not satisfy the requirements of prophecy, because Revelation 17:8, 11 indicates that the Roman Empire is to be revived. The beast was, is not, and is *yet to come* to the amazement of the world. A revival will have to occur in order that the return of the Lamb as "Lord of lords and King of kings" may crush the Roman Empire. It is *that* event, the Parousia, which crushes the Roman Empire (Rev. 17:14 with 19:11-19).

To avoid the problem that a return of Christ did not occasion the fall of ancient Rome, Payne equates the beast of Revelation 13 and 17 with general political power, which will be destroyed at the second advent.[10] It is true that the harlot Babylon represents the city of Rome specifically (Rev. 17:18) and that the beast upon which she rides is a wider concept. But we cannot generalize the beast to the extent that it becomes political

---

[8] Pp. 108, 121.
[9] *Pace* Payne, 147.
[10] P. 174.

power in general, for the beast dies and revives in such a way as to amaze all except the elect (17:8, 11). The old Roman Empire expired, but general political power did not. Thus we may expect the Roman Empire to revive as did the beast representing it in John's vision. *The city itself* falls under the judgment of the seventh bowl in connection with the yet future Battle of Armageddon (Rev. 16:12-21). In the corresponding vision of the image in Daniel 2, the taking of two forms by the Roman Empire, first the legs of iron and then the feet and toes of iron and clay mixed, indicates two phases. The Messianic kingdom smites the feet of the image, the later form of the Roman Empire, and replaces the image. Only with difficulty can it be said that the Messianic kingdom supplanted ancient Rome. Hence, both the Messianic kingdom and the second form of the Roman Empire destroyed by it are future.

Imminent posttribulationism lacks historical perspective. Although it disowns the fantastic spiritualizing interpretations of older historicists, the view must maintain that some such interpretation may be correct. Payne gives us a detailed example of potential-historical interpretation in his discussion of Revelation 11.[11] Jerusalem will fall after three and one-half years of destruction (A.D. 66-70? vv. 1, 2). The law and the prophets in the witnessing Church (the two witnesses) are condemned by the world with martyrdoms (vv. 3-10). Verses eight and nine may refer specifically to Stephen's death at Jerusalem (Acts 7:58) and to his exposed body (Acts 8:2). But if the forty-two months in verse two refer to the three and one-half years preceding the destruction of Jerusalem in A.D. 70, to what do the 1,260 days (three and one-half years) of witnessing in verse three refer? Was the Church to witness and endure martyrdom for only three and one-half years of this age? Did not "the law and the prophets" cease with John the Baptist (Matt. 11:13)? Has the Church destroyed her enemies as do the two witnesses supposedly representing her (v. 5)? What plagues has the Church inflicted on her enemies (v. 6)? Did the Roman Empire (beast) destroy the Church (two witnesses, v. 7)? Rather, has not the Church outlived ancient Rome? The Church in general does not fit the picture of martyrdom, for the two witnesses die *in Jerusalem* (v. 8). Nor does the church in Jerusalem during

---

[11] Pp. 118, 119, 173.

A.D. 66-70, for the Christians escaped to Pella. The historical interpretation does not withstand scrutiny.

Finally, historicism fails to provide an adequate interpretation of the Olivet Discourse, according to which the second advent "immediately" follows a period of intense tribulation involving the abomination of desolation in the temple. Holding that Matthew 24:4-22 concerns the destruction of Jerusalem, Payne notes that harmonies of the gospels place Luke 21:24 (concerning A.D. 70) after Matthew 24:22 and Mark 13:20. Matthew 24:23-31 then refers to the second advent and an immediately preceding period of tribulation so short that it does not materially affect imminence.[12] Here again Payne is working on the basis of his denial of double fulfillment. The very fact that the verses which follow the shift from A.D. 70 to the second advent speak of the tribulation which has been described *before* the shift and state that the second advent will take place immediately afterward—this fact requires a double fulfillment. It is noteworthy that the interval Payne puts between verses 4-22 and verses 23-31 is like the interval he denies between the sixty-ninth and seventieth weeks of Daniel—except that the peculiar wording in Daniel suggests an interval, whereas no hint crops up in the gospels.

In Matthew 24:29 Jesus speaks of "the tribulation of those days." Payne refers the expression to verses 23-28, not to verses 4-22 descriptive of the fall of Jerusalem. But in verses 23-28 no tribulation is described, only deception. The reference has to be to the only tribulation described, that in verses 4-22. Yet Payne must disjoin these verses from the end of the age in order to maintain that the fall of Jerusalem exhausted them and at the same time escape the fact that Jesus did not return "immediately after" A.D. 70—just as many pretribulationists disjoin the exhortations to watch (24:32-25:13) from the preceding context (and are criticized by Payne for so doing[13]). Retaining the continuity of the passage, we should rather say that "the tribulation of those days," "immediately after" which Jesus returns, has to do with a period of persecution and upheaval connected with a yet future abomination of desolation and only foreshadowed by the events during A.D. 66-70.

Potential historicism incorrectly infers imminence from the

---

[12] Pp. 116, 152, 153.
[13] P. 56.

terms used for watching, misses the signalling nature of events immediately antecedent to the second coming and their consequent obviousness to the saints, fails to see double fulfillment and a revival of the Roman Empire, demands possible historical interpretations as forced as those of the old historical school, and ignores the continuity of the Olivet Discourse, which describes a complex of events immediately preceding the return of Christ.

Addendum on Midtribulationism

Midtribulationists place the rapture at the halfway mark in Daniel's seventieth week. To them the tribulation comprises only the latter three and one-half years. The seventh trumpet will sound in the middle of the week. This will be the "last trumpet," at which our translation and the resurrection of the dead in Christ will take place. At that time "the mystery of God" (Rev. 10:7), which is taken to be the Church, will reach completion. The resurrection and catching up of the two witnesses in Revelation 11 become symbolic of the rapture.

In its view of the second coming as two phases separated by an interval of some length, midtribulationism stands with pretribulationism. For that reason most arguments against standard pretribulationism likewise militate against midtribulationism, which lacks some of the consistencies of pretribulationism. In its placing of the rapture at the seventh trumpet and in its putting of the Church in the first half of the seventieth week, midtribulationism tends toward posttribulationism. Essentially, then, midtribulationism is an unstable view with tendencies in opposite directions.

Besides the arguments against pretribulationism in general, we may note a couple of other objections to midtribulationism. The seventh trumpet will sound at the end of or after the seventieth week, not at the half-way mark. And allegorization of the two witnesses as the Church is fanciful. The measurement of the temple and altar, the holy city, the sackcloth, the dead bodies, and numerous other details cannot be regarded as figurative without doing violence to the passage. Furthermore, the very fact that the two witnesses will exercise their ministry during the forty-two months in which the holy city will be trodden under foot by the Gentiles requires this to be the latter half of the week. For not until the Antichrist breaks his covenant favorable to the Jews will the holy city be trodden down by the Gentiles.

Addendum on Partial Rapturism

Partial rapturists hold that only spiritual, mature Christians who are watching for the Lord's coming will be raptured before the tribulation. Remaining Christians will be left to go through the period. Everything to which pretribulationists object in posttribulationism is likewise objectionable to them in partial rapturism. Contrariwise, every argument against a pretribulational rapture of the whole Church militates against a pretribulational rapture of part of the Church.

Moreover, partial rapturism has weaknesses peculiar to itself. (1) Exhortations to watch, which contrast true believers and false professors, are made to refer instead to mature and immature believers. But "watching" in the NT perspective characterizes *all* true Christians. (2) Partial rapturism rests on legalism by regarding the rapture as a reward rather than the inheritance by faith of all true believers. (3) The distinction between children in their minority and adult sons (Gal. 3:23-4:7) contrasts saints under the old covenant and saints under the new covenant, not immature and mature saints of the present age. (4) By dividing the body of Christ, partial rapturism does not take account of the "we all" in 1 Corinthians 15:51, "the dead in Christ" of 1 Thessalonians 4:16, or the identity of those translated with those who "believe that Jesus died and rose again" (1 Thess. 4:14). (5) In viewing the tribulational period as a time of purgation for living believers who failed to qualify for the rapture, partial rapturism logically demands a purgatory for deceased believers who died in a state of Christian immaturity.

Addendum on Strombeck's View
of the Parousia

Strombeck seeks to establish the term "Parousia" as Christ's pretribulational coming and hidden presence in the clouds during the tribulation, followed by His manifestation at the close of the tribulation. " 'They were eating and drinking, marrying and giving in marriage' [Mt. 24:38]. These words describe a normal condition of life from the earliest days of the human race."[1] He concludes therefore that the Parousia will begin before the tribulation, because during that period normal conditions of life will be upset.

But are we to think that people in the tribulation will stop eating and drinking, marrying and giving in marriage? The emphasis in the words of Jesus does not fall upon a normal condition of life, but upon the unexpected suddenness of His advent to those who will be engaged otherwise than in watching for Him. Strombeck wrenches these verses out of context and applies them to a pretribulational event totally unmentioned and unhinted at in that part of the Olivet Discourse which gives the chronological succession of final events (Matt. 24:3-31). Moreover, Jesus has just applied the word "Parousia" to His posttribulational advent (v. 27).

Strombeck sees a distinction between the Parousia of the *Son of Man,* which will be His pretribulational coming and presence in the clouds during the tribulation for judgment on the earth, and the Parousia of the *Lord Jesus Christ* for the rapture of the Church. Christ is not the Son of Man to the Church because "from now on we recognize no man according to the flesh" (2 Cor. 5:16).[2] But the Christ who walks among the seven candlesticks, *which are the seven churches,* is designated "one like a son of man" (Rev. 1:13). Again, Jesus calls Himself "the Son of Man" in the Upper Room Discourse (John 13:31). The first martyr of the Church saw "the Son of Man standing on the right hand of God" (Acts 7:56). The title which particularly ex-

---

[1] Strombeck, 69.
[2] Strombeck, 64-68.

presses Christ's relationship to Israel is "Son of David." "Son of Man" designates Jesus as the eschatological and representative man and carried no special dispensational significance to the exclusion of the Church.

Strombeck quotes OT passages which describe the day of the Lord as cloudy. Taking these expressions quite literally, he argues that the clouds will hide Christ from the world's view as He and the Church hover in the skies throughout the tribulation.[3] But Strombeck is assuming that the cloudy day of the Lord is the tribulation; whereas we have seen that that day will not begin till after the tribulation. Strombeck also urges that the posttribulational "*manifestation* of His Parousia" (2 Thess. 2:8; cf. Matt. 24:27) means that the Parousia, which will arrive before the tribulation and continue in the sky throughout the tribulation, will be unveiled as the clouds part and Jesus, who has been there all the time, is revealed to the world.[4] This is an ingenious way to evade the force of the posttribulational references of the Parousia. However, "the manifestation of His Parousia" need not be the outshining of a presence which has been hidden. It is better taken as the manifestation which *is* His Parousia (genitive of apposition; cf. "the gift of the Spirit"). Even if the genitive be taken objectively, it is not necessary to make the coming of the Parousia prior to its manifestation. The Parousia after the tribulation is not an appearance alone. It is a coming, an arrival, for Jesus and Paul use ἔρχομαι (*come, arrive*) interchangeably with Parousia in referring to the posttribulational advent (Matt. 24:30, 42-44; 25:31; Mark 13:26; Luke 21:27; 2 Thess. 1:10; cf. Rev. 19:11ff.).

---

[3] Strombeck, 80ff.
[4] Strombeck, 78, 79.

Bibliography

N.B.: This bibliography is intended as a guide only to those works to which reference is made in this book. Extensive bibliographical material on the rapture and related eschatological matters may be found in the books listed below under the names of Ludwigson, Stanton, Douty, and Culver. Works concerning which, for purposes of the discussion, bibliographical information has already been given in the body of this book (see the last part of the chapter "Historical Confirmation") do not appear below.

Aldrich, Roy L. "The Transition Problem in Acts," *Bibliotheca Sacra*, 114 (1957), 235-242.

Alford, Henry. *The Greek Testament.* Fifth edition. Cambridge: Deighton Bell, and Co., 1871.

Anderson, Sir Robert. *The Coming Prince.* Grand Rapids: Kregel Publications, 1954.

Armerding, Carl. "The Coming of the Son of Man," *Moody Monthly*, 51 (1951), 787, 788, 809.

———. *The Olivet Discourse.* Findlay, Ohio: Dunham Publishing Co., 1955.

———. "Will There Be Another Elijah?" *Bibliotheca Sacra,* 100 (1943), 89-97.

Barnhouse, Donald Grey. "Early Premillennialism," *Eternity*, 9 (1958), 31, 32.

Bauer, Walter; Arndt, William F.; and Gingrich, F. Wilbur. *A Greek-English Lexicon of the New Testament and Other Early Christian Literature.* Chicago: The University of Chicago Press, 1957.

Baxter, J. Sidlow. *Explore the Book.* Edinburgh: Marshall, Morgan & Scott, Ltd., 1955.

Biederwolf, William Edward. *The Millennium Bible.* Chicago: The Glad Tidings Publishing Co., 1924.

Bullinger, E. W. *The Apocalypse.* London: Eyre & Spottiswoode, 1909.

Cameron, Robert. *Scriptural Truth About the Lord's Return.* New York: Fleming H. Revell Company, 1922.

Chafer, Lewis Sperry. *Systematic Theology.* Dallas: Dallas Seminary Press, 1948.

Cremer, Hermann. *Biblico-Theological Lexicon of New Testament Greek.* Translated by William Urwick. Edinburgh: T. & T. Clark, 1954.

Culbertson, William, and Centz, Herman B., eds. *Understanding the Times.* Prophetic Messages Delivered at the Second International Congress on Prophecy, New York City. Grand Rapids: Zondervan Publishing House, 1956.

Culver, Robert D. *Daniel and the Latter Days.* New York: Fleming H. Revell Co., 1954.

Deissmann, Adolf. *Light From the Ancient East.* New York: Harper & Brothers, 1922.

Douty, Norman F. *Has Christ's Return Two Stages?* New York: Pageant Press, Inc., 1956.

Ellicott, Charles J. *St. Paul's Epistles to the Thessalonians: with a Critical and Grammatical Commentary, and a Revised Translation.* London: Longman, Green, Longman, Roberts & Green, 1866.

English, E. Schuyler. *Re-Thinking the Rapture.* Travelers Rest, South Carolina: Southern Bible Book House, 1954.

Frost, Henry W. *Matthew Twenty-Four and the Revelation.* New York: Oxford University Press, 1924.

Gaebelein, Arno C. *The Harmony of the Prophetic Word.* New York: Our Hope, 1907.

————. *The Revelation.* New York: Our Hope, 1915.

Giblin, Charles H. *The Threat to Faith. An Exegetical and Theological Re-Examination of 2 Thessalonians 2.* Analecta Biblica, 31. Rome: Pontifical Biblical Institute, 1967.

Graham, James R. *Watchman, What of the Night?* Los Angeles: Ambassadors for Christ, n.d.

Gray, James M. *Synthetic Bible Studies.* New York: Fleming H. Revell Company, 1923.

Harrison, William K. "The Time of the Rapture as Indicated In Certain Scriptures," Parts I-IV, *Bibliotheca Sacra,* 114 (1957), 316-325; 115 (1958), 20-26, 109-119, 201-211.

Hatch, Edwin, and Redpath, Henry A. *A Concordance to the Septuagint.* Oxford: Clarendon Press, 1897.

Ironside, H. A. *Lectures on the Revelation.* New York: Loizeaux Brothers, 1919.

Ketcham, Robert T. *Pre, Mid or Post Tribulation Rapture?* R. T. Ketcham, Dept. B, 608 South Dearborn, Suite 848, Chicago 5, Illinois.

Kittel, Gerhard, and Friedrich, Gerhard, eds. *Theological Dictionary of the New Testament.* Translated and edited by Geoffrey W. Bromiley. Grand Rapids: Wm. B. Eerdmans Publishing Co., 1964-.

Klausner, Joseph. *The Messianic Idea in Israel.* Translated from the third Hebrew edition by W. F. Stinespring. London: George Allen and Unwin Ltd., 1956.

Ladd, George Eldon. *The Blessed Hope*. Grand Rapids: Wm. B. Eerdmans Publishing Co., 1956.

Liddell, Henry George, and Scott, Robert. *A Greek-English Lexicon*. Revised and augmented by Sir Henry Stuart Jones with the assistance of Roderick McKenzie. Oxford: Clarendon Press, 1948.

Linton, John. *Will the Church Escape the Great Tribulation?* Published privately by the author, 328 Belle Isle View, Riverside, Ontario, Canada, 1961. (Originally a series of articles in the *Sword of the Lord*, but with two additional chapters.)

Ludwigson, R. *Bible Prophecy Notes*. Grand Rapids: Zondervan Publishing House, 1956.

Mason, Clarence E., Jr. "The Day of Our Lord Jesus Christ," *Bibliotheca Sacra*, 125 (1968), 352-359.

Moffatt, James. *The Revelation of St. John the Divine. Expositor's Greek Testament*. Vol. V. W. Robertson Nicoll, editor. Grand Rapids: Wm. B. Eerdmans Publishing Co., 1951.

Moulton, James Hope, and Milligan, George. *The Vocabulary of the Greek Testament*. London: Hodder and Stoughton, Limited, 1952.

New Bible Commentary: Revised. D. Guthrie, J. A. Motyer, A. M. Stibbs, and D. J. Wiseman, editors. Grand Rapids: Wm. B. Eerdmans Publishing Co., 1970.

Payne, J. Barton, *The Imminent Appearing of Christ*. Grand Rapids: Wm. B. Eerdmans Publishing Co., 1962.

Pentecost, J. Dwight. *Things to Come*. Findlay, Ohio: Dunham Publishing Co., 1958.

Rand, James F. "A Survey of the Eschatology of the Olivet Discourse," Part II, *Bibliotheca Sacra,* 113 (1956), 200-213.

Reese, Alexander. *The Approaching Advent of Christ*. London, Edinburgh: Marshall, Morgan, and Scott, Ltd., 1932.

Robertson, Alexander, and Donaldson, James. *The Ante-Nicene Fathers*. New York: Charles Scribner's Sons, 1908.

Robertson, Archibald Thomas. *A Grammar of the Greek New Testament in the Light of Historical Research*. Third edition. Nashville: Broadman Press, 1934.

Sauer, Erich. *From Eternity to Eternity*. Grand Rapids: Wm. B. Eerdmans Publishing Co., 1954.

Scofield, C. I. *The Scofield Reference Bible*. New York: Oxford University Press, 1945.

Scott, Walter. *Exposition of the Revelation of Jesus Christ*. London: Pickering & Inglis Ltd., n.d.

Smith, Wilbur M. "The Church: The Tribulation and the Rapture," *Moody Monthly*, 57 (1957), 26-28, 30-32.

————. "In the Study," *Moody Monthly*, 58 (1957), 46-49.

Stanton, Gerald B. *Kept From the Hour*. Grand Rapids: Zondervan Publishing House, 1956.

Strack, Hermann L., and Billerbeck, Paul. *Kommentar zum Neuen Testament aus Talmud und Midrasch*. Vol. IV, Part 2. München: C. H. Beck'sche Verlagsbuchhandlung, 1922.

Strombeck, J. F. *First the Rapture*. Moline, Illinois: Strombeck Agency, Inc., 1950.

Tenney, Merrill C. *Interpreting Revelation*. Grand Rapids: Wm. B. Eerdmans Publishing Co., 1957.

Thayer, Joseph Henry. *A Greek-English Lexicon of the New Testament*. A translation, revision and enlargement of Grimm's *Wilke's Clavis Novi Testamenti*. Fourth edition. Edinburgh: T. & T. Clark, 1953.

Thiessen, Henry Clarence. *Lectures in Systematic Theology*. Grand Rapids: Wm. B. Eerdmans Publishing Co., 1951.

————. *Will the Church Pass Through the Tribulation?* New York: Loizeaux Brothers, Publishers, 1941.

————. "Will the Church Pass Through the Tribulation?" *Bibliotheca Sacra*, 92 (1935), 39-54, 187-205, 292-314.

Tregelles, S. P. *The Hope of Christ's Second Coming*. Los Angeles: Ambassadors for Christ, n.d.

Walvoord, John F. "Christ's Olivet Discourse on the Time of the End," *Bibliotheca Sacra*, 129 (1972), 20-32.

————. "The Church in Heaven," *Bibliotheca Sacra*, 123 (1966), 99-103.

————. *The Millennial Kingdom*. Grand Rapids: Zondervan Publishing House, 1959.

————. "Millennial Series" (various titles), *Bibliotheca Sacra*, beginning in 106 (1949) but with specially pertinent articles in 111 (1954), 1-10, 97-104, 193-203, 289-301; 112 (1955), 1-10, 97-106, 193-208, 289-303; 113 (1956), 1-15, 97-110, 193-199; 114 (1957), 1-9, 97-101, 193-200, 289-307; 115 (1958), 291-301.

————. "The New Covenant with Israel," *Bibliotheca Sacra,* 103 (1946), 16-27.

————. *The Rapture Question*. Findlay Ohio: Dunham Publishing Co., 1957.

————. "The Resurrection of Israel," *Bibliotheca Sacra,* 124 (1967), 3-15.

————. "A Review of 'The Blessed Hope' by George E. Ladd," *Bibliotheca Sacra*, 113 (1956), 289-307.

————. *The Thessalonian Epistles*. Findlay, Ohio: Dunham Publishing Co., 1955.

Wood, Leon J. *Is the Rapture Next?* Grand Rapids: Zondervan Publishing House, 1956.

Wuest, Kenneth S. "The Rapture—Precisely When?" *Bibliotheca Sacra*, 114 (1957), 60-69.

Scripture Index

Index to Other Ancient Literature

Index of Authors and Subjects